MIDDLE WAY MIND TRAINING

THE ART AND SCIENCE OF
UNCOVERING AND EXPERIENCING
THE HAPPINESS
WE HAVE WITHIN

FRANK NAVRATIL

MIDDLE WAY MIND TRAINING

THE ART AND SCIENCE OF
UNCOVERING AND EXPERIENCING
THE HAPPINESS
WE HAVE WITHIN

www.middlewaymindtraining.com

First Edition
Published by Frank Navratil
Purkynova 1246/9
Ricany, Czech Republic

ISBN 978-80-88022-23-7

Beginner's Mind

I was once the maestro

rigid and unyielding

blinded by my expertise

oblivious of my fatal delusion

a restricted mind

traversing narrow alleys

only to encounter

barricades of resistance

my mask of brilliance confined

within closed doors of

ignorance

Now, I cultivate a beginner's

mind

an open inquisitive sky

without clouds of arrogance

a wisdom in uncertainty

breath of virgin air

I graciously accept

all that I will never know

always the apprentice

never the master

willing to learn

willing to step forward

the innocence of a child

a clear untainted vision

soft and malleable

full of wonder and excitement

free from opinions and views

free from misconceptions

no expectations no convictions

empty of any judgment

With an expansive mind

I am open

to infinite possibilities

like empty pages of a book

I wait to be written

I listen more deeply

I see more clearly

I understand so much more

my cup filled with curiosity

as I follow my intuition

detached from the grips of ego

my beginner's mind

stays forever present

and wide awake

to the full experience

that awaits me

Frank Navratil

*(from Stranded on a Desert Island by
Navratil, 2022)*

For Jana

CONTENTS

ACKNOWLEDGEMENTS

First and foremost, an incredible amount of gratitude goes to my wife Jana, for her never-ending support, acceptance and encouragement while writing this book and the sacrifices she had to make for me so I could complete this project. Without her generous encouragement and unconditional love, this book would never have been written. Thank you with all my heart.

I would like to thank the Buddha, for his teachings and his infinite wisdom that has transcended time, will forever be my guide, my illuminating light along the middle way, to enable me to navigate in peace and harmony through this world and beyond.

I would like to thank all my teachers: the Dalai Lama, Thich Nhat Hanh, S.N. Goenka and all the Buddhist writers, scientists, scholars and monks, who have given me an intellectual understanding of Buddhist philosophy and science.

Amongst my teachers I also include any enemies I may have made along my path and all those who have disappointed me, hurt me, or showed ill will towards me. They have taught me about patience, understanding and compassion.

I would also like to thank all my patients over the years who have given me an extraordinary first-hand opportunity to learn about the healing process of the body, mind and spirit.

Finally, I thank all of you, whether you know it or not, you are all a part of me and I am a part of you. We are all waves that move across the same ocean and we will be forever inter-connected. I share this incredible journey we call human life with you all.

PREFACE

I am not some kind of spiritual guru, and you certainly should not blindly take the advice that I have presented in this book. I do not claim to know all the answers. The Buddha certainly made this profound statement very clear in his teachings; do not believe anything unless you can experience it yourself firsthand. We really should try to maintain a beginner's mind in whatever we attempt to do. Never claim to be the expert, always remain the apprentice. So all I can ask is that you try to keep an open, inquisitive mind, test the methods out yourself, and use the results to form your own opinions. Take this book as an invitation to participate in a scientific experiment on your own mind. Ask yourself all the questions, examine the research, establish your own hypothesis, test this hypothesis on yourself and make your own observations. Only then will you be able to adequately analyze the results and come to your own conclusions.

I am just an ordinary person, like you. I just reached a point, years ago in my life, where I started to question all those inbred and conditioned expectations that we have placed on ourselves and began to search for a way to relieve the immense pressure of having to carry that overwhelming burden on my shoulders. All I humbly claim to be is just a diligently attentive observer who wishes to share the realization that his own ongoing struggle up that endless precipice of life that often manifests itself like an insurmountable mountain is common to each and every one of us.

My first exposure to Buddhist philosophy began with listening to the Dalai Lama in Sydney, Australia in the early 90's. Coming from a fairly conservative Catholic upbringing, this encounter was like a breath of fresh air, a new way of seeing things and certainly challenged the way I had been living my life up to that point. It also brought a welcomed sense of humor about the absurdities that we often find ourselves struggling with.

Thus began my often painful journey of self-reflection and my ongoing endeavor to battle against the wind, to veer away from traditional beliefs, to think outside of the box and to risk stepping into an open unknown expanse of space that holds unlimited potential.

Initially, with the death of my mother to cancer at a relatively young age, I was in retrospect able to appreciate early on that life is really precious, fragile and often unpredictable. I suppose I have her to thank for the change in my plans. Instead of pursuing classical allopathic medicine, a dream since childhood, I went against the grain choosing instead a path least trodden on. I began my study of alternative medicine and became a naturopathic doctor.

Naturopathy forced me to look at health in a natural and holistic way. I was encouraged to look for causes of disease and to use only natural drug-free treatments. These causes were often not related to the body, or from a lack of adequate nutrition, but very often transcended into the realms of the mind and the spirit.

After years of experience dealing with thousands of patients, it became undeniably clear to me the intricate connection between the mind and the body and the ultimate consequences for health. Physical health alone did not guarantee a sense of well-being. If the mind was not in the right place, a favorable environment for physical healing was very difficult if not impossible to achieve.

I guess this was my first inkling of an enlightened realization that everything truly begins in the mind.

However, nevertheless, during that time, I personally still became victim to the grasps of ambition, greed, obsessive goal setting and the futile attempts to continually satisfy my ego-driven needs for success, status and self-worth. With every success and achievement of a goal, I found myself setting another higher one, never really feeling completely fulfilled or satisfied. Any fleeting feelings of happiness I would experience were never really sustainable.

Years later, the seed of dharma that was first planted in my mind after seeing the Dalai Lama in Australia, found some fertile ground and began to sprout, and I began to study Buddhist philosophy with renewed fascination. It seemed to fill that dark empty hole in my life, and offered a sense of direction and a path to better understand the frustration I was going through. I was intrigued how it made so much sense and how it started to make my mind feel at ease, almost immediately.

I started to read every book on the subject that I could get hold of, including those written by the Dalai Lama, Thich Nhat Hanh, Bhikkhu Bodhi, Alan Watts, Jack Kornfield, Sharon Salzberg and many, many others. I also began my first attempts at practicing meditation which provided an oasis of refuge, far removed from the hectic stressful lifestyle in which I was deeply entrenched. I even enrolled in a course on Buddhism, and started regularly going to a Buddhist meditation center. I decorated my home with Buddha statues and found that they reminded me of the philosophy behind them, which further set my mind at ease.

Coming from a science background in university, I was naturally always somewhat skeptical of anything of any flighty, esoteric or intangible character, and at first, Buddhism was no different. Yet, as I immersed myself deeper into the philosophy, I could not help but clearly come to the conclusion how much correlation it had to logical reasoning and science.

One of the strongest arguments for Buddhist philosophy that convinced me of its merit was its insistence that you should not believe in something just because you have read about it, heard about it, if it has been passed down by tradition or even if you have been taught about it from the greatest masters. It should become the truth only if you are able to directly experience and internalize it. This struck a very positive chord in me, seeing that most of my life up to that point I had been inundated with dogma and blind faith.

Buddhism I discovered was free of dogma, at least in its original form. There was no blind faith or even belief in God, as found in most religions. Buddhism actually was not by definition, a religion at all, but more of a philosophy or science about a practical way of life whose main goal was to reduce suffering and increase happiness.

In this way, I believe the basic teachings of the Buddha maintained their pristine form for 2500 years and are as relevant today as they were in Buddha's time. The Buddha has been proven to be one of the greatest scientists and psychologists when it comes to the workings of the mind. In fact, the modern trends of meditation and mindfulness all have their origins in Buddhism. It is no wonder that scientists, psychologists and psychotherapists are now going back to the original teachings of Buddhism to learn more about the workings of the human mind. The emergence of new innovative and effective methods to deal with psychological disorders such as Mindfulness-based Cognitive Therapy (MBCT), Mindfulness-based Stress Reduction (MBSR), and Buddhist Psychology and Psychotherapy are testament to this.

My fascination with Buddhist philosophy in accordance with science along with the health and psychological benefits I witnessed with meditation and mindfulness training, led me to develop a holistic mind training method, based on the noble eightfold path or middle way as it is often called. I decided to call it Middle Way Mind Training (MWMT) and it is the subject of this book.

When I looked at existing methods such as mindfulness training and other related interventions, although very effective, I felt they only utilized a portion of the noble teachings of the Buddha and a more holistic and complete method was needed. As the Noble Eightfold Path is considered to be one of the most profound fundamental teachings in Buddhist philosophy, it seems that every one of the eight principles is essential in order to achieve true and sustainable happiness and freedom from suffering.

Hence my long journey has brought me here to this very place to share with each one of you, a practical method that I have developed based on 2500 years of Buddhist science, utilizing scientifically backed techniques, called Middle Way Mind Training. Think of it as the art and science of uncovering and experiencing the happiness you already hold within. The training of the mind can be likened to an intricate surgical operation that slowly but surely uncovers and eradicates old negative habitual patterns, those that are not allowing you to experience sustained happiness. It requires a dramatic paradigm shift towards a new way of thinking. Ultimately, it has the power to shape the way you respond to and experience life. It is not an easy path and requires a lot of dedication and discipline but the rewards are immeasurable. Understanding what happiness is and how you can actually achieve it and sustain it is a gift that I believe everyone on this planet needs and truly deserves.

The results I have witnessed using this method have been nothing less than transformational. I sincerely hope that Middle Way Mind Training will help each one of you to dramatically increase the level of happiness in your lives. Perhaps you too, will discover that the happiness you have been searching for outside of yourself has always been deep within and just waiting to be uncovered and experienced.

Frank Navratil

PREFACE

PART I

IDENTIFYING THE REALITY OF OUR UNHAPPINESS

Pain is certain, suffering is optional.

– The Buddha

BEGINNER'S MIND

In the beginner's mind there are many
possibilities, but in the expert's there are few.

— Shunryu Suzuki

As we begin our journey to explore the human mind to better understand the art and science of uncovering happiness, there seems no better way to approach this monumental task than with the way we approach learning. We start with one of the most critical and necessary surgical operations of the mind, the cultivation of a beginner's mind.

This seems like a very strange concept, since most of us have had instilled since childhood, the pursuit to become the best we can be, to become experts in our field, to become presidents, managers, CEO's, Olympic medalists, Nobel Prize winners, or members of the scientific elite. However, our attachment to the role of being an expert is often unfortunately one of our greatest hindrances in the learning process, not to mention its ability to dramatically reduce our level of happiness.

An expert's mind implies in some ways an end of a process. For example, the end of our training, when we are now an expert or the end of our education, where we have now achieved all we can learn. Being an expert creates boundaries and division. It creates a full mind which has no more room for expansion in contrast to an empty and open mind, where there is still so much more to be learned.

Shoshin or Beginner's mind is a Zen Buddhist term and was popularized in the book, "Zen Mind, Beginner's Mind," by Shunryu Suzuki (Suzuki, 1970). It is interesting that even Steve Jobs of Apple Inc, a long-time Zen practitioner, was said to be a fan of this concept.

In a true beginner's mind, all self-centered thoughts such as those of what we have accomplished in life are extinguished. Self-centered thoughts of achievement and how we can benefit ourselves only, limit our vast mind. When we are true beginners, we can really learn something. The beginner's mind is in essence a mind of compassion. When our mind is compassionate, it has no boundaries.

When we can see things with a childlike wonder, with non-judgmental awareness and approach learning with an eager, open attitude, we become much more creative and innovative. The possibilities become infinite. What always seemed impossible before suddenly becomes very possible.

Part of the reason we cannot be happy, is because we continue this charade of playing the role of an expert, the "know it all", where ego holds onto our pride for dear life. This places us under a lot of stress in order to maintain this state, but also prevents us from making intelligent choices.

This practice is often especially difficult for people in leadership positions, such as managers and advisors. This is because they are expected to always know what to do and will often pretend to know something even if they do not, in order to avoid appearing weak or stupid.

A beginner's or a "don't know it all" mind cultivates patience and activates our ability to listen, to look at all views, not just our own. It is these very strongly-held beliefs that often hold us back from learning new things. A beginner's mind is one of wisdom. When we are able to evaluate all sides of the story and listen to all opinions and views without personal judgment or ego getting in the way, we are much better able to learn and make a wise and intelligent decision. Just think how much more effective we could be as a manager if we really listened to the ideas from our subordinates, or how much more effective we could be in life, if we at least actively listened to ideas and opinions of friends and loved ones around us. There are so many mistakes we have all made or continue to make. Cultivating a beginner's mind could surely prevent many of them.

I often receive comments from clients from courses and consultations asking, "Why should I go back to being a beginner again, when I have invested so much time in education and work experience? Am I not supposed to become good at what I do?" The goal is certainly not to undo what we have learned or experienced in our life. The goal has to do with our approach to learning. If we approach our work and our life with a beginner's mind, we open up our mind in a way that we are able to welcome new learning experiences no matter how many times we have performed the same task. We never become bored because each time is a brand new experience, one that is open to new possibilities and outcomes. We will notice the beauty in every moment and each moment is never the same. We will remain patient with others and with ourselves because we will always keep an open mind.

The other revelation that we will soon realize as we read further into this book, is that our mind cannot always be trusted. There is a danger when we have strong attachments to our opinions and views, as they are carefully guarded by our ego. This often blinds us to the reality that really exists. This means that the opinions and views that we hold onto so close, may not even reflect reality and may not even be beneficial to ourselves or to others around us. How many times have we passionately believed we were right, and found out later that we were dead wrong? How do we really know if our view is right? I am sure that even Hitler believed that he was right with his distorted view of eliminating Jews and creating a New World Order, or terrorists who perform suicide attacks with the belief of achieving political or religious aims.

In the development of a beginner's mind, it is important to put aside all preconceived ideas about the world and about our self. We need to let go of any judgments that we have on our self, on people we know, or on the world around us. We should take a look at any strong opinions that we have and let them go. For every strong opinion or view there is always another alternative view, a different opinion or a different way to look at things.

It is always fascinating for us to look at young children and admire how unconditioned they are, how they see things with wonder for the very first time. We can cultivate these qualities by training the mind. Our life can become a playground of adventure, creativity and an arena of new discovery.

A beginner's mind allows for a shift in the world around us, allowing a new transformation to occur. Our conditioned, expert mind has only made things difficult for us. It has created divisions amongst our friends and separated us from family and co-workers. It has also stunted our capacity to grow and learn from our mistakes. Most importantly, it has taken away a lot of happiness that we deserve. The more fluid our beliefs, the more fluid our reality becomes. Our beliefs create our reality. As we change our point of view, our world around us changes as well.

To begin to develop a mind of wisdom, a beginner's mind, some important thoughts are:

- Try to imagine looking at a situation that is important to you from the point of view of someone else.
- Try to keep an open mind, in this way you open your mind to infinite possibilities.
- There will always be another way to look at things, which is different to your way of thinking.
- Let go of any fear or wall of pride that you have built around you and become more accepting and more understanding.
- Try to adopt a mind of curiosity and play, in all your activities in your work and relationships.
- Try to do something new every day in your daily life, no matter how small.
- Embrace the unknown and try to make a habit of breaking old routines.
- Imagine you are doing everything for the very first time.
- Try to maintain a beginner's mind while reading this book.

The Science behind a Beginner's mind

Researchers say that there are many cognitive benefits including enhanced memory from training a beginner's mind, achieved both by learning new skills and with extensive meditation and mindfulness exercises. People who score high in this trait tend to have a richer and happier life experience. Here are just a few of the many published research studies on this fascinating subject.

A research study published in Journals of Gerontology (Lazar, et al. 2020) offers some compelling evidence. The question was addressed whether learning new skills in an encouraging environment leads to cognitive growth in older adults. A group of adults, who were aged 58 to 86, were encouraged to take three to five new classes that they had never taken before (which was comparable to an college course load of about

15 hours a week) for three months. As most of the adults were fearful and unsure about this challenge, they were also given additional and motivational one-hour sessions that included learning barriers, the value of learning new skills and resilience in aging. Researchers measured their changes in short-term memory and other cognitive tasks. Results showed that the participants, who were engaged in learning new skills with the right environment and motivation, increased their cognitive ability to levels of adults 30 years younger after only 45 days. It seems that the secret to their success was that they got out of their comfort zone while at the same time were supported to reduce any fears and insecurities.

Sara Lazar PhD, a neuroscientist at Harvard has examined the brains of people with extensive mindfulness and meditation experience. She has shown that meditation slows down or even prevents age-related thinning of the frontal cortex (Gard, Holzel, Lazar, 2014). Most of us when we get old tend to get more forgetful and our cognitive capacities decrease. Her research studies showed that those who meditated in their forties and fifties had the same amount of grey matter as those in their twenties and thirties.

THE IMPORTANCE OF DIRECT EXPERIENCE

When our beliefs are based on our own direct
experience of reality and not on notions offered by
others, no one can remove these beliefs from us.

— Thich Nhat Hanh

Knowledge is knowing that a tomato is a
fruit. Wisdom is knowing not to put it in a fruit
salad.

— Brian Odriscoll

I recall a relevant humorous story, called Swimology, that was shared by S.N. Goenka from a 10-day Vipassana meditation retreat I attended years ago, from a book, based on his teachings, The Art of Living (Hart,1987).

There was once a young professor who was travelling on a ship. He was very highly educated having a list of letters after his name and multiple PhD's. He did not however, have much experience in life. On the same ship there was also an illiterate old sailor, who would come to the professor's cabin to listen to the lectures that he was presenting. One evening after the lecture, the professor asked the sailor,

"Old man, do you know geology?

"What is that sir?" he replied.

"Old man, geology is the science of the earth."

"Sir, I have never been to school. I have never studied geology."

"Old man, you have wasted a quarter of your life."

The old man returned to his quarters with a very long face. He thought to himself that if such a learned person says so, it must be true, so I have wasted a quarter of my life."

The next evening the professor delivered a lecture on oceanography. At the end of the session, the professor asked the sailor again.

"Old man, do you know oceanography?"

"What is that sir?"

"Old man, it is the science of the ocean."

"No sir, I have not studied oceanography."

"Old man, you have wasted two quarters of your life."

The old man left with an even longer face. He thought to himself if such a learned person says so; I surely have wasted two quarters of my life.

The next evening the professor delivered a lecture on meteorology. After the lecture, the professor asked the sailor,

"Old man, do you know meteorology?"

"What is that sir?"

"Old man, it is the science of the weather, the wind and rain."

"No sir. As I told you before, I have never been to any school. I do not know meteorology."

"Old man, you do not know geology, you do not know oceanography and you do not know meteorology? You have wasted three quarters of your life."

This made the old man very unhappy. He thought to himself, when such a learned person says that I have wasted three quarters of my life, it surely must be true.

The next day, the old sailor came running to the professor's cabin in a panic and asked,

"Professor, do you know swimology?"

"What is that old man?"

"Do you know how to swim, sir?"

"I do not know how to swim, old man."

"Professor, you certainly have wasted all your life. The ship has hit a rock and is sinking. Those who can swim can get to the nearby shore. Those who cannot will drown with the ship."

In order to make a sustainable change in our life when it comes to happiness, not only do we need to use a beginner's mindset, as we learned in the last chapter, we also need to directly internalize or experience what we are about to learn. The importance of direct experience in this process cannot be underestimated. No significant or lasting change can be made without it.

There have been a multitude of books written on the subject of happiness. There have been many theories presented on what happiness really is and how it can be achieved. There are a number of speakers that speak on the topic around the world. Every year there are reports listing the happiest countries or cities to live in, theories on why these people or those cultures are happier than others and theories on which activities bring the greatest happiness.

Achieving knowledge can be gained from listening to others or intellectually analyzing a subject, but true wisdom is developed from direct, personal experience. We may listen to the greatest gurus about how to attain happiness or read all their books but it will be to no avail, as this offers us only an intellectual understanding of the subject. One should not believe in something because someone said it or if it is found in a book or even presented by the greatest teachers. One should not believe in traditions just because they have been handed down from generation to generation. What we believe in, should be based on our own direct experience. The Buddha emphasized this important concept often in his teachings.

As we will soon discover, everything that is taught in this book can be reproduced and verified by our own direct experience. There is no blind faith involved. That is the essence of Middle Way Mind Training.

2500 YEARS OF BUDDHIST SCIENCE

If science proves some belief of Buddhism wrong,
then Buddhism will have to change.

— His Holiness the 14th Dalai Lama

As we know, the only way to truly understand reality and happiness for that matter as it truly is, is to understand the mind through our own experience. Buddhist science has been teaching this and passing it on through its lineages for 2500 years. Many of us associate Buddhism with a religion, but if we strictly dissect what the meaning of a religion really is, there has to be a belief in a central higher power or a God. This important definition is not found in Buddhism. When Buddha was asked anything about God, he chose to remain silent as he did not want to get entangled in a debate where there could never be any resolution. He never stated that there was not a God, and never said there was, he just refused to get into an argument that could not be proved.

Therefore, Buddhism has often been compared to more of a philosophy, a way of life or a practice, or what I like to call it, a science of the mind. So, personally I prefer to refer to Buddhism as Buddhist science as it steers away from its often misleading religious connotations. Buddhism is based on pursuing and realizing the truth about reality, it is not based on blind faith or any dogma or rigid beliefs. Buddhism, like science, is open to change and they are both strongly interconnected.

Even Albert Einstein, one of the greatest scientific minds this world has ever seen, valued Buddhism over every other belief as he saw it was most appealing, relevant and logical to intellectual minds. He believed that the religion of the future must be a cosmic religion, free of dogma and theology, that it should transcend a personal God, and that it should unify all things that are natural and spiritual. He stated that only Buddhism answers this broad description as it is able to cope with modern scientific needs.

When Einstein was in Japan in November 1922, shortly after he had been informed that he had won the Nobel Prize, he stayed at the Imperial Hotel Tokyo as he was in town to give a series of lectures. A courier came to his room to make a delivery and perhaps Einstein did not have any small change to give him for appreciation or the bellboy refused a tip, but he gave him a note instead that he wrote in German on a piece of hotel stationary. On the note he wrote his theory of happiness, "A calm and modest life brings more happiness than the pursuit of success combined with constant restlessness." He told the bellboy to save the note, that it could be valuable in the future. It certainty proved to be just that. In 2017, in an auction in Jerusalem, Einstein's note on happiness sold to an anonymous European buyer for 1.56 million USD. (New York Times October 25, 2017)

Buddhism's close association with science, unlike other religions, has also been demonstrated extensively by Tenzin Gyatso, the 14th Dalai Lama and spiritual leader of Tibetan Buddhism, who has engaged with scientists for decades. His strong engrained belief that Buddhism should be supported by science has led him to even state that, "If science proves some belief of Buddhism wrong, then Buddhism will have to change." No leader of any major world religion has ever proclaimed anything like this where they have placed such an important emphasis on science.

Ancient Buddhist scriptures have always promoted an empirical investigation and have invited followers to put the teachings of the Buddha to the test before accepting any of them. The *Abhidhamma*, one of the three baskets or collections of these ancient Buddhist texts that comprise the *Pali Canon*, describe the nature of experience, focusing on the essence of reality and presenting an elaborate analysis of the mind. The text describes the nature, origin, and interaction of all psychological and material phenomena, including human consciousness itself. Today, many scientists, psychologists and psychotherapists study the *Abhidhamma* for new insights on how the human mind operates (Bodhi, 2003).

Buddhist science has influenced the development of many new cognitive therapies, including mindfulness-based cognitive therapy, mindfulness-based stress reduction and Buddhist psychology and psychotherapy. These methods based on Buddhist science have been scientifically proven to be very effective in treating depression, anxiety and stress as well as many other psychological disorders. The modern trends of meditation and mindfulness we see today that have now begun to be practiced in corporate environments, all have their roots in Buddhism.

Buddhist concepts have been found to be in various degrees compatible with many scientific fields, including evolutionary biology, quantum physics, cosmology and psychology. While science mainly focuses on the objective material world, Buddhism delves primarily into the subjective consciousness, the science of the mind. While science deals with the objective and conceptual scientific method, Buddhism uses non-conceptual intuitive understanding that develops as a result of the practice of training the mind in meditation.

In fact the Dalai Lama has given many speeches to neuroscientists and has engaged in many scientific discussions on cognitive neuroscience and physics. He was instrumental in setting up the Mind and Life institute in the 1980s, which for the first time brought together world renowned scientists and philosophers with the wisdom practices of Buddhism. Today the institute continues its noble mission, "to bring science and contemplative wisdom together to better understand the mind and create positive change in the world." The Dalai Lama has also promoted scientific education amongst Tibetan Buddhist monks.

Today, modern Buddhist literature includes many books about Buddhism and the brain, meditation and mindfulness, showing the compatibility of Buddhism with modern science.

While most of the discussion between Buddhism and science has generally focused on ways in which Buddhism can adapt to modern science or how science can study the efficacy of Buddhist practices, perhaps it's more significant future developments lie in the potential that Buddhism has to provoke rethinking and ultimately transformation within science itself.

The complexity of the ancient Buddhist scripts to this day, still challenge even the greatest Buddhist scholars themselves. This is testament that it is not possible to only intellectually understand the mind with scientific concepts that are known today. The only way to fully realize the potential of Buddhist science in my opinion is to turn inwards, and fully experience and appreciate them though the process of training the mind.

The exciting developments that have been due to revelations from Buddhist science show the incredible universal wisdom that the Buddha developed through his own experience and that which he shared with the world. As more and more new research results unfold, it is becoming increasingly evident that adopting the principles of Buddhist philosophy in our life has immense benefits and truly holds the key to our happiness.

In the next chapter, we will learn about the original founding pioneer of Buddhist science, the Buddha himself.

THE BUDDHA

The thought manifests as the word;
The word manifests as the deed;
The deed develops into habit;
And habit hardens into character;
So watch the thought and its ways with care,
And let it spring from love
Born out of the concern for all beings…

– The Buddha

Every one of us can become a Buddha. The word "Buddha" is a Sanskrit term and means "awakened or enlightened one." The Buddha was just a human being, an extraordinary one, but still a human being, none the less, just like us. While most people associate the Buddha as the originator of the Buddhist religion or philosophy, I consider him to be one of the greatest scientists or psychologists that ever lived.

Before he became enlightened or a Buddha, he was Siddhartha Gautama who was born over 2500 hundred years ago, sometime during the 5th century BC in ancient India, now modern day Nepal. He came from a wealthy family, was a prince, the son of a king, but at the age of 29, after being moved by suffering in the world, decided to leave his lavish lifestyle in search for the truth and denounce his kingdom to become an ascetic.

He spent many years searching, meditating and experimenting with many spiritual practices of the day including self-mortification but realized and promoted what would be called the Middle Way, a way of life based on a balance between the extremes of pain and indulgence. It is said that after six years of searching and experimenting, and at the age of

35, the Buddha achieved enlightenment while meditating under a Bodhi tree.

But what is really meant by enlightenment? In scientific terms, it means seeing reality as it actually is, not as we would like it to be. It means to be awakened from our deep sleep or lack of awareness of primarily living in the past and the future and not in the present moment. In Buddhist terms, it means to achieve a deep state of meditation, the final goal which is called nirvana, a state of mind that frees us of all suffering.

After his enlightenment, the Buddha then spent the next 45 years until his death at age 80, travelling and teaching across central India. The teachings of the Buddha, what he personally discovered, are called in Buddhist philosophy the Dharma or universal law of nature. They include detailed explanations of how the mind is constructed and methods of how to eradicate suffering.

His path to enlightenment, the doctrine leading to it, has been passed down through numerous unbroken lineages of teachers and has spread through many countries. Many of these lineages still flourish to this day.

There is a reason why, for thousands of years, mankind has built statues and shrines in Buddha's honor all over the world and why to this day, his presence adorns millions of homes, offices and centers the world over. He has become a symbol of inner peace, harmony and happiness and statues of him seem to appear wherever there is a need to be reminded of the importance of attaining these precious inner qualities.

The seed of Dharma planted first in the East by the Buddha himself, more than 2500 years ago, has now spread all over the world and is quickly becoming popular in the West, demonstrating that it holds universal application for everyone. It is now up to each and every one of us to learn and internalize the fundamentals of Buddha's teachings and apply them to the science of training the mind. This is the goal of Middle Way Mind Training.

If there was anyone in the history of mankind that deciphered the meaning and path to happiness, and who devised a practical and scientific way to eradicate suffering, it surely had to be the Buddha.

Today, Buddhism has branched into many types of schools or traditions, including Mahajana, Theraveda and Vajrayana Buddhism. Each claim that their view is close to the original views of the Buddha.

Although they may each differ in some ways, what they all have in common are Buddha's fundamental teachings; the Four Noble Truths. These, the subject of the next section, remain the core of Buddhist philosophy and their importance in understanding the path to happiness cannot be overemphasized.

BUDDHA'S FIRST TEACHING -
THE 4 NOBLE TRUTHS

Both formerly and now, it is only suffering that I
describe, and the cessation of suffering.
— The Buddha

uddha's first important revelation to his followers after he achieved enlightenment was his teaching of the Four Noble Truths. They are considered noble because the Buddha said they are real, infallible and do not change. They have withstood the test of time and are as applicable to our lives now as they were 2500 years ago. Why are we delving into these ancient Buddhist teachings? I really believe that they are instrumental to gaining knowledge of why we suffer and why we are not so happy. I consider them a formula for understanding and attaining happiness as they are directly relevant and crucial to our understanding of the human mind. Buddha's sole mission, as we know was to discover how to end suffering and these four sacred truths really comprise the basic foundation of Buddhist philosophy.

The Buddha has often been compared to a great physician or psychologist. In many ways his teachings are very similar to medical science. His Four Noble Truths consist of identifying an illness, finding the cause or diagnosis, formulating a prognosis and giving a prescription or cure. Let's take a look at each one of them.

The first of the Four Noble Truths has given Buddhism quite mistakably, a bad reputation. I can certainly understand why. The First Noble Truth is the truth of dukkha or suffering. Suffering is an inescapable part of life or an innate characteristic of human existence. Who really wants to hear all that pessimism and gloom and why should we even dwell on human suffering? For this reason, because of this First Noble Truth, Buddhism is often perceived as a negative philosophy.

Nothing could be further from the truth. First of all, the Pali word "dukkha" used in the First Noble Truth is often conventionally translated to English as "suffering." It is often difficult to accurately translate the Pali and Sanskrit language, so to understand a more appropriate meaning of dukkha is to think of it as a form of dissatisfaction, or that human life is incapable of satisfying us completely. Since all beings experience pain and misery during their lifetime, this statement is a fact of life and the First Noble Truth acknowledges this fact. Birth is pain, old age is pain, sickness is pain, death is pain; sorrow, grief and anxiety are pain. Contact with the unpleasant is pain. Separating from the pleasant is pain. Not getting what one wants is pain. These are all sources of pain or suffering that all of us experience during our human existence.

This is not a pessimistic outlook. The Buddha emphasized it as it is a realistic view. In some ways it comes with the realization that suffering or dissatisfaction is a natural part of our lives. It is like a sickness that we need to first identify and understand in order to move on to finding the cause. This leads us to making a diagnosis or in essence the Second Noble Truth, the cause of suffering.

The Second Noble Truth states that there is a cause to the suffering that humans endure. The Buddha taught that the cause of our suffering is desire or craving. Our incessant desire to always have more of what we want or less of what we don't want, are cravings that create suffering or dissatisfaction in our lives. The bitter reality is that we can never completely satisfy our desires so we can never really be one hundred percent happy.

The Third Noble Truth erases any negative connotations associated with Buddhism as it states that there is a solution or a way to end all this suffering. The Buddha made a prognosis, if we can stop our desires and cravings, then we can stop our suffering. In other words, he stated that there is a possible cure to our illness.

The Fourth and last Noble Truth revealed by the Buddha, is his cure or prescription on how to practically deal with this disease or human affliction. It is called the Noble Eightfold Path or Middle Way. The Buddha outlined a path that includes 8 areas that we as humans must develop in order to extinguish suffering in our lives.

Middle Way Mind Training draws on these 8 areas of the Noble Eightfold Path and brings them into the context of modern science. We will learn about each of these areas in greater detail as we progress along our journey into understanding happiness. This chapter serves as a short introduction to the Four Noble Truths. We will investigate each of these Four Noble Truths in much more detail later in future parts of this book.

The Buddha often compared his teachings or the dharma to a raft that is needed to be able to cross the river of ignorance. Let's get on board this raft and see where it takes us next.

WHAT IS REALLY HAPPINESS?

Our idea of happiness may be the very thing that
is preventing us from being happy.

Thich Nhat Hanh

According to Aristotle, the famous Greek philosopher, everything we do is for the sake of happiness. The ultimate goal of human existence is happiness. Let's think about this for a moment. When we search for a life partner, we look for someone who will make us happy, right? When we associate with this person instead of that person or choose who our friends become, we do it to make us happy. We educate ourselves in college as it will lead to work that will make us happy. We apply for that job, so we can make money and be fulfilled in order to make us happy. When we think about it, every action and everything we do, is in some way a move to make us happy.

Now, if this is actually true, it means that if we spend all our time trying to make ourselves happy, we really should know what happiness is, right? Wrong. Most people, when asked what they think happiness is, may have a general idea, but very rarely can they give the specifics of what happiness actually means.

So our journey to unlocking the mystery of happiness includes identifying, understanding and learning how it can be experienced. Common questions you may be asking yourself are: What is really happiness? Where does it come from? What do we have to do to get it?

When I tried to find a definition of happiness in dictionaries or on the internet, I only found the following vague explanations. Happiness is: a state of well-being or contentment, a pleasurable of satisfying experience, a state of being happy, subjective well-being, the opposite of sadness, a state of being satisfied that something is good or right. One alarming and surprising definition I encountered was: Happiness is the subject of debate on its meaning! It seems that we really do not accurately understand what happiness really is.

Happiness is often included as a component of well-being. Well-being is defined as a state of being comfortable, healthy and happy or the experience of health, happiness and prosperity. We understand what healthy means, we understand prosperity but very few of us have ever given much thought to what happiness really means.

If everything we do is because we want to be happy, we honestly need to know more about this mysterious desired emotional state. The Buddha said that we as humans have two basic wishes, to be happy and to be free of suffering. So these are both very important aspirations that motivate the majority of our behavior throughout our lives.

While happiness may be the subject of debate on its meaning, one thing I am sure we can agree on, is that it is a pleasant feeling that we experience and that the majority of us prefer. Very few of us wake up in the morning and say to ourselves that we want to have a life full of unhappiness and suffering. So naturally, happiness is a preferred feeling. It is something that we seek, search for or strive to attain. Well, most of us don't go out and seek unhappiness in what we do; we tend to have an aversion to unhappiness or suffering and tend to move away from it as much as possible.

The media tend to distort our meaning of happiness as seen in their relentless efforts to advertise products and services that promise to make us happy. From anti-aging creams that promise to make us look young to luxury goods to satisfy our need for status and prop up our self-worth, the list is endless, but do they really make us happy?

Every year the World Happiness Report ranks the world's happiest countries using statistical analysis. When we don't find our country is at least in the top 10, we feel that we must be doing something wrong, or it must be the government, economy, environment or social welfare system that is to blame. Will changing countries make us happier?

The Science behind Happiness

Who do you think is happier, a lottery winner or a paraplegic? Most people would instinctively say the lottery winner of course. A classic 1978 USA study (Brickman et al. 1978) compared 22 lottery winners to 22 who did not win any money (the control group) and to 29 people who were paralyzed due to accidents. Research showed that within a couple years both paraplegics and lottery winners return to their baseline level of happiness. This means that tragedy does not stop us from being happy and great luck does not keep us happy. The lottery winners reported getting less enjoyment from simple pleasures in everyday life like having breakfast or talking with a friend. The control group did not differ significantly from the lottery winners. Winning the lottery did not increase happiness as they thought and experiencing a catastrophic accident didn't make people as unhappy as they thought. The thrill or happiness of winning a lottery will eventually wear off, same as the shock of unhappiness after a tragedy.

Another study (Kuhn et al. 2008) of Dutch lottery winners showed similar findings. The researchers found that people have a set point of happiness, like a thermostat. When they experience a major event like winning a lottery or becoming paralyzed, their thermostat may temporarily move up or down but over time, it returns to its usual setting.

Finally, it is also interesting to note that Aristotle's view of happiness differs from the Buddhist view. While Aristotle claimed that happiness is the central purpose in life and a goal in itself, the Buddhist view is that it is something we already have and does not have to be achieved.

WE ARE NOT AS HAPPY AS WE WOULD LIKE TO BE

Do not desire happiness, because it creates only
unhappiness and nothing else.

— Osho

*O*ur misguided efforts to identify what happiness is and our futile attempts to achieve it, often lead us into states of increasing frustration and sadness. The inability of many of us to deal with unhappiness and tragedy in our lives has lead to increasing rates of drug and alcohol addictions, suppressed emotions, stress, anxiety, depression and many other psychological problems.

Mankind has progressed immensely with numerous technological advances. The advent of computers, the internet, smart phones, electric vehicles, lithium batteries, renewable energy and medical advances are just some of the many achievements.

Unfortunately, although we now have many more comforts in life, can now live much longer and have more opportunities, these technological improvements have not coincided with any real dramatic increases in our levels of happiness. In fact, statistics show that the exact opposite has occurred, we are certainly not as happy as we would expect or like to be. The truth is there has been very little progress in happiness.

This is becoming very evident as studies have found that up to half of the general population will suffer from a major psychological disorder at some time in their lives. Millions around the globe suffer from addiction, substance abuse and self-destructive behavior. Half of us will seriously contemplate suicide at some point in our lives. More than half of absenteeism at work has been attributed to stress. Most of us will experience a chronic feeling of being unsatisfied many times during our lives and very few of us can really say that we are always happy and fulfilled. These are staggering statistics.

Over the last forty years in every wealthy country on the planet, there has been a startling increase in depression. This illness is now ten times more prevalent than it was in 1960. Depression is really threatening to become the plague of the 21st century. Not only are we not as happy in recent times, but we are now much more depressed.

It is common to hear people comment and say "that's life" when something goes wrong. This implies that it is common knowledge to most people that a lasting form of happiness is just not possible in life. According to Buddhist science however, this is only a distorted view. A sustained source of happiness is possible but one has to know where to look to find it.

It takes courage and wisdom to identify a problem and recognize where there is a need for improvement. As we can surely see, the world is full of suffering and happiness is becoming very difficult to find. Everywhere we look, someone is dealing with problems in their life. We will soon learn how important it is to identify this problem in order to initiate the process of transformation in our mind.

The Science behind Unhappiness

There have been several research organizations and scientific experiments and surveys made on measuring levels of happiness and well-being in the world. Here are just a few of the many studies on our unfortunately declining state of happiness.

An interesting study made in 2012, published in the Journal of Affected Disorders (Brandon et al. 2012) evaluated the effect of modernization on the current epidemic of depression and found that several factors that may contribute to poor physical and mental health, especially to depression include malnourishment, a sedentary lifestyle deficient in sunlight, lack of sufficient sleep and social isolation.

As digital media has increased, adolescents spend less time interacting with each other personally. They have less time for socializing with friends or going to parties. In fact a study made in 2019, (Twenge et al., 2019) comparing adolescents in the 1980s to those in the 2010s, found that on average they now spend at least an hour less each day interacting face to face than they did in the 1980s. There has been a significant shift in social interaction going from face to face social contact to online activities, but as a result, it is coinciding with declining happiness.

Other studies on digital media and young adults have found a reported sense of lower well-being for those who spend a lot of time on digital media. (Booker et al., 2015); (Lin et al., 2016); (Twenge & Campbell, 2018). A couple examples include girls spending 5 or more hours a day on social media are three times more likely to be depressed than non-users, and heavy internet users (vs. light users) are twice as likely to be unhappy. Some studies have shown that activities linked to cell phones and digital media lead to more unhappiness and activities that are not linked to technology, lead to more happiness.

A study of 1000 adults (Tromholt,2017) who were instructed to randomly cease using social media for a week or to continue using in normally, found that those who gave it up reported more happiness and suffered less depression at the end of the week.

A study on college students in 2018 (Hunt et al.,2018) who were told to limit their social media time to 30 minutes a day and only 10 minutes a session, found that they reported less loneliness and depression over the next few weeks.

The General Social Survey which has been measuring social trends among Americans since 1972 indicates long-term declines in the level of happiness and increased unhappiness especially from 1988 to present times (Twenge et al., 2016).

The World Happiness Report in 2019 reported several research studies that showed sharp increases in depression, self-harm and thoughts about suicide especially amongst adolescents since 2010. They also indicated that negative feelings such as worry, sadness and anger have been rising around the world, up 27 percent from 2010 to 2018. This has resulted in an epidemic of addictions and self-harm behavior (Twenge, 2019).

THE FIRST NOBLE TRUTH

What is the noble truth of suffering? It is the
suffering of birth, the suffering of old age, the
suffering of sickness, the suffering of death, the
suffering of separation from loved ones, the
suffering of facing unwanted phenomena, and the
suffering of not getting what one is seeking. In
brief, every aspect of the five aggregates is
suffering.

—The Buddha

*I*n this section, we will go over the First Noble Truth in much
more detail than we did when we first introduced it as the first of
the Four Noble Truths. The Truth of Dukkha or suffering was part of the
first teaching that the Buddha made and he emphasized it because it
needed to be fully understood and internalized. He highlighted a
fundamental truth of our existence that suffering or dissatisfaction is a
part of human life. Like a truly skilled physician, the Buddha precisely
identified and dissected a common illness that is common to all of us.

The origin of the word "*dukkha*" came from the ancient Aryans who
brought the Sanskrit language to India and they were a nomadic horse-
and-cattle breeding people who travelled in horse or ox-drawn carts or
carriages. The prefix "*du*" means bad and "*kha*" is originally a word for
hole, in particular an axle hole of an Aryan carriage. Together "*du-kkha*"
meant "a bad axle hole." As we know an unbalanced and poorly rounded
axle hole results in a very uncomfortable ride, hence its relation to a form
of discomfort or suffering.

The term "*dukkha*" as we mentioned before has been translated in the
West to mean "suffering" but in Buddhist science it has a much wider
range of meaning and can refer to anything from pain, discomfort,

misery, distress, unease, stress, dissatisfaction, imperfection or even incompleteness.

Part I of this book is primarily about understanding the reality of our unhappiness. Yes, at first glance, quite a morbid, depressing topic, but as I mentioned before, a much needed positive step to initiate the process of transformation in our mind at the start of our journey to discovering the secrets of happiness.

For most of us, our natural tendency is to ignore suffering, push it away, avoid and suppress it, and really if we can help it, not give it much thought at all. Our culture generally teaches us to keep this truth deep in our minds most of the time, in a place where it is kept far from our sight. For us, suffering is negative and we try our best to avoid seeing it, even though we are constantly experiencing it. We do not want to accept our true character, the fact that life is impermanent, continually changing and has unavoidable and inevitable suffering. According to Buddhist science, this is termed ignorance, is not wise and leads to unnecessary suffering.

Through the First Noble Truth, Buddha first asks us not only to see the momentary and suffering character of the world, but also to have tolerance in accepting suffering as a natural component of life, not as a negative aspect. Only then will we have the capacity to work towards the solution of discovering happiness. If we can recognize the character of worldly pleasures as suffering, transitory and illusory, the grip of our ego will loosen and afflictions of our mind will subside spontaneously. The ability to see and internalize the sufferings of the world without being overwhelmed by them will only come through proper understanding, determination, and strength of the heart. It also most certainly requires transformation of the mind and that is where Middle Way Mind Training can play an important role.

However, Buddhism also teaches, that while the true character of our human world is suffering, how it affects us depends on our way of perceiving and feeling it. For people who have non-virtuous emotions and negative habitual patterns, it causes unhappiness, while for those who have virtuous ones, it causes happiness.

According to Buddhist science, there are three root sufferings of living beings: ordinary suffering, suffering produced by change, and the pervasive suffering of conditioning. Although we may temporarily fulfill our worldly desires, physical, emotional or mental suffering is inevitable and unavoidable.

There are eight major sufferings particular to human beings. They are the four major experiences of suffering of human life: the suffering of the process of taking birth, of old age, of sickness, and of dying and death. They are accompanied by four secondary sufferings of human life: the sufferings of worry about facing harsh situations, about separation from loved ones and desirable things, about not achieving what one wishes, and about encountering unwanted situations.

Let's discuss the three root types of dukkha according to Buddhist science.

Dukkha-dukkha

Dukkha-dukkha is the ordinary suffering of the body and mind that is associated with unpleasant feelings. It refers to any physical and emotional pain or discomfort that we as humans experience in our lives. It stems from the reality that we all are born, we all age, we eventually get sick, and then we die. Even though we realize this fact intellectually, our common response is usually aversion to these unpleasant experiences and that creates this suffering.

A newborn baby cries when it is born and is obviously in a state of distress or discomfort in its first moments during birth. This is our first experience of suffering as we all undergo birth. Many of us suffer when a loved one passes away or when we get a terminal disease or even as we ourselves begin to age and we see our first grey hairs and wrinkles. All of these inevitable processes are common to us as humans and every one of us will experience them at some point in our lives. Other examples of this type of suffering are injuries, diseases and psychological issues like depression, stress, loneliness, emotional pain and sorrow.

Viparinama-dukkha

Viparinama-dukkha is the suffering of change that results from our response to pleasant experiences as we crave for them to continue. It refers to the suffering that arises from our inability to accept change. When pleasant or happy experiences cease, this is unpleasant for us.

Even the most pleasurable things, no matter how enjoyable or blissful, are not lasting, and they all fade away.

Take your favorite desert as a simple example. When you crave for a slice of chocolate cake and take your first bite, it tastes delicious. When you reach for a second piece, it tastes good but not as good as the first. After a few more pieces, your craving for the cake changes to aversion; you get sick of it and don't even want to see it anymore. Another example: you have been craving for a new car, you have saved for it for a long time and once you finally buy it, you have a wonderful, pleasant feeling. After a few weeks, this feeling fades, and soon you start craving for a newer model with more features, and on and on it goes.

This type of dukkha demonstrates the imperfection and incompleteness of pleasant moments, and how they are ultimately unsatisfying. People cling to pleasurable experiences and feel sad or experience negative mental states when they pass, and they cannot accept the truth of their impermanence.

Viparinama-dukkha is related to the profound human experience that many things in life cannot be owned or possessed forever. Material things, people, and situations often change and can often be lost. Examples include material wealth that can be lost, valuable objects can be destroyed or deteriorate such as a car or house. Friendships can start in good faith and then end. Positive feelings, such as warmth, trust and intimacy can often change to painful feelings after a breakup in a relationship.

Samkhara-dukkha

The first two sufferings we discussed, ordinary suffering and suffering produced by change, are easier to understand than Samkhara-dukkha, which is the pervasive suffering of conditioning. It requires a deeper appreciation of Buddhist science.

The suffering of conditioned reality is associated with an inherent phenomenon, associated with each moment of our existence. When we are born, many things are out of our control, we inherit genes that constitute our body composition and inherit diseases, so we are conditioned by something which is out of our control. This brings a degree of uncertainty and unreliability.

Buddhist philosophy teaches that as long as we wander in this human realm with a biological body, we always have the potential for many things to go wrong such as to get sick, to be caught in a pandemic that suddenly arises, injured in a car accident or killed in a war that starts to name just a few examples. We are always to some extent vulnerable. We are dependent on many things and this conditioning brings with it this type of suffering. As this conditioned state is imperfect and inherent, it is a fabric of reality or a statement of how things actually are. Most of us do not realize our inherent nature and constantly undergo this type of pervasive suffering. It is a basic un-satisfactoriness due to the reality that all forms of life are changing, are conditioned by a variety of factors beyond our control, that everything that arises, passes away and decays, or lacks any stable core or substance. This suffering that we experience creates a sense that things never measure up to our expectations or standards.

The First noble truth is a call to become aware of the negative aspects of life and to be able to detect and identify them. Only if we understand these types of dukkha, will we be able to uproot, remove and overcome them. The method Buddhists use for this are techniques of meditation and mindfulness, analytical thinking with sharp discerning, as well as intellectual activity and development. Even negative feelings are impermanent and can be transformed into positive ones through personal growth and development and mind training.

We often feel that we are the only one suffering, and frequently ask ourselves why is it happening to me? The universal truth of suffering is common to everyone. No matter how rich we are, how famous we are, how successful we are or how many friends or loved ones we have, dukkha is a common aspect we as humans all share. The positive side of this reality is that we do not have to feel that we are alone in our suffering. Everyone on this planet is in the same boat as us, floating on the same ocean.

PART I: IDENTIFYING THE REALITY OF OUR UNHAPPINESS

PART II

THE CAUSE OF UNHAPPINESS

There is no fear for one whose mind is not filled
with desires.

– The Buddha

OUR FUTILE SEARCH FOR

HAPPINESS

All joy in this world comes from wanting others
to be happy, and all suffering in this world comes
from wanting only oneself to be happy.

— Shantideva

In Part I, we focused on identifying the reality of our unhappiness as a part of our human nature. We discussed how dukkha or suffering is in many ways with us throughout our lives and being able to accept this reality is important for us to move on to developing our understanding of happiness. In Part II, which begins here, our aim, is to discover the true cause of our suffering.

I hope we can all now appreciate that the world is full of suffering. Everywhere we turn, we can see it clearly before our eyes. Friends get into arguments and turn to enemies, relationships fall apart, wars begin, people do not achieve what they want, businesses fail, people get cancer and other diseases, we age, friends and relatives die, disappointments occur in life, in situations and with people as well as so many other sources of suffering.

But why are we so unhappy? What actually causes this unpleasant feeling we call unhappiness?

It may be better to start with the way we approach happiness. We all have a tendency to look for it or to search for it. It has become a goal to achieve and is an inherent motivation in everything we attempt to do. But herein lies the problem. According to Buddhist science, our view or approach to happiness is distorted. We fail to see reality the way it really is.

A common formula for achieving happiness is to look for ways to make ourselves happy. Most of us are unsatisfied with many aspects of who we are, what we have achieved or where we are at, and we desperately desire to change our situation. We instill fixed ideas in our minds that constitute a plan for attaining the happiness that we crave and when our plan fails it becomes a reason for why we are unhappy. When we analyze ourselves, most of us hold onto such a life plan that includes a collection of our dreams, our goals or our ambitions.

Remember what Aristotle said, everything we do, we do for happiness. We are all seeking it, in everything that we do. It also implies that we have not found it. We do however; convince ourselves, that there is a way to achieve it, with what I call our perceived formula for happiness.

If I were _X_, had _Y_, and achieved _Z_, this would equal (=) happiness for me.

Let's take a look at some common examples that we commonly use. If I were rich, famous, smart, better looking, talented are just some of the few words that could fill the X blank. If I had more money, a better place to live, a great idea, a different relationship, a better job could all fill the Y blank. If I achieved a college degree, a better position, fame, or great wealth could all fill the Z blank.

As you can see, we make the mistake of predicting we will be happy when....... this or that happens.   When we retire, when we make a million dollars, when we win the lottery, when we find our soul mate, when we buy a nicer house, when we buy a better car, when we finish our degree, and when we get a better paid position, we will be happy and the list goes on and on and on.

The truth is, and the science even backs this up, we are always wrong. We are never as happy as we predicted we would be. We may be wrong a million times, yet we still continue to do it. We turn a blind eye to the actual reality. Why we persist in pursuing the very things that fail to bring us happiness is a core issue in Buddhist science. Daniel Gilbert a professor of psychology at Harvard University has researched this topic to great extent (Gilbert and Wilson, 2005). Almost all our actions such as decisions to have children, to buy a house or get a better paying job are based on predictions of the emotional consequences of these events. The imagination of our mind however, often leads us astray. Gilbert and his collaborator Tim Wilson refer to an "impact bias" that we have, meaning the gap between what we predict and what we ultimately experience, constituting the error we make in our estimation of the intensity and duration of the emotions we expect.

We keep assuming that because material possessions aren't bringing us happiness, they're the wrong things, rather than recognizing that the pursuit itself is futile. When we reach a certain material goal, such as making a certain amount of money, we find it doesn't bring us the happiness we thought it would, so we assume we haven't earned enough and we probably need to earn more. Likewise, the Mercedes is not enough, it must be the Ferrari, my partner is not exciting enough, so I should get a new one. We refuse to see the reality that regardless of what we achieve in the pursuit of things or experiences in our external world, it is never going to bring about an enduring happiness. Buddhist science teaches us that our perceived outcome from this pursuit is only a delusion.

As humans, we also have a common flaw that makes us prone to a lot of misery. Our strong misguided belief that we are special and unique often makes us blind to other's advice. We tend to self-teach ourselves rather than learn from other's experiences.

Our existing emotional condition also heavily influences our predictions of the future. Our brains often fall victim to a wide range of biases that cause our predictions of the future (as well as our memories of the past) to be inaccurate. Because of these mental errors, it is remarkably difficult to predict what will really make us feel happy. Our lack of awareness of how our mind works, leads often to our brain "filling in" all sorts of missing information each day. We make assumptions about things that we predict, based on the previous experiences we have had or heard about before. As we will learn shortly, our memories can also be great deceivers when making future assumptions, which can lead us to make the wrong decisions.

Think about it for a minute. We dream about buying a new car, we save up for it for years, then when we finally buy it, yet the thrill of ownership fades away very quickly. In no time we are back to where we started, craving for the next best thing. In a few weeks, we may see that our neighbor has a better newer model, and our happiness gets quickly deflated or even turns to jealousy. We construct the idea in our mind that we need a better, newer car and again believe that it will make us happier. Another example, we fall in love, we believe we could not have found a better partner but in time though, the intense feeling wears off and we start to notice our partner's faults and perhaps start to feel unsatisfied. We may begin to argue and even ask ourselves why our partner is not the same as when we met them.

In many ways, our minds are caught up in a rat race. We are heavily influenced by what we see or hear. We also naturally compare our level of happiness to the delusion of what happiness should be. We look at others who we assume are happier than us. We look up to and aspire to be like the rich, the successful or the famous. They become our role models. We admire business men, famous actors and celebrities. We constantly compare ourselves to others and we convince ourselves that their lives are much better than ours. The brutal truth is that others are suffering the same as we are. Billionaires are not free of suffering, nor are famous actors. They all have the same core problems that we do. If they have a lot of money, they worry about losing it or crave to accumulate more, or if they have world-wide fame they suffer when they do not get the attention they had before. As we surely know, many rich and famous people are not happy at all and frequently suffer from depression or have contemplated or committed suicide.

We fall for these delusions all the time and make these fatal mistakes over and over again. If the achievement of our goals has the high expectation that it will sustain our desire for happiness, we are looking down the wrong path. In other words, by doing these very actions, we are constantly setting ourselves up for unhappiness.

The underlying conclusion to this behavior and the reason that we are not happy, according to Buddhist science, is because most of us suffer from a basic flaw. That basic flaw is that we are looking for sustained happiness in places where it cannot be found.

THE EXTERNAL WORLD

We can never obtain peace in the outer world until
we make peace with ourselves.

— His Holiness the 14th Dalai Lama

*I*n the last sections we alluded to the probable conclusion that we tend to look for happiness in places where it cannot be found or in places that it at least cannot be sustained. What do these places usually all have in common? They are all part of the external world around us.

Let's examine this external world and how our mind makes sense of it all. Remember that all sensory input from our outside world is processed in some way in our mind. Our relationship with the external world, for most of us, is that it is the only source where we feel that we can find happiness. The external world where we usually seek happiness from generally includes material possessions, our relationships, our work, as well as all our experiences. Our lives are full of attempts to manipulate our external environment to achieve all our goals, dreams and ambitions which we believe will bring us happiness. However, if our happiness really depends on the external environment, we are setting ourselves up for a great deal of unhappiness. The reason being is that we cannot control the externals. What do we mean by this? Let's looks at a few examples.

Our external world is full of factors which we really cannot control. If we say to ourselves for example, that we will only be happy if it is sunny outside, we will probably be very disappointed most days, especially if we live in a rainy climate like England or Ireland. Obviously, we cannot control the weather. If we can only be happy if we have perfect relationships with people around us, we will have a difficult time as we cannot control situations where our friends may betray us, or our partner may fall in love with someone else. Our external environment is always changing. We cannot control the economy, we don't know if a war will erupt, or the stock markets will crash, or new technology makes our inventions obsolete or our business goes bankrupt. We can only control our health to a certain extent. We do not know if we will catch an infectious disease, get cancer, have a serious accident or get Alzheimer's. So many things can happen in our external world that are beyond our control and that is what we have to come to grips with as human beings. As we all know, our plans and goals often do not materialize the way we expect, so being too strongly attached to them, can lead to unnecessary disappointment and unhappiness.

Buddhist wisdom teaches that there is no sense grasping onto our external world for dear life, when the reality is that it is constantly changing and out of our control.

The other side of the argument is that there are so many things and experiences in our external world where we do find examples of happiness. The birth of a child, the success of landing a great job, our wedding day, strong friendships, the love from our family are just a few of the joys we get in our lives from our external environment.

Buddhist science does not claim that there are no sources of happiness in our external world, only that they are not sustainable, and eventually in an untrained mind will lead in one way or another to dukkha or a sense of dissatisfaction or suffering. The happiness of witnessing the birth of your child can change to heartbreak when your child gets a terminal disease or becomes a disappointment for you in later years. A beautiful relationship with a soul mate often turns into a bitter divorce. A disagreement with a friend can turns them into your worst enemy. We have all experienced many of these outcomes or others that are similar. We have already seen that we are not as happy as we expect when we crave and achieve material possessions. Science also shows us that those who make money a high priority in their lives have a greater risk for depression, anxiety and low self-esteem. Success and fame certainly do not guarantee happiness as we can see from many celebrities and their battles with drug or alcohol abuse or even suicide.

Along with every external experience, there is an underlying dissatisfaction. That is what Buddhist science teaches. Are we supposed to push away all material possessions, the people around us or the activities we experience? No, we certainly need material things and people in our lives in order to survive in this world. Buddhism only conveys the wisdom that we should not grasp and hold on to these things at all costs because everything in our external world changes and much of it is beyond our control. We can still live a happy and fulfilled life, realizing life as it actually is and not what we would like it to be. Ultimately we will save ourselves a lot of unhappiness if we accept this reality.

I hope you have come to the realization that lasting happiness is not something we should search for outside of ourselves through external sources. If we cannot get happiness from our external world, then where can we find it? To find the answer means we need to turn inwards, into the depths of the mind itself.

THE PRESENT MOMENT

Realize deeply that the present moment is all you
have. Make the Now the primary focus of your
life.

— Eckhart Tolle

*H*ave you ever given any thought to where your mind is usually at? A group of psychologists at Harvard did and found out that our untrained mind wanders almost fifty percent of the time. That means that almost half our lives are spent dwelling on the past or dreaming or worrying about the future. This astonishing scientific study revealed that half our lives are being played out or actually wasted, outside of the present moment. This means that we are not really living one half of our lives. The implications of this are profound. Just imagine if we could learn to train our minds to live more in the present. We could all accomplish so much more and become much more aware of the present reality around us. By not being aware of the present moment, we miss so much of life that passes us by unnoticed. It is no wonder we tend to be much more prone to getting into accidents, our ability to listen effectively is reduced and decision-making skills are substantially compromised when our minds are elsewhere than in the present moment. Learning to savor each moment as we live it is a skill that can certainly be trained and improved.

As we begin to take the first preliminary steps and begin to focus inwards instead of out to our external environment in order to understand happiness, it will become increasingly important to be able to take notice of or observe our thoughts. We live in an age of distraction. The phone is always ringing, we are bombarded with emails and texts, advertisements capture our attention in all media, not to mention the thousands of thoughts that pass through our minds continuously. Our lives are in a constant state of chaos. We are always doing something, always much too busy. There is very little time for relaxation or time out from our hectic lifestyle. What we do not realize though, is one of life's sharpest paradoxes. A happy future hinges on our ability to pay attention to the present.

The present moment is the only time that we are alive. All life unfolds in the present. To really appreciate this fact, we need to understand what is meant by the past and the future. When we recollect experiences or moments in our past, we are actually only piecing together stories, using our memory and we are doing this of course while being in the present. When we dream, plan or worry about the future, again we are painting a picture of what we anticipate but what has not been realized, again while being in the present.

Even though life presents itself in the present, we often let it slip away. While time passes by unobserved, we squander away a large proportion of our lives when we worry about the future (what has not happened) or ruminate about the past (what is already gone and cannot be changed).

According to that Harvard study in 2010 (Killingsworth and Gilbert, 2010), psychologists Matthew Killingsworth and Daniel Gilbert experimented on 2,250 subjects, recording what they were doing during random moments, what their mind was focused on, and what made them most happy. They found that people were happiest when they were focused on doing things in the present moment and even though their minds were wandering half the time, this activity consistently made them less happy. It was interesting to note that their study concluded that even thinking or daydreaming about something pleasant tended to make them more miserable. While human beings have the unique ability to reflect on the past and learn from it, as well as plan for the future or imagine things that may never happen, this same ability is often used in non-productive ways and can be quite detrimental to happiness.

As Buddhist science has taught us for 2500 years, a wandering mind is an unhappy mind. Our human cognitive achievement comes unfortunately at an emotional cost. Regretting the past or worrying about the future takes away a lot of our happiness. The reality is that we cannot suffer the past or the future because in reality they do not exist. What we are really experiencing as suffering is only our memory and imagination.

If we are not in the present moment, we are either looking forward to the uncertainty of the future or dwelling back on pain and regret from the past.

It seems that people are much happier when living and experiencing things in the present moment, than when their mind is wandering in the past or the future. This has been further presented in research data from 15,000 people across 80 countries of various ages and income levels by Matthew Killingsworth. His studies suggest that mind wandering has a much more significant effect on our happiness than external factors such as income, marital status or education and that experience brings more happiness than possessions (Killingsworth et al, 2020).

Science today is slowly catching up and confirming what Buddhism has been teaching for over 2500 years. As I hope you are slowly starting to realize, happiness has a lot to do with our state of mind.

STRESS IS CREATED BY OUR MIND

Stress is caused by being here but wanting to be there.

— Eckhart Tolle

We have seen in the previous chapter that our inability to live in the present moment can affect our level of happiness. Being unable to accept the present moment as it is, leads us to a state of unhappiness that we all know very well, stress.

It seems that everyone is stressed out these days. We complain about stress in the workplace, the increasing and unrealistic workloads that are constantly placed on us, the strained relationships with our boss or co-workers, or the never-ending demands from our customers. We face stress in our personal and family lives when we have to deal with difficult partners or conflicts with family members and friends as well as misbehaving children. At times it seems there is no escape. Most of us accept stress as something we have to learn to live with. When stress is repeated or prolonged it becomes chronic and a syndrome called burnout can occur, which often leads to apathy, anxiety, depression and lethargy. Stress and burnout are becoming major problems in the modern workplace and are now the leading causes of absenteeism. The physical effects of stress include fatigue, heart problems, backache, headaches and many other related diseases.

When asked where this stress is coming from or who is to blame, we are quick to point a finger at anyone in the nearest vicinity and in the line of fire, except of course ourselves. While stress seems to be a common subject of conversation and may even sit on top of our list of daily concerns, it seems most of us know very little where it really stems from.

What actually causes stress? Most of us can quickly name a certain external situation or a specific person that is the cause of our stress. However, situations and people are all external factors. Does stress really come from the external environment, outside of us? Most of us, feel that this is the case but is it really true and do we have any choice in the matter?

Buddhist science teaches that stress is internal and only created by our mind. If stress was caused by the external environment, then everyone would get stressed out from the same person or the same situation. We know this is not the case. We may say our boss stresses us out, but as we know, not everyone will feel the same way towards him or her. The same goes for certain situations in our lives, which may cause us intense stress but for another person they have no effect. Here we come to another very important realization. The person or situation is not the cause of our stress; it is our mind's response to it. So our mind is actually creating the stress. Stress is created by our mind.

Once we can accept that the stress that we are feeling is not due to external factors and we stop blaming things or people outside of ourselves, we will be in a much better position to initiate a dramatic transformation in our mind and reduce our levels of stress significantly.

What happens to us during a stressful event? Let's compare it to a common situation in life. Say we are late and running to catch a train or bus. We know that we just have to catch this one; otherwise we will be late for our meeting. As we frantically sprint to attempt to catch it on time, just as we get there, the doors close right in front of us. Most of us will automatically react and cry out "No!" Then we will then look around in disbelief and turn towards the driver or conductor with often an angry look as if the driver intended to close the doors on purpose. We may then spend the next few minutes or more in a negative state of mind, going over the unpleasant situation again and again in our minds. This event may even put us in a bad mood for the entire morning or afternoon.

So, what actually happened in our mind during this stressful event? We wanted something to happen (catch the bus) but something else happened (the doors closed in front of us). We rejected what took place. We didn't want to accept the reality that we missed it. Then anger arose and we fixated on the problem, exaggerating it (the driver did it to me on purpose), which produced unnecessary tension, pain and suffering. We got trapped in a negative cycle of mind. This tension between what we wanted to happen and what really happened created the stress we experienced.

In this situation and in many similar to it, our minds are like untrained wild horses. We overreact to situations irrationally rather than respond to them reasonably. We go through life with the brakes on, fighting against reality as it unfolds before us, wanting to be somewhere else than where we actually are. Our natural reaction is to blame our external environment. As you already know though, we cannot control the external environment. It is constantly changing. That is the reality of life. That is the reality that we need to accept.

A Buddhist scientific approach means training the mind to accept every situation with a solution-oriented mind without externalizing the problem. As difficult situations in life are always bound to occur, and are unavoidable, we need to confront them in a realistic way. We need to respond positively, not negatively to a stressful situation. Buddhist wisdom teaches that we should look at difficult people or situations as a unique opportunity to train our patience. When we think about it, patience is the nature of acceptance. When we cultivate patience, we learn to accept reality as it is. Difficulties will always be encountered in life, that is a given. It is how we react to them that matters. Our mind creates our reality, so to deal with stress, we first need to recognize or identify what is happening in the mind. We can only change the external environment so much as we know, but we can completely and utterly transform our mind. Why is it so difficult to stay with a peaceful and happy mind? Because delusions of attachment such as anger arise and steal away our attention and then we lose our peaceful state because we become agitated. Our anger in our mind, created by our inability to accept reality as it is, is creating our stress.

If we go back to the missing the bus example again, a wise approach would be after the doors shut in front of us, to accept the situation as it is. I was late, I missed the bus. It is no one else's fault but mine. The solution is I will either catch the next bus and accept being late or find an alternative way to get to my destination faster perhaps by taxi so I can arrive at my meeting on time.

As I am sure you are all saying to yourself now, this calm, cool and collective response rather than reacting irrationally and crazy is obviously logical but is much easier said than done. We have a lot of habitual patterns engrained in our minds over the course of our lives. As we also learned at the beginning of this book, transforming the mind involves much more than just an intellectual understanding, it requires internalization and this means sufficient training of the mind.

CAN WE TRUST OUR MIND?

When sitting in meditation, say, "That's not my
business!" with every thought that comes by.

— Ajahn Chah

*I*t seems an odd question to ask ourselves, whether we can trust our own mind, as most of us consider our mind to be our internal master, a sacred temple of refuge or our personal and reliable intimate guide throughout all of our life. Surely our mind plans and chooses what direction we take, tells us what is right and wrong, makes decisions and comes up with all our great ideas, right? I mean, who else can we trust, if we cannot trust our own mind? Certainly, if we don't have trust in our mind, we have probably lost our mind and we would be considered a lunatic or to say the least, someone who must be in some way psychologically unbalanced, deranged or psychotic.

While modern psychologists or psychotherapists target their treatments and methods specifically on those with concrete psychological problems or mental disorders, the science of Buddhist psychology has a much broader approach. The Buddha taught that due to our ignorance of the way reality really is, we are all in some way suffering from delusion. Our untrained minds are not seeing reality the way it really is and trusting such minds one hundred percent, is one of our greatest fatal mistakes.

While thinking and planning and remembering are necessary functions in our lives, our thoughts and ideas about issues are generally always more one-sided than we realize and should be taken more lightly rather than rigidly. Moreover, our thoughts and emotions are constantly changing. The problem is that we usually completely believe them and react accordingly. Buddhist science however, teaches us about the nature of thoughts, to question them and ask ourselves whether we are absolutely certain that what we think or what our opinions are, are actually in touch with reality. Strong beliefs in our own thoughts and opinions can lead us to make the wrong decisions. No matter how strongly we believe our side of the story, there are always other ways to looks at the same thing or other points of view.

Take for example a terrorist who is convinced that his act as a suicide bomber is the correct decision to make, or Adolf Hitler who was convinced that Jews had to be exterminated to create his New World Order. Those are of course examples of very extreme situations, but even in our everyday lives we often get caught up with strong opinions that are later proved to be completely wrong. Our minds can be easily manipulated by our emotions and those around us or by memories of past experiences. We may have strong undeserved prejudices on an entire certain race just because we had one bad experience with one individual in the past.

Our mind constructs views of what we think is right or wrong. As we learned at the start of this book about the Beginners Mind, a lot of our suffering comes from how strongly we hold on to our beliefs, opinions and thoughts. Buddhist science teaches an analytical approach and forces us to ask ourselves, "Is this really true?" or "How do we really know that this is true?"

Training the mind through specific meditation techniques teaches us that through stillness and inner peace, we are able to observe the transience and imperfection of our thought processes. We observe how thoughts arise like clouds in the sky and pass away in the same way. We learn to not cling onto our opinions or strong beliefs for dear life, as they are prone to change just like everything else.

The Buddha taught that mind consciousness is always continuing, like a stream of water. Mind consciousness is our "working" consciousness that makes judgments and plans; it is the part of our consciousness that worries and analyzes. Thinking, worrying, and planning take quite a lot of energy. Meditation and mindfulness training methods, which we will learn about in future sections of this book, keep us in the present moment. They allow our mind consciousness to relax, become more aware and let go of wasted energy worrying about the past or predicting the future.

Some scientific conclusions have been found about the way our mind often operates. One of the most damaging flaws is our tendency to think that we are right, even in the face of contradictory evidence. We need to realize that our mind often jumps to conclusions and quickly seeks a solution without seeking alternative answers or exploring other possibilities.

The mind also sees what it wants to see and tends to filter out information that contradicts our view of the world and only allows entry of that which supports it. If you have ever had friends tell you repeatedly that your partner is cheating on you and you were the last to find out, then this is a prime example.

Another flaw is that the mind distorts information so that it can align with our beliefs and attitudes. As we will learn in much more detail in a later chapter, even our memories are often distorted, influenced and reconstructed and can be entirely fabricated, without us even realizing. Many studies have shown that witnesses of a crime that occurred often recall their experience completely differently than what actually in reality happened. Our mind has also been found to make up its own narrative in the absence of information and then convinces itself that something is true.

It seems that we are not really well designed for multi-tasking in our fast-paced world, even though our mind tries to convince us otherwise. Studies have shown that multitasking increases stress and makes us less creative and efficient. Our mind also has a habit to stick to what it is familiar with, even if old ways are no longer working. This pertains to a lot of situations that are not necessarily good for us, such as staying in damaging relationships or accepting bad working conditions.

The beginner's mind has taught us that our mind more often than not, has too much confidence in its abilities, and tends to play the expert. Experts have a habit of blaming their mistakes on outside factors that are out of their control, not on their own thinking. It definitely pays to step back whenever our mind insists it is right because we have always done something that way and look at the situation with a new perspective.

Most of us do not undertake the task or ever even have the opportunity to observe our thoughts in true awareness. Rather, our thoughts tend to influence and control us. Without training, our minds are inundated with constant thoughts, without even our realization. This very lack of awareness makes us prone to often making the wrong decisions or holding wrong views or opinions. Buddhist science postulates that our thoughts are not really us and that we often mistakably associate ourselves or identify solely on that inner ongoing commentator, our mind. If we do not have any control or awareness of our thoughts, then when they arise, we grasp onto them with strong conviction based often on delusions, only to realize later that we made fatal mistakes. As we have seen, most of the science supports the fact that our mind is very malleable and very easily manipulated or prone to delusion. One can only come to the startling conclusion that an untrained mind is a mind that we really cannot trust.

THE SIX SENSE DOORS

Come, live with the doors of the senses guarded,
diligent and mindful, vigilant and mindful, with
the ways of the mind well watched, possessed of a
mind that is awake and observing.

–The Buddha

The Buddha placed a great importance on the way that we open up the mind to the awareness of our external and internal environment and for a very good reason. He taught that there exist six internal sense bases or sense doors, gateways that humans possess. They enable us to connect the world around us to our sensory organs, and allow the entry of everything we consciously can experience. They define the totality of our experience, meaning that every moment of our lives involves experiences that are known by way of one of these sense doors. They include our sight, hearing, smell, taste, touch and thought. While they are essential to allow us to navigate our environment and bring feeling to our experience of the world, they are also unfortunately the source of a lot of our unhappiness.

Each sense door is composed of a sense organ and a sense object and when they come into contact with each other, consciousness is activated and the mind is made aware of the object. If the sense object and sense organ do not come in contact, it is not possible to activate consciousness. For example, our sight is made up of our eyes and visual objects. When our sense organ, the eye comes in contact with its visual object, our sense consciousness is activated, in this case our visual consciousness. This contact allows us to see or to become visually aware of the object.

Hearing is made up of our ears and sound waves. When the ears come in contact with a sound, our auditory consciousness is activated and we are made aware of a sound.

Smell is made up of the sensory organ, the nose and scents and odors. When the nose comes in contact with a scent or an odor, our olfactory consciousness is activated and we are made aware of a smell.

When another sense organ, the taste buds of the tongue come in contact with a taste, our gustatory or taste consciousness is activated and we are made aware of a taste.

Similarly, when our body comes in contact with anything tangible, our tactual consciousness is activated and we are made aware of touch.

Finally, the mind is considered the sixth sense door. If we were to close off all the five previous senses, our thoughts still remain. When we think of something, such as from the past or the future, or when we concentrate on our thoughts or emotions, these thought processes arise in the mind through the mind door, not through seeing, hearing, tasting, touching or smelling. For example, we can imagine the taste of a lemon in our mind without using our tongue sensory organ to actually taste it. In this way, thought is also considered a sense door in Buddhist science. So, when our mind comes in contact with a mental object, our mind consciousness is activated.

The process of activating mind consciousness is most notable when we are shut off from external stimuli such as during meditation. When our mind is concentrating on our breath or thoughts or even emotions such as anger or fear, these thought processes are predominantly through the mind door. We are seeing them not through our eyes or ears but with our mind's sense. The mind door includes our imagination, such as thoughts that we are imagining now or when we retrieve memories from the past or speculate about the future. The mind is considered to be a sixth sense door because it can allow entry of thoughts that originate from within itself without the need for external stimuli. As we know, thoughts constantly arise and pass away in our minds. Without our mind sense door, we would not be even able to even construct abstract ideas or contemplate our existence.

Why did the Buddha find these gateways and the consciousness they activate so important? Because that is the place where all thoughts originate. He stressed the need to be mindful of each stage of our mind process, to guard the sense doors in order to be able to take control of our thoughts. If we can accomplish that, we can certainly eliminate a lot of unnecessary suffering in our lives.

Once any of the sense consciousnesses are activated, the next stage of processing in the mind is perception, whose job is to recognize, such as what smell? what sound? what image? what taste? It also evaluates the sensory information, being influenced by all experiences as well as memories from the past. Perception then gives rise to feelings that we judge. We either like something, dislike it, or are neutral towards it. Buddhist science claims that feelings arise along with associated sensations in the body, which can either be pleasant, unpleasant or neutral. For example, you may hear a song on the radio, your perception identifies it as a song that you have heard before, your mind may identify the song with a particular event in your life in the past and it evokes a feeling in your mind along with sensations in the body. If these feelings and sensations are repeated enough, the mind reacts and constructs conditioned mental formations that can even lead to habitual patterns if the ego gets involved. If the feeling is pleasant the mind reacts with craving, "I like this song", "I want to hear it again", "It reminds me of a happy time in my life" and positive mental formations are imbedded in the mind. If the feeling is unpleasant, the mind reacts with aversion, "I can't stand this song," "It reminds me of a bad time in my life," "I don't want to hear it," and negative mental formations are imbedded in the mind. If the feeling is neutral, "I am indifferent about this song" then no specific feelings of craving or aversion are activated and the song is ignored.

The same process applies to any of the other sense doors. When something arises in the mind, it follows the same pattern: a thought arises, we perceive it, the perception gives rise to feelings and sensations in the body, we judge these feelings as pleasant or unpleasant or neutral, and then we react to those feelings.

The important lesson to learn from our six sense doors is that while they allow the entry of information of the world, they are also subject to manipulation by our mind. We need to understand our experience as it really is, bringing awareness to every moment because without it, we become only creatures of mental conditioning, constantly trying to manipulate our experience in order to increase our pleasure or minimize our pain. It is critical to be mindful throughout this process when our sense doors are open.

The Buddha taught that we need to guard our sense doors and be especially mindful of them, noting what mental states arise, otherwise our untrained mind will lead us to extremes of desire and aversion, both of which have the potential to cause us a great deal of suffering in our lives. Remember from the previous chapter, you cannot trust the mind. Our senses are all influenced by previous experiences, individual preferences, and these also can change with time.

To simplify things, different people have different tastes in food, some are attracted to a smell and some are disgusted by it, some love a type of music, others the opposite. We can crave for the taste of a piece of chocolate cake, thoroughly enjoy the taste of the first piece, then desire another piece, enjoy the taste somewhat less and then perhaps after a third piece, become totally averse to the taste of chocolate cake. We can even lose our desire for it even for future months at a time, based on that experience.

What this implies is that our reaction to information that enters our sense doors is very fluid, is manipulated, subject to change and often may not even be indicative of reality. Someone will see an ordinary wooden stick on a pathway in the night and believe it's a snake because they have an extreme fear of snakes which can evoke a false feeling of fear or panic in that person. Another person feels nothing when they pass the same stick. A particular bad experience with one individual from a certain race can make us racist towards all members of that race, and we can feel anger or aversion every time we see such a person. Does this reflect true reality? No. It is our conditioned mind that reacts to a thought process that is left unchecked. We are being fooled by our mind. So our senses are conditioned and do not always reflect reality. That is why we need to train our minds to be aware of the entire thought process.

So, when we use any of our sense doors such as when we see a visual image, hear a sound, smell an aroma or odor, taste something, touch something or think a thought, we cannot allow our mind to get too caught up with it. We cannot get fixated or captivated by it to such as extent that it gets out of our control. If we leave the mind unattended and uncontrolled, negative mental states such as greed, desire, anger, hatred or disgust will inevitably arise. We then set up the possibility that they can invade and dominate the mind, which can lead to negative habitual mental formations and patterns.

We really need to keep all our six sense doors in check. Just like we wouldn't blindly let strangers in our door without first being aware who they are before we let them in. By monitoring each seed before it enters and grows inside our mind, we can prevent any mental defilement such as greed, desire, anger or aversion to take hold there. As we will learn in future chapters, these are all causes of our unhappiness.

OUR MEMORY IS DISTORTED

We all have memories that are malleable and
susceptible to being contaminated or
supplemented in some way.

— Elizabeth Loftus

I remember as a child, a particular incident that happened to me, that was quite traumatic. Our family was at a lake and my father was playing in waist deep water with my younger brother, swinging him around. I was nearby, wading in shallow water and eventually I got into water over my head, and started drowning. My father was not aware of this, as he was engaged with my brother and I remember that a lifeguard had to pull me out and rescue me. In my younger adult life, when I became a lifeguard myself I would often tell this story as the reason why I became a lifeguard. The strange thing though is that my parents never remembered this incident. When asked about it, they could not recall any time where a lifeguard rescued me. This was a mystery to me because the memory stayed with me my entire life, yet my parents claimed it never happened. Now, after reading a lot of scientific literature on memory, I have to ask myself, did this incident really happen or did my mind just make it up?

People commonly say that they have trouble remembering names or where they put their car keys, and as people age, their memories often get worse and diseases like Alzheimer's may ensue, further degenerating memory with time. There is a lot of research on forgetting, but what research is there on remembering things that never really happened, or remembering things that were different than how they actually happened? One of the most renowned researchers in this field is Elizabeth Loftus, an American research psychologist, who has spent her life studying false memory. She has been involved in many trials including famous court cases for O.J. Simpson, Michael Jackson, Harvey Weinstein, Rodney King and many others.

She has studied hundreds of innocent defendants who were convicted of crimes that they did not commit, and many who even spent decades in prison for the crimes. After DNA testing proved that they were innocent, she found that three quarters of those cases were due to faulty memory by eyewitnesses. While most people believe that memories are just stored like a recording device, with recorded information just called up when you want to play it back, Elizabeth Loftus and her scientific studies have shown that this is just not the case. Memory is not fixed; it can be constructed and reconstructed. It can be changed and many other influences can alter it as well. She found that if you feed suggestive information to someone such as misinformation about an experience they have had, you can distort or contaminate or even change their memory. It seems misinformation is around us everywhere. We can contaminate our memories with misinformation. For example, this can happen if we are asked about an incident that happened to us with strong leading questions or if we talk to other witnesses that give us different information about the incident we witnessed. Even seeing media coverage about the incident opens up the opportunity to distort the memory of the real event. It has been demonstrated when a crime occurs and there are several witnesses, each witness can recall the incident in differing ways that vary tremendously and which may completely deviate from reality. I am sure you may have memories of some event that happened that was shared with your friends and when you get together years later, each of them may recall something significantly different from your recollection.

Elizabeth Loftus has also shown in many experiments that it is possible to plant certain false memories such as a desire for a certain food, which will play out and can affect behavior long after the memories take hold (Bernstein and Loftus, 2009).

We can also lie to ourselves or about ourselves enough that we can honestly begin to believe what we say, even though it may be completely fabricated. It can become our reality and remain engrained in our memory. People can say things with total confidence, include all the intricate details and even display lots of credible emotion, but it can be totally false. Unfortunately, contrary to what we believe, we just cannot distinguish false from true memories. Memory, like thoughts or any of our sensory doors is fluid; it can change with time, be manipulated, conditioned and may not even reflect reality. Memory is prone to embellishment, is very selective and can be distorted by a narrow focus, colored by our feelings, influenced by who we talk to, what we see and what we bring into our minds.

What does our knowledge of the science of memory say about the mind and what can it tell us about happiness? If our memories cannot even be trusted, how can we be sure that we see a true reality? According to Buddhist science, our untrained minds do not see reality as it is and we are all considered to be living under a delusion. Since our mind creates our reality, it can also be the source of our happiness. It really comes down to training the mind to live in the present moment, to be aware and mindful of each thought and event as it presents itself in our lives, to guard our sense doors and emotions very carefully as to not allow our memory to become contaminated. As we will soon see, mind training can help us to see and remember the reality that is truly unfolding before us.

THE MARKS OF OUR EXISTENCE

Devotion to truth is the sole justification of our
existence.

— Mahatma Gandhi

To move towards a deeper understanding of the cause of our unhappiness, we really need to appreciate our human condition and the nature of our reality. The Buddha taught that all phenomena that form our physical world, including all our psychological experiences and mental activities, have three innate characteristics. These three marks of existence, as they are often called, are the basis of the Buddha's wisdom about the world. They are in a way, natural inherent characteristics of our human condition. The marks are common to every single one of us, and there is no escaping them if we have chosen to be a member of the human race.

The three characteristics of our human reality are **suffering**, **impermanence** and **non-self**, which correspond to the Pali words; *dukkha*, *anicca* and *anatta*. At first glance, these three marks of existence seem quite negative and depressing. I mean in simple terms, they infer that we are doomed to suffering, nothing in life is permanent and in reality we have no identity or self. If that is what life is all about then most of us I am sure would rather not hear about it. I mean, our natural reaction is to show aversion, to move away from such thoughts since they are not thoughts we wish to associate with and certainly not very pleasant. But according to the view of Buddhist science, the very essence of our ignorance or lack of understanding of these concepts is the very reason we are suffering in the first place. The three marks of existence really tell us a lot about the nature of our reality as human beings and our ability to be aware of them and understand them are crucial to our investigation of the cause of our unhappiness.

Suffering (*dukkha*)

We are already familiar with the first mark of existence, *dukkha* or suffering as we have covered it in some detail in an earlier chapter as the first of the Four Noble Truths. *Dukkha,* as we know, refers to the realization that our human existence is prone to suffering or dissatisfaction. We learned that *dukkha* is a part of human existence and our efforts to hide from that reality tend to make matters worse. We also create a lot of unnecessary *dukkha* in our lives such as when we crave for things that are unachievable or worry about things that cannot be changed. Since we have investigated *dukkha* or suffering to some lengths already, let's delve into the other two marks of existence; impermanence and non-self.

Impermanence (*anicca*)

The concept of impermanence or *anicca* in the Pali language is also very significant in Buddhist science. We may have heard of the saying, "you can't step into the same river twice." *Anicca* is the concept that everything around us is always changing. Everything in the world is in constant flux. The law of impermanence is a natural phenomenon; everything arises and passes away. One of the reasons we suffer is because we do not accept this reality and we expect things to stay the same or we hold on to things that we will lose. We see this with our own bodies, as they change and age and eventually die, which is certainly not permanent. We see this with our relationships, as they can often change with time; marriage can turn to divorce, friends become enemies or vice versa. We see it with our feelings and opinions that often change with the weather. In fact even those things that we consider permanent like mountains and oceans are also impermanent as they too will eventually erode and change with time. Impermanence teaches us that no matter how much money we accumulate in our lives, no matter how many friends or family members we have, no matter how much success or status we achieve, or how much material wealth we accumulate, we will one day lose it and have to let it all go. It is not permanent just like everything else in the world. The Buddha taught that our attachment to our world and our inability to accept its impermanence is a great source of pain and unhappiness for us.

Non-self (*anatta*)

Another strong sense of attachment that we have is our attachment to our <u>self</u>. In Buddhist science, this concept is considered an illusion as the <u>self</u> in reality does not exist, at least not in the way we think it does. This third mark of our existence is the concept of non-self or *anatta* in the Pali language. This is quite an advanced and profound Buddhist teaching which is often misinterpreted or misunderstood but is one of the greatest causes of our unhappiness. The fact that we cling to a permanent self that in reality does not exist creates many problems for us in our lives, creates a duality that separates us from the world and from others around us, and leads us often to feelings of isolation and loneliness.

We tend to attach fixed identities to our self, and this identity becomes who we are or who we believe we are. For example, we may say we are a teacher, or a writer, but is that really who we are?In life we have many roles; we can be a wife or husband, a mother or father, a friend, a daughter or son, an employee, business person etc., but these are just roles that the mind identifies as our self. These roles are subject to change just like everything else. We can change our profession, marital status and relationships with others, so these identities are not really something inside us that have any permanent continuity. They are not something we can really call a permanent self. We may consider someone an easy-going person, impatient person, difficult person or aggressive person, but even these characteristic labels can often change in that person from one day to the other.

The Buddhist view is that there is no sense of continuity in attaching an identity to a self. When we take away all the labels and identities we associate with as our <u>self</u>, we can see there is no real <u>self</u> left. So, who are we? What part of us can we really say is our <u>self</u>? By conventional reality, without closely analyzing or investigating, we feel very strongly that a self or sense of "I" truly exists and to us there is no argument. We feel that this is true, but upon investigation and close analysis, it is not possible to find what part of us is really our self. If we break our body down, we discover that for example, our hand is not our self and neither is any other part of the body. We cannot really locate the self. Buddhist science indicates that the reality or existence of "I" can only be established within a conventional framework, one which is unanalyzed or unexamined. If we go deeper and search for an essence of "I" by analysis or close examination, we just cannot find it. This is what we call the ultimate reality of non-self.

From the Buddhist point of view, a permanent self is just an illusion that our mind desperately and mistakably grasps onto. Our bodies are continuously changing, evolving; cells are being replaced or lost, thoughts, opinions, and feelings are changing from minute to minute and day to day. We are not the same person physically or even mentally that we were yesterday. Since everything is impermanent and constantly changing, we can view our self as constantly changing. It would be more accurate to refer to ourselves as a process, one that is changing with everything around us. There is really no permanent self we can find in a world that is constantly changing. We will also see in future chapters that we are all interconnected with others and the world around us, as quantum physics is suggesting. We are in fact more like a wave interconnected to a vast ocean.

So, how can an understanding of the three marks of existence help us with happiness in our lives? Well, as I mentioned earlier, the very things we tend to push away are the very things that are creating our unhappiness. The more we accept reality the way it really is, not the way we want it to be, the more we will be able to increase our happiness levels. This means accepting some aspects of *dukkha* or suffering with the human condition as inescapable consequences in our lives. For most of us, this involves acceptance, relinquishing control, letting go and becoming much more flexible and playful with our lives. This is obviously not an easy transformation, and requires quite a lot of awareness and mind training. We all know that planning our lives is subject to so many changes that it makes more sense not to plan too far in advance. Being open to change is our best approach or we will be disappointed a lot of times, especially if we hold on to our plans too tightly. Sticking to a fixed plan can also leave us unable to see new opportunities as they arise and take advantage of them. The path in life changes so frequently because of the natural law of impermanence. If we really understand it, accept it and internalize it, then we can avoid a lot of problems and suffering in the future. Lastly, holding onto the illusion of a fixed and permanent self that does not exist opens up our lives to unnecessary conflicts, obstacles and difficulties. The concepts of impermanence and non-self are so instrumental to our understanding of Buddhist science and discovering why we are unhappy. I have therefore dedicated the next two chapters to go into much more depth on the significance of each of them.

THE NATURE OF

IMPERMANENCE

When you see and accept the impermanent nature
of all life forms, a strange sense of peace comes
upon you.

— Eckhart Tolle

I wanted to dedicate an entire chapter to impermanence as it is fundamental in understanding the core of Buddhist philosophy and science. One thing I have observed about human behavior and I am sure we all have as well, is that generally, people are averse to change. Usually they try to resist it, at least initially. Most people find it difficult to change anything in their lives, such as their jobs, their relationships, their opinions or even just the regular habits they engage in during the day. This applies even if they work in terrible conditions, have a toxic relationship or very negative or destructive habits. This is not to say they won't but many will opt not to do so. Many have a fear of change based on the uncertainty and instability it brings and most would rather remain in a familiar, comfortable and safe environment that they think they know or understand. When change is brought on people, many find it very difficult to accept or adapt. As the old saying goes, "Old habits are hard to break." The reality however with this common approach to life is that whether we like it or not, nothing is really permanent and change as we know is constantly occurring with every breath and during every minute we are alive.

Think about it for a minute. As much as we would like to believe that we have control over our lives, our life is already full of uncertainty. We do not know when we will die, but in reality it can be at any time. We can die in our childhood, in our twenties, or in our nineties. We can suddenly die in an automobile or plane accident. We can get a cancer diagnosis or contract a terminal disease tomorrow. Our good health is only temporary; we will eventually age, get sick, and die, as will our friends, enemies, relatives, and strangers. Human life is unfortunately very brief.

We can't predict whether our marriage will last or whether our partner falls in love with someone else and leaves us. We don't know if we will be laid off or replaced by someone more competent than we are and we don't know if our business will go bankrupt due to poor unforeseen economic conditions. There are so many factors beyond our control.

We already live in a world of impermanence or *anicca* as it is commonly referred to in the Pali language of Buddhism. Our lives are in a constant state of flux where nothing ever stays the same. We can easily see it in nature with the change of seasons; we see it in the progressive wrinkles on our face and in our declining health as we age. One of the fundamental teachings in Buddhist science is that everything changes. The world may appear solid and unchanging, but in reality the entire universe is in a process of arising and passing away. In other words, with impermanence, there is a strong sense of unreliability in the world around us. The reality is that we just cannot rely on things ever staying the same.

Even though impermanence is a natural universal law according to Buddhist science, we still do not take kind to change. Our behavior shows that we attempt to do what we can to resist change. We try to resist aging through our obsessive desire to stay young as seen in the dramatic growth of cosmetic surgery, but eventually our bodies will decline and decay. Many of us find it very hard to accept when someone who is close to us passes away even if they are very old. Some people never get over a death of a loved one, even though death at any time is a natural consequence of the human condition.

Impermanence can be seen in our mental attitudes which often change. Emotions such as excitement or anger often arise in us for some time, only to fade away with time. We can have very strong opinions or attitudes towards something which are also subject to change at any time.

A lot of problems can arise when we resist change or fail to accept impermanence. When we crave or cling on to things of this world which do not last forever, we inevitably suffer. Here we can see that impermanence (*anicca*) is intimately related to the other mark of our existence, suffering (*dukkha*). An untrained mind that believes to have control over everything in our external environment reacts to impermanence usually in a negative way. If we do not understand and internalize that impermanence is a natural part of our lives, we tend to respond by blaming things and people for the unwanted changes that occur. We get involved in conflicts and we suffer unnecessarily. A lot of our happiness is taken away.

Training the mind to accept and internalize impermanence can reduce a lot of unnecessary suffering that we endure in our daily lives. It serves to loosen our attachment to the world as it is and helps us to comprehend that things are not permanent.

Buddhist science teaches us that it is important to accept change that occurs the way is actually presents itself, not in a way we want things to play out. All conditioned phenomena are always changing. There really is no point to crave and cling to things when eventually we will have to let them go. Our opinions and strong beliefs are also not permanent and as we have seen, will often change. Trying to go against the wind, against the laws of nature, is clashing with reality and with the natural law of impermanence. As a result, we often miss out on a lot of potential happiness.

WAVES IN THE OCEAN

Enlightenment is when a wave realizes it is the
ocean.

— Thich Nhat Hanh

$\mathscr{W}$estern psychology has focused a lot of effort on maintaining, satisfying and strengthening the self. It has attempted to understand the way the self works by using mainly an individualistic approach. This is certainly evident in the numerous formulations of the self in the West with the majority being constructed on the basis that there is an "I" entity. Take the examples, self-esteem, self-awareness, self-confidence, self-defense, self-control, self-image or self-identity to name just a few. I am sure you can also attest to the countless thousands of self-help books that adorn our book stores. All of these self terms are predominantly centered on a central "I" in the human equation.

The ego engages in several psychological activities that tend to construct and strengthen the self, applying principles to consistently seek pleasure and avoid pain. It seeks enjoyment from sensual pleasures from our six sense doors. In the pursuit of acquiring material possessions, financial security, fame or power, our mind experiences only short-lived happiness that never lasts. In addition, desire is nearly always centered on the self and this can lead to extremes such as selfishness which can be detrimental to our own happiness. In this way, the ego becomes the center for our psychological activities hence its connection with self centeredness, self-interest or egocentrism. This results in the inclination to consider our own condition as being more important than that of others. It also leads to an identity that perceives itself not only as being unique but fundamentally separate from others. It creates the duality of me and you, mine and yours, as well as the concept of inside and outside of us.

Death seems to be the greatest threat or challenge to the self or to the identity of a human being. Most of us fear death. Just the mere realization that we will all die one day means that the self we know will disappear. The self requires a way to cope with the inevitability of death. It is interesting that some scientific psychological theories such as Terror Management Theory (Greenberg et al., 1986) argue that all of our human activities are motivated by avoidance of death anxiety, that lingering fear about our impending death that is present in our conscious and subconscious mind at all times. The theory claims that in order to combat death anxiety, we tend to strengthen our self-esteem or sense of personal self-worth. We need to feel significant, be remembered or see ourselves as a contributor to a life that is meaningful and has value. All our human activities reflect this behavior. Perhaps we are motivated to become the best at what we do, to become world-class athletes or famous personalities, or other achievements that we can attain that can outlive us. Our self needs to be somehow remembered. The problem arises though, that the self requires to be propped up constantly by the ego. It requires constant support and that is never sustainable. We may then eventually succumb to the effects of death anxiety which can include negative emotions that can manifest in anger, greed, anxiety, depression, unhappiness, hatred or fear.

Contrary to Western Psychology, Buddhist science has a different perspective on the self. It claims it is only a delusion. This last mark of our existence, referred to as non-self or *anatta* in the Pali language, is probably the most difficult concept to understand and digest. It is however, one of the most significant and profound teachings in Buddhism and its lack of deep understanding is deemed a primary cause of our unhappiness.

Stating that our self does not exist in the way we think it does, goes against what most of us have been conditioned to believe. For many people initially, it may be an unsettling or even frightening concept rather than a liberating one. The term non-self refers to the realization that the self or the "I" lacks any intrinsic existence. By understanding that everything in the world is impermanent and constantly in a process of arising and passing away, we can get closer to an understanding that even our body and mind are not permanent. The concept of emptiness is often mentioned in Buddhist science and relates to impermanence as everything is empty of any solidity. We are undergoing change continuously, rather than having any fixed identity, fixed body or fixed mind. This is not a loss of the self, it continues to exist but we arrive at the conclusion that the view that we have of it is only an illusion and we gain insight that the self is not the body and the mind. The Buddhist view holds that our personal identity is delusional, as a self in reality does not actually exist and is certainly not permanent, the way we feel it is. Clinging to this delusional self is a major cause of our suffering. The aim of Buddhist wisdom is to minimize or extinguish the self, avoid clinging on to desires, leading to the dissolution of the ego. Buddha's teachings aim at attaining a true and lasting happiness by cultivating a transformation from the self state to the non-self state.

What does it mean to transform into a non-self state? According to the Buddhist view, our identity or self is constructed by egoistic behavior that seeks out pleasurable stimuli, leading to a sense of satisfaction which creates a sense of identity or uniqueness and a feeling of ownership of the body, mind and external world. As I mentioned already several times, Buddhist science views this feeling of self as just an illusion of the mind.

Finally, as we will discover in the next chapter, the Buddhist view of the self and reality is beginning to show striking parallels to quantum physics, which so far has come the closest to explain matter and reality than any other modern scientific field we have ever known. While the Buddhist concept of anatta or non-self teaches that we are not really self-entities, it does not mean we do not exist at all; it just means we exist in a way that is probably much different to what we might believe.

Just as individual waves have a common field, the ocean, which links them all together; Buddhist science seems to point to the reality that we more or less co-exist with others and our common world. We are different, yet one and the same. It may just be that modern science may soon be able to explain and prove what the Buddha discovered years ago, that we are not just lone souls drifting through life, but somehow universally interdependent and interconnected with each other and the world around us.

QUANTUM PHYSICS AND

BUDDHIST SCIENCE

The total number of minds in the world is one.

– Erwin Shrodinger

As we continue our examination and understanding of the mind and how we view and perceive reality, we cannot help but notice that Buddhist science shares quite a few parallels with quantum physics, the study of the physical properties of nature at the smallest subatomic level. I have mentioned several times that I consider Buddhism a science of the mind and it is very interesting that as discoveries in quantum physics emerge, they are confirming many concepts of the ancient 2500 year old Buddhist understanding of the mind. Buddhism resonates quite strongly with the latest scientific discoveries in quantum physics (Ricard and Thuan, 2001). The goal of Buddhist science is to view the truth about reality, the way reality really is. The question that comes to mind is, do we see reality as it is, or is it just an illusion. We have seen in previous chapters that we cannot completely trust our untrained mind as it is so often conditioned. There is certainly a large discrepancy between how we perceive reality and how reality actually exists.

What quantum physicists have found regarding the nature of reality and what mounting evidence now seems to support, is that everything at the most fundamental level is primarily energy. This means that at the subatomic level, nothing is really tangible. How can that be possible? I mean what gives us the impression of touching an object then? According to quantum physics, we have never actually touched anything in our lives. What gives us the impression of touch is really just an illusion in our mind. The objects around us, including our own bodies, appear solid but under a microscope, atoms which constitute matter are in actual fact 99.999999999999 percent empty space.

This forces us to redefine how we see ourselves and the world around us. The apparent feeling or solidity of objects that we touch is only a conventional reality. In actual fact, we do not touch anything with our hands or fingertips. It is physically impossible. What gives the impression of solidity is the repulsion of other sets of atoms, similar like the actions of magnets that repel each other. For example, when we sit down in a chair, the electrons within our body are repelling the electrons that make up the chair. In reality, we are hovering above the chair at an unfathomably tiny distance. The sensation of touch is a grand illusion, created by the brain's interpretation of the interaction between the electrons and the electromagnetic field.

What really holds everything together and makes things appear solid, is a sea of fluctuating energy, not actually anything physical. Everything we see, experience and interact with is predominantly empty space. So what we and the objects around us really consist of is invisible energy, not tangible material. There is therefore no practicality or reason to be attached to material possessions or our own bodies for that matter. Quantum physics indicates we are only grasping onto objects which are empty of any inherent solidity as well as being impermanent and undergoing a constant dynamic flow of change.

The Buddhist view is that everything in the universe does not stand alone as we perceive it to be and is not separate from its surroundings. Everything is intimately interconnected and interdependent. As we have learned, the idea that we are a separate entity from each other and the world around us is considered only an illusion. Quantum physics helps us to come closer to this realization, so that we can move away from a self to a non-self view as well as an interconnected realization of our true place in the world.

The state of oneness with the world joins all of us together and reaffirms that we are not alone. The illusion that we are separate entities, according to Buddhist psychology creates feelings of isolation and loneliness. On the other hand, the understanding that we are all interconnected contributes to inner peace and happiness.

Buddhist science teaches that our mind is the center of reality. It is not just a part of our reality but it creates our reality. Similar to the way our mind creates our dreams. The idea that there is a world outside our mind or separate from our mind is a concept in Buddhist science that is considered incorrect. Quantum physics seems to be coming to the same conclusions that were presented 2500 years ago by the Buddha.

Let's look at a few principles of quantum physics and see how they parallel the Buddhist view of reality.

One of the fundamental concepts in quantum physics is that matter exists as a wave and a particle, known as wave-particle duality. Relating to the Buddhist point of view of impermanence, this means that particles, which in classical physics were once regarded as little pieces of matter, are now also regarded as processes consisting of continuously evolving and changing wave functions. These processes only give the appearance of discrete and localized particles at the moment they are observed.So particles are forever changing, and lack any inherent existence or solidity independent of the act of observation. This also gives new insight into the Buddhist view of emptiness. Reality is defined by the mind that is observing it. Reality is only a projection of the mind. Consequently, everything composed of particles is also impermanent and continually changing, and no static, stable basis for its existence can be found. Therefore, at a much generalized level, the scientific view of the world seems to converge with the Buddhist view. Buddhism is a philosophy based also on process for which the underlying basis of reality is change and impermanence.

Quantum physics demonstrates that energy is beyond everything tangible and material. Buddhism has always defended this idea and prioritized the need to transcend the physical in order to give our consciousness more relevance. At the end of the day, our mental impressions are what shape and form our reality. We are what we think, and what we think shapes our surroundings.

Another prominent discovery in quantum physics is the concept of quantum entanglement. We can think of quantum entanglement as a very serious long distance relationship. No matter how far away we are from each other, we are still connected. This sense of oneness, which Buddhist science teaches, is the idea that everything in the universe is interconnected; therefore the idea of being separate from the matter we see around us is considered an illusion. This point of view is mirrored in a phenomenon in quantum mechanics that is called quantum entanglement. When two particles interact with each other, they form a special relationship with each other or become entangled. A very strange phenomenon then arises as a result of this entanglement. No matter where or how far the two particles are separated in space and time, even if they are hundreds of light years away, they remain forever interconnected. Each will reflect anything that is done to the other; they seem to behave like one object, instead of separate from each other. If we go back to our long distance relationship analogy, this means that whatever we think, feel or experience is also experienced by our partner on the other side of the world. This quantum concept also means that before the Big Bang, our entire universe was condensed to a point smaller than an atom and contained all matter and energy that we experience. This matter and energy was entangled and always was and will be forever interconnected. Perhaps this can explain the mystery why and how flocks of birds can fly together in perfect V-formation without colliding and can turn in an instant all together, almost as if they were one entity, the whole group of birds interconnected in some way.

One cannot help but parallel this to Buddhist science which points to a reality of true oneness in the universe. Quantum physics demonstrates how sensitive atoms may be to everything we do and gives new meaning to thoughts and emotions that define our reality. The quantum field seems to be a sea of energy that connects us to all things around us. If everything we do reverberates in the entire universe, the whole idea of cultivating compassion transforms from just a nice idea to a matter of life-changing proportion. The Dalai Lama has often been quoted saying, "My religion is very simple. My religion is kindness." Perhaps this simple teaching of compassion emphasized by the Buddha 2500 years ago, and now possibly rediscovered in concepts of modern quantum physics, can not only alter our own experience of happiness but really change the world in ways we never dreamed possible.

ADVANCED CONCEPTS IN

BUDDHISM

Searching outside of you is Samsara (the world).
Searching within you leads to Nirvana.

— Amit Ray

I wanted to include a few advanced concepts in Buddhism, most of which have not been scientifically confirmed or supported by modern science because they are important to at least consider as possibilities in our study of the science of happiness. My aim is definitely not to preach any religion or push any dogma. I am certainly opposed to that way of thinking. However, just because they have not been scientifically proven by our current available scientific methods to this day, doesn't mean they will not in the future. I mean, take for instance, in the West it has taken 2500 years for meditation and mindfulness to reach the masses and capture the attention of the scientific community.

At the very beginning of this book, I wrote about the beginner's mind and I sincerely hope that you can keep your mind at least partially open as to not miss out on a deeper understanding of the whole picture of Buddhist philosophy as it relates to happiness. As you know, I come from a science background and am naturally very skeptical of concepts that rely solely on faith and you should definitely be too. The Buddha himself stressed that you should not blindly accept anything unless you have the wisdom to experience it for yourself. Your natural reaction should be to always question all theoretical truths and thoroughly investigate and experience them, testing any beliefs before you accept and internalize them. However, these advanced concepts are worthy to at least be included here because for one thing, they have been handed down from the Buddha's teachings. We cannot deny that so far, as we as we have seen in previous chapters, a lot of what he passed down is slowly proving to be accepted and confirmed through quantum mechanics, not to mention the thousands of years of reported experiences passed down by Buddhist monks and their lineages around the world. As many of his teachings about the workings of the mind are only now being revisited and showing parallels to modern science and psychology, it would be a serious mistake not to at least give them some room for thought.

Let's take a look at some of the more profound advanced concepts central in Buddhism. They include *samsara, dependent origination, karma* and *nirvana*. The difficulty of explaining these advanced concepts using the scientific method stems from the fact that modern science relies on studying matter that is generally outside of us. What objective method then do we use to prove that karma, interdependent origination, rebirth, or nirvana exists? These concepts are generally outside of our sphere of scientific understanding, and certainly at this time tend to lean more towards spirituality and religious faith rather than pure scientific fact. What approach can we use then to confirm that they exist? While there are several scientific studies supporting rebirth and theories on dependent origination, the concepts of karma and nirvana are ones that must really be experienced personally firsthand. To do this, it requires training the mind to achieve a deep state of meditation that leads to enlightenment and seeing reality as it really is, which is certainly not easy to attain.

The Buddha taught that only by reaching these advanced enlightened states of mind, can we see our previous lives, understand the role of *karma*, escape the cyclical human existence called *samsara* and reach the final goal of Buddhism, the extinguishment of all suffering, or *nirvana*. It is worthwhile to be familiar with these concepts as each of them are invariably related to one another and present possible valid explanations to what may be missing links to our understanding of reality. We shall discuss each one of them, as well as mention any supporting scientific evidence if any is available. For many of us, these Buddhist concepts provide a way to understand the meaning of our existence, often leading to greater happiness in our life.

Samsara

According to Buddhism, the Sanskrit word *samsara* refers to the predicament that we are trapped in a world where we live, die, and experience rebirth repeatedly over and over again. We live in a world of suffering or dissatisfaction (*dukkha*), one that is endless and has no beginning and no end. The concept of *samsara* is not exclusive to Buddhism but has its roots also in Hinduism and other Indian religions. Beings are driven from life to life in this system of *samsara* by *karma*, which is activated by our good or bad actions that we commit in this life as well as in previous lives. *Samsara* is also the opposite of *nirvana*, a condition of being free from all suffering and the cycle of rebirth. In the state of *samsara* we are bound or trapped by greed, hatred, and ignorance of the true reality that exists. Buddha taught that we continue to wander in *samsara* from life to life until we can find awakening through enlightenment. Several realms exist in *samsara* other than our human realm, such as the animal realm and other higher or lower dimensions. The human realm is considered a precious realm where we as humans have a possibility to attain enlightenment but we can wander or experience rebirth through a number of realms other than the human dimension. To understand *samsara* you need to understand the other concepts such as *dependent origination, karma* and *rebirth* as they are closely interrelated.

Dependent Origination

Dependent Origination or dependent arising is the Buddhist doctrine of causality. It maintains that nothing has been created but that all things in the world arise or come into existence by causes. The Buddha taught that when we are able to fully see the arising and cessation of the world, that nothing is really permanent, we are said to be endowed with perfect view or with perfect vision. This means that we are able to see that everything is interconnected, nothing is separate and nothing stands alone. In other words, everything affects everything else. We are a part of this dynamic system or process of dependent origination. These are causal relationships affected by everything that occurs around us, which in turn affects the world that we live in.

Take the example of an apple tree. In order to bear fruit, it requires more than just a seed. That seed requires proper conditions such as enough sunshine, the right climate, adequate nutrients and moisture from the soil. If any of these conditions are not present or not in the proper amount, it leads to a different outcome. This can result in poor quality of fruit or perhaps no fruit at all. When we begin to view all phenomena in the world with awareness that no entity can be sustained or exist independently without fulfilling a variety of different causes or conditions, then we can see the interconnectedness of the world. This insight originates from the Buddhist concept of dependent origination.

The concept states that phenomena arise from pre-existing phenomenon and that current phenomenon conditions future phenomenon. This is occurring moment by moment in our minds, consciousness and in all our experiences. Dependent origination is a view on how our world is created and what happens in our consciousness with each moment. We become a conscious participant in the world that we create. When we understand it, we can begin to understand that life is a continual process, it is not static or fixed but alive and constantly changing with every moment. Scientific evidence related to this concept was discussed in the last chapter on quantum physics in regards to parallels to the quantum field, wave-particle duality and quantum entanglement.

Karma

When we can see the causality of all phenomena in the world as in dependent origination, we can see how *karma* fits into the picture. The law of *karma,* according to Buddhist philosophy is considered one of the natural laws of causality, much like gravity or thermodynamics. In Buddhist terms it is not a God-like or religious belief but a law that follows nature. Most people have heard or used the word karma and most have heard of these related phrases, such as "What goes around, comes around" or "as you sow, so shall you reap." *Karma* is a Sanskrit word meaning "action" or "doing." In Buddhist science it means actions or deeds driven by intention, through body, speech and mind that lead to positive or negative consequences in the future. Buddha stressed that it is the intention that creates the quality of the *karma,* not the outcome. We can compare a murderer who uses a knife to stab a person with the intention to harm and kill them, to that of a surgeon who unsuccessfully uses the same knife to operate on a person with the intention to save their life. In both cases the person dies, but in the murderer's case, negative *karma* is generated, in the surgeon's case, positive *karma*. Buddhism teaches that if intentions are rooted in greed, hatred and ignorance, it leads to suffering but if rooted in compassion, patience, generosity and wisdom, it leads to greater well-being.

The concept of *karma* brings new light to how we should live our lives as well as how we can maximize our happiness. If we wish to enjoy happy and pleasant experiences in our present life or in future lives, then according to Buddhist views, we need to engage in thoughts, words and deeds that are beneficial to ourselves and to others around us. By engaging in thoughts, words and deeds that are harmful to ourselves and to others around us, we will suffer unpleasant experiences. So it is often said that if you want to know what your future will be in this life or in the next life, just look at the way you are behaving in your present life right now.

Karma also dispels the need for acts of revenge or fights for justice, as each and every one of us will suffer the consequences of our negative actions, even though we may be under the illusion that we got away with something. *Karma* makes us accountable for every action that we take. Buddhism states that the fruits of *karma* can ripen at any time in this life or in future lives so we can never know when it will play out. Every action creates a karmic seed which is stored in the consciousness. This seed can come to fruition in our present life, in the next life or any future life. Positive or negative experiences in our present life are also influenced by our past *karma* in our previous lives. In Buddhism, a favorable or unfavorable rebirth in our next life will depend on the positive or negative *karma* we generate in this life. Scientifically, the concept of *karma* is obviously difficult to prove, but I think intuitively many of us already somewhat may know or have experienced its effects, at least in some subtle way.

Rebirth

Rebirth is often used interchangeably with the well known term "reincarnation" but Buddhists generally prefer the term "rebirth" to differentiate between the Hindu and Buddhist views. The concept of reincarnation generally refers to the transmigration of a soul, from lifetime to lifetime. This is the Hindu view, and it is how reincarnation is generally understood in the West. Buddhism, as we know teaches the doctrine of non-self, which says there is no permanent, unchanging entity such as a soul. This means that in reality, we are an ever-changing collection of consciousnesses, feelings, perceptions, and impulses that we only hold together to maintain the illusion of a self. With rebirth, the driving force or *"karma"* is carried forward from life to life, which has been compared to a flame from a candle passed on to another candle. There is certainly debate even amongst Buddhist traditions about whether consciousness is transferred or not. Some traditions liken rebirth as more like a stream of consciousness that has some maintenance of continuity. The Buddha himself was said to have been able to recall a number of his past lives as well as specific details about them when he attained enlightenment.

There are some interesting scientific studies that support the idea of past lives. One of the most prominent psychiatrists in this field was Dr. Ian Stevenson, a Professor of Psychiatry at the University of Virginia School Of Medicine. His main claim to fame was his meticulous scientific studies of children's memories of their previous lives. In fact, he claimed to have found over 3,000 examples of reincarnation during his time which he shared with the scientific community. His work established that the statistical probability that reincarnation does in fact occur was overwhelming, and that there was so much evidence that it stood up to mostly all branches of science. Stevenson's most known colossal body of work, the 2,268 page, two volume, "Reincarnation and Biology" in 1997, established him as a leader in this field (Stevenson, 1997). It included 225 detailed cases of children who remembered their previous lives and who also had physical birthmarks or birth defects that matched those previous lives and that were located on the same part of the body. Some of the evidence and details were even confirmed by the dead person's autopsy records and photos. The results he discovered were amazing. Another observation that he found was that children's memories of their past lives are usually only remembered when they are between the ages of two and five.

Dr. Jim Tucker, a child psychiatrist, also worked with Ian Stevenson and took over after he retired. He has also conducted several decades of research on reincarnation by scientifically investigating children's memories of past lives and has published his research results which show compelling evidence (Tucker, 2006).

Another noted American psychiatrist and hypnotherapist is Dr. Brian Weiss, who specialized in past life regression. He has studied hundreds of patients by hypnosis and although a huge skeptic initially, these patients have made him believe that past lives do exist. He has found that trauma experienced in past lives is often related to phobias that people experience in their present lives (Weiss, 1988).

Nirvana

In Buddhist philosophy, *nirvana* is a transcendent state of enlightenment or awakening where there is complete cessation of suffering, desire and sense of self. It is a state where one is released or liberated from the effects of *karma* and *samsara*, the cycle of death and rebirth. It is the final goal of Buddhism and of Buddha's Noble Eightfold Path. The Sanskrit word *nirvana* literally means "blowing out" as in the extinguishing of the fires (greed, hatred and ignorance), those which cause us suffering and imprison us in endless cycles of human existence.

Nirvana is what the Buddha achieved through meditation on the night of his enlightenment at age thirty five. He spent the rest of his life teaching and helping others to arrive at that same freedom. There are many interpretations of *nirvana* in various Buddhist traditions. It is often described as a way out of our endless cycle of death and rebirth, a state that exists beyond space or time, of perfect peace and happiness and one which is impossible to describe. In some schools it is referred to as realizing ones innate or basic nature, one that is cloaked in ignorance.

There is no scientific proof of *nirvana*. We know of *nirvana* through the teachings of the Buddha and other Indian religions. It is not a place, but a state of mind or awareness. It can only be experienced. *Nirvana* is the ultimate sustained level of happiness that we can ever hope to achieve. For most of us, unless we are a dedicated monk, attaining *nirvana* is probably not a reachable goal in our present lifetime. However, although we may not reach this complete state of mind, we can certainly achieve a taste of *nirvana* in our current lifetime by decreasing unnecessary suffering and greatly increasing our level of happiness.

THE SECOND NOBLE TRUTH

The root of suffering is attachment.

–The Buddha

*I*n the first section of this book, we learned that the first of the Four Noble Truths was about the inherent suffering of our human existence and that it was important to accept and thoroughly understand it in order to progress along our journey of discovering the reality of uncovering happiness. Like a skilled physician, we needed to be able to first identify this prevalent disease and accept that it really exists, before we can make an accurate diagnosis.

The Second Noble Truth, as taught by the Buddha, is the truth of the origin or cause of suffering, or using our physician analogy, his diagnosis of the disease. He revealed that the cause of our suffering, is craving, translated from the Pali word, *tanha* which literally means "thirst." Our thirst or cravings, in other words our desires, are at the root of our discontent and suffering because of the reality that they can never be fully satisfied. The Second Noble Truth is about recognizing these desires and understanding the detrimental effects of becoming attached to them.

As we discussed earlier in a chapter on the six sense doors, when we see, hear, taste, smell, feel or imagine something we like, a pleasant feeling arises in our mind. If we are not careful, which is usually the case in an untrained mind, we immediately get attached to these feelings and we react by clinging and grasping on to our desires. No matter how often we satisfy a desire, it is never enough and we want more of the same or something better. These desires tend to exert a strong power over us and when we react to them with a form of attachment by clinging or grasping, we succumb to this delusion over and over again. It is a vicious circle that according to Buddhist science is responsible for feelings of discontent and suffering in our lives. The Buddha attributed this to our ignorance. This does not mean that we are stupid or lack intelligence. It is the ignorance of our true reality that forces us to become such hopeless victims of desire.

The whole reason why the cause of suffering is craving is because we act out of line with reality. Grasping or clinging on to objects of desire, goes against this sense of order. It is not in line with the law of impermanence. Remember our world and everything in it, is constantly changing, everything arises and passes away. Nothing is permanent and there is no inherent self. Forming strong attachments or clinging on to thoughts, feelings, experiences or material possessions is futile as they are impermanent and like everything subject to change. When we hold on tightly to things, feelings or thoughts that will by nature eventually pass away; we inevitably suffer, as we set ourselves up for disappointment. The act of clinging and not letting go is the reason. So our ignorance, based on a misunderstanding of reality, is what makes it very easy for us to react to desires by craving.

According to Buddhist science, the most sensible solution is to be in touch with reality. The Buddha saw in his wisdom, the ineffective outcome in attempting to manipulate our external world by trying to get what we want or pushing away what we don't want. Getting what we want just leads to an increase in wanting. Not getting what we want, leads to suffering. Craving is habitual. It is unfortunately never enough. This sets us up in such a way to always fail. When we want or desire things, we try to change the externals by pushing or pulling, to make things change according to our desires. As we know the external environment has too many variables that constantly change beyond our control. Training our mind to be more mindful, can transform the act of grasping and clinging to accepting, understanding and adapting. We can then begin to see reality as it really is. Through the process of letting go of our incessant desires, we immediately receive relief from suffering.

We have to note that there are two forms of desires, ones that are selfish and those that are non-selfish. Not all desires lead to suffering. Non-selfish desires are not driven by the ego or by pride, or by an addictive attachment and are beneficial to others, such as a genuine desire to help people, without expecting anything in return. As this stems from our true nature as compassionate beings and aligns with the reality that we are all interconnected, we do not suffer but benefit as a result. Selfish desire on the other hand is like a thirst that is impossible to quench, it temporarily satisfies but as we have already mentioned leads eventually to discontent and suffering.

The Buddha taught that there are three kinds of cravings that lead to suffering. The first is the **craving for pleasure of the senses**, or *kama – tanha* in the Pali language. This includes the cravings that result from sense objects that enter our doors of sight, sound, smell, taste, touch and thoughts. The second is the **craving of becoming or of existence**, or *bhava – tanha* (Pali). This is the craving to become or continue to be, or become something other than we actually are. It is a craving for a fixed identity or existence such as becoming or remaining rich, famous, praised, beautiful, young, healthy, strong or respected. We do not want our life to end; we crave for continued existence and immortality. There is attachment to identity or status, to ambitions and personalities, without the acceptance of impermanence. The final type is **craving for non-becoming or non-existence**, or *vibhava – tanha* (Pali). This is the desire to cease to exist or not to continue, such as the desire for suicide, craving to avoid pain and suffering, or craving for not becoming things such as sick, poor, weak, ugly, lonely, unsuccessful, criticized or despised. It is also the desire for things not to be, or things that one has an aversion to such as when we say, "I wish I was not so short", "I wish I was not in this situation", or "I wish this would end."

The Buddha elegantly laid out the reality when it comes to the cause of suffering. His diagnosis was simply that craving, in all its many forms is the fundamental root cause of our dissatisfaction, the basis of all our suffering in this life. However, in simple terms, wisdom is required before craving can be abandoned. There is a need to be able to see reality as it really is, in order to find the sustained happiness that we all have the potential to discover in ourselves. The Second Noble Truth leads us to the possibility that we may be able to alleviate the suffering in our human lives. This is the subject of the next part of this book.

PART III

UNCOVERING THE HAPPINESS
WITHIN

Happiness is like a butterfly; the more you chase
it, the more it will elude you, but if you turn your
attention to other things, it will come and sit softly
on your shoulder

— Henry David Thoreau

OUR MIND CREATES OUR WORLD

Your entire universe is in your mind and nowhere
else. To expand the universe, expand your mind.

— Deepak Chopra

We cannot help but wonder how reality for us really exists. The greatest philosophers and scientists have attempted to answer this question throughout human history, yet most of everything we have learned has really only been interpreted through observations that enter our sense doors from the external environment. With quantum mechanics, modern science has come closer to realizing our true reality, yet so many questions still remain unanswered. We have come closer to the understanding that we may be more of a process than a specific concrete unchanging identity and that we are much more connected to others and the world around us than we had ever imagined. However, it seems that the scientific method, despite the fact that it has served us immensely well in so many of our innovations and understanding of our world, has its own limitations. It still unfortunately, suffers from a reliance on information from our external world that must enter our mind through our sense organs. As we know, this information can often be distorted, biased and cannot always be trusted to reflect true reality.

The Buddha advocated a different approach. His method to understand our true reality was to direct our efforts inwards and to explore and analyze our mind. In this way the mind could be trained to achieve clarity in order to be able to view reality the way it really is, not how we would like it to be.

Nowhere is it more apparent that we are not in touch with reality, than in the way we react with our external world. Believing that we have the power to manipulate it so that we can find lasting happiness there has been our fatal delusion. When we are unhappy, we are quick to place the blame on people outside us, on the situation itself or on conditions surrounding it, but rarely do we see the truth. What we envision our reality to be is only a construct of our mind. That reality is constantly being shaped and altered by past experiences, habitual patterns, emotions and biases. Our untrained mind will react accordingly, often in ways that are not beneficial to ourselves or to people around us. Our untrained mind is unable to clearly see reality.

We have seen how the internal struggles that we have in our mind and our attachments can lead to stress and unhappiness. Our inability to accept reality as it is in the present moment and refusal to let go of our grasping behavior is a major reason for these outcomes. The law of impermanence shows us that our external world and we ourselves are constantly changing and this is beyond our control. A trained unobscured mind will have the ability to possess this clarity and awareness, accept reality and avoid impulsive negative emotional reactions that often ensue.

There is an enormous power that we hold in our mind. The mind really creates our perception of the world. Unfortunately the untrained mind is very susceptible to becoming easily deluded. Very few of us are able to objectively view the world and experiences as they truly are without being influenced by our ego-driven opinions, emotions or our past memories. We can liken this to perceiving things through rose-colored glasses, or not being able to see the actual true reality. Scientists have learned that the brain even tends to fill in the blanks or constructs missing pieces of information together when it comes from what passes through our sensory organs (Smythies, 2005). Through evolution we have created these abilities to perceive our external world but it is more of a convenient relative reality that is presented in our mind rather than an ultimate or absolute reality. Evolution is primarily concerned about passing our genes on to the next generation, a survival of the fittest, natural selection type of mentality at whatever cost is necessary. In the process, evolution does not concern itself very much about our happiness.

As we proceed throughout this part of the book, I will endeavor to uncover the mystery according to Buddhist science, of uncovering and realizing our true happiness. Hopefully, we will arrive at the conclusion that our only barrier to overcome if we want to achieve this goal is our mind.

RELEASING THE GRIP FROM OUR EGO

The ego seeks to divide and separate.
Spirit seeks to unify and heal.

— Pema Chödrön

popular Buddhist-themed parable that is obviously not authentic but certainly relevant is this one: A man once told the Buddha, "I want happiness." He replied, remove "I": that's ego. Then remove "want," that's desire. Now what you're left with is "happiness." In a previous chapter we discussed cravings and desires and how according to Buddhist science, they are the primary cause of suffering and detract from our happiness. In this chapter, we will go over another mental construct, the infamous ego and how it relates to the strong identification with our self.

Ego usually has bad connotations associated with it and it is most often linked to words like arrogance, megalomania or vanity. Strictly speaking *ego* is a psychological term popularized by Sigmund Freud, meaning awareness of one's identity, the concept of the self or the part that we consider our self. Ego is often associated with our sense of self-esteem or self-importance.

Our ego is created from early childhood when we begin to first construct our identity. We are given a name to identify who we are; we receive feedback from our parents, teachers and others around us on what we are good at and what we are not. We form attachments to these opinions. Our likes and dislikes are shaped through our interaction with the world. Slowly we begin to build or construct an image of who we believe we are. Certainly this behavior has many limitations as we generally start to see ourselves unfortunately as permanent fixed entities.

We begin to form an illusory concrete self, born from our attachment to our identity. However this self that we construct doesn't really have any solid basis. In Buddhist science, as we know, we refer to this as the concept of non-self.

It is very helpful to go through the following mental exercise. Ask yourself, what part of you is really you? Are your hands really you? If you lost your hands in an accident would you still be you? What part of your body if it was removed would be you? If you say your brain is what makes you, you, ask yourself what part of your brain is it? If you say your personality, then ask yourself if your personality has changed from when you were a child to now in the present. Of course it has. What about your memory? Are your memories what make you, you? We know that memories can often be distorted. What if you lose your memories as you age as in senility or Alzheimer's disease? What about your skills, do your skills make you who you are? If you are a singer who loses his or her voice or a dancer who becomes paralyzed, are you still the same person, if you lose your skills?

It seems that the things that we think make us who we are, are only parts of who we are or roles that we play, but as we go through this mental exercise, we cannot actually find one part of us that we can say is actually us. What we are is more like a stream of changing experiences.

This is what is meant by the Buddhist concept of non-self. It demonstrates that a true independent self really does not exist. In reality, we are not permanent entities and we are also not independent from everything around us. We are interdependent with others and the world around us, a world that is constantly changing. The concept of non-self is a great tool for releasing the grip of the ego. The ego, just like everything else is not who we are. According to Buddhist science, the ego is just a mental fictitious construct, a mere illusion.

Neither Buddhism nor Freud's psychotherapy have ever sought to eradicate the ego. Doing so would render us most likely helpless or even psychotic. Evolution has enabled our ego to be able to navigate the world around us, to regulate our instincts, to protect us from immediate dangers and to mediate the conflicting demands on the self. Our society usually promotes a strong healthy ego, rather than a conscious de-escalation of the ego. There is a lot of encouragement in our culture for developing a stronger sense of self. Most of us identify with aggressively meeting our needs, hence the importance of developing self-love, self-esteem and self-confidence. As important as these accomplishments may be, they are not enough to guarantee our happiness and well-being.

Ego is one affliction we all have in common. Because of its relentless pursuit of attention and power, we suffer. Our efforts to become better, richer, stronger or more attractive force us in an unsustainable direction, as we are never sure if we have ever achieved enough. This endless obsessive ambition, leads to inevitable consequences. Common reactions of disappointment, bitterness and anger arise when things do not work out as we planned. And they never do as we all know, since our external environment is often beyond our control. The ego's permanently selfish agenda always claims to have our best interests in mind, but that is certainly often not the case.

The construct of the ego breeds fear and isolation. Once we can understand that we are not an isolated independent self but in reality a part of an interconnected world, we feel less fear and isolation and the grip of our ego subsides. As our awareness grows, the ego begins to dissolve. Its grasp becomes weak as we let go of the notion of our illusory self.

In order to observe or even recognize the ego, we need to be in the present moment. Since we are generally present only half the time our ego is often left free to reign. The ego has properties of always looking to the future or dwelling on the past, while constantly seeking and trying to find something better, and never being satisfied in the present moment. With an ego that is left uncontrolled, there is no possibility for sustained happiness. If we are relentlessly searching for something better and never ultimately satisfied our mind is unable to find peace and we cannot be happy. On the other hand, if we are in full awareness in the present moment, the holding patterns of the ego become harmless and we are no longer possessed by its power. Remember that our ego is just a fictitious construct in our mind, a mental formation that we have the ability to control and overcome.

Buddhist science teaches us to be aware of our ego and to question and doubt its motives. If we want a more satisfying and happier existence, we have to understand how to loosen its grip. The very ego whose fears and attachments drive us in our lives is also capable of a profound and far-reaching development. As conscious and self-reflecting individuals, we do have the capacity to talk back and interact with our ego. Instead of focusing solely on pursuing success in the external world, we can opt to direct our efforts inwards.

There are many things in life that we cannot control, such as natural events, sudden illness, accidents, loss, and circumstances in our childhood, but we do have the capacity to train and transform our minds. How we interact with our ego is up to us. People who give in to their ego may have a strong sense of self but they still are prone to suffer. They may appear on the outside that they are in control. Inside, however, they are unable to relax, be compassionate or sympathize with others if they are primarily focused only on themselves.

Simply building up the ego leaves us stranded and isolated. It is interesting that the most important events in our lives, such as falling in love, giving birth to a child or facing death, require our ego to let go of its grasp. There is a profound sense of freedom and happiness during this process. The mind learns to relax when it is no longer fighting against the strain of the ego's perfectionism. I am not saying we cannot pursue and enjoy the pleasures of life, but we can enjoy them without attachment to the ego.

Buddhist science with its many meditations and mindfulness techniques as we will soon see, teaches us to watch our own mind and not be tricked in believing everything we think. It teaches us to also be aware of the present moment, much more than we have been in our entire lives. In this way we do not fall victim to the selfish impulses of the ego. Observing the mind also allows us to see the true reality of our identity, which comes as a welcome relief, as opposed to the habitual ego-driven state we are often entrapped in.

THE PLACE WHERE HAPPINESS IS FOUND

Why wander all over the world looking for
something you already have? You are already the
richest person on Earth.

— Thich Nhat Hanh

The amount of our time that our minds spend wandering in the past or dreaming about the future is over forty-eight percent as we have previously discovered according to Harvard researchers (Killingsworth and Gilbert, 2010). That means that our minds spend just a little over fifty percent of the time in the present. As we have learned, we can only really live in the present. On top of that, we spend most of our time seeking happiness from the external environment, a place that due to the law of impermanence, we unfortunately really cannot control. Time and time again we become disappointed and discontented even when we achieve our goals. Even modern scientific studies confirm these outcomes. The bottom line is that we seem to be on a misguided path when it comes to our search for happiness, and wasting valuable time during the process. We should not worry if we feel a sense of hopelessness in our discussions so far after analyzing our human predicament that arises from the First and Second Noble Truths. There is a light at the end of our tunnel. To come this far in this book, we are now much better equipped on our journey to discover the true source of happiness.

The Buddha was adamant in his warnings to be mindful of our sense doors because, as we have learned, craving inevitably ensues. An unguarded mind leads to clinging and grasping to our external world, a world that is impermanent and cannot offer us sustained happiness. It is our ignorance of reality that puts us in this predicament and it is only by training the mind that we can escape its deceptive hand.

I hope you can appreciate by now that one of our fundamental problems that we have is that we are looking for happiness in places where it cannot be found. I will repeat that again because it is vitally important to come to this realization. We are looking for happiness in places where it cannot be found. Allow this profound thought to sink in and internalize. We are looking for happiness in places where it cannot be found.

If happiness is not found in our external environment, then where can we find it? The Buddha taught that our source of happiness is inside, specifically in our mind and not based on external conditions like wealth, success, fame, power, position, knowledge, or relationships. He taught that it in only in the mind, where we can find the true source of happiness.

If suffering and discontent is constructed in our minds and the cause which is craving is also constructed in the mind, then we need to turn inward if we are to understand where happiness is really found. We need to seek happiness from a different source. So far mankind has not been very successful in this endeavor. Our growing rates of anxiety, depression and psychological disorders can attest to this failure. We are constantly driven, as we have learned, by our ego to our external environment for the source of our lack of happiness. That is also unfortunately the same place we point our finger to blame when we get disappointed or when we suffer. It is time to take personal responsibility, because each one of us is personally responsible for our own happiness. We can certainly be influenced in our decisions that we make in life but when it comes down to it, the decision to change our mind is entirely up to us. We are the masters of our destiny and ultimately of our own minds. The enlightening outcome that emerges from this inner awareness is that we can now fully open up our minds to unlimited transformation.

What about our clouded minds and unreliable judgment? I demonstrated already several times how we cannot trust our minds, that information from our sense doors is biased and distorted and often does not reflect reality. If happiness is to be found in our minds, with all this going on, how can we sort out what is true and what is false? Yes, our minds are clouded with a multitude of conflicting thoughts that we cling to and which distort our judgments and prevent us from seeing reality as it truly is playing out. However, we will soon appreciate in future parts of this book, the important role of mind training that will result in a mind that is able to view our reality much more clearly.

The interesting irony to our futile search is that according to Buddhist science, happiness is not something that we need to seek; it is something that we already have. Why then, do we search for something that we already have? This is quite a radical mindset to most standard ways of thinking because it goes against our habitual ego-driven mechanism to search for happiness outside of ourselves. The more we seek happiness, the more it eludes us. If we can learn to uncover the happiness we already hold within, then we can stop trying to desperately extract it from external sources.

A more progressive Buddhist way of thinking is to realize that happiness is within and we can bring this happiness out to our external world, to our relationships, to our working environments and to each and every situation that we experience.

INNER PEACE

I have no money, no resources, no hopes. I am the
happiest man alive.

– Henry Miller

We are hopefully closer now to the realization that our mind is the center of our suffering and discontent, and the place where the illusion of our identity is created that is subject to the whims of the ego. It is also the place where all cravings develop.

This means that the mind is really the source of all suffering. We cannot blame it on situations, people or anything in our external environment. It is the reaction in our mind to what occurs in our life minute by minute that is to blame. If our grasping mind reacts with aversion, we suffer. If our mind reacts with craving and attachment, we also suffer. At the same time, our mind is also our source of happiness. As we know everything happens in the mind, not outside. Since happiness and suffering are just states of mind, their causes are also states of mind.

Let's go back to our definition of happiness which we explored in the beginning parts of this book. Society generally evaluates happiness on external factors such as achieving a certain amount of success, good economic conditions, a reliable social system, good friends and family etc. We have seen how these external variables do bring some happiness but usually it is not sustainable and subject to so many influences that are beyond our control.

How then, are we expected to achieve happiness when our external environment is constantly changing and there is no certainty of things staying the same? As we know most of us are looking for happiness in places where happiness cannot be found, that is, in the external environment. Happiness is not found out there, it is found inside the mind. It is often very difficult for people to grasp this concept. Remember how we defined happiness. We explained earlier that happiness is a feeling but how can we achieve this feeling while not relying on our outside world to give it to us.

Think about the times when you feel really happy. You don't feel happy when you are under stress, when you are worrying about the future or regretting the past. Usually, the times you are most happy, is when you have no cares, no worries, when you are not dwelling on the past or worried about the future. When was the last time that you felt that way? Maybe it was on the beach, or while you were on vacation or perhaps watching a sunset or having a cup of coffee in the morning, reading a book, or having a great conversation with a friend. What do all these experiences have in common? They are times when we feel at peace with ourselves. Nothing is pushing us to hurry, there are no demands placed on us, no deadlines, we are not stressed out or worrying about finances. We are not agonizing over problems in our families or relationships, or dealing with difficulties at work. In times like this, we have no agitating thoughts that stir up our mind. Our mind is at peace. Could happiness really be that simple?

Happiness, according to Buddhist science is when we are free of suffering and that is when we have inner peace within ourselves. It is a time when our ego is not in control and trying to push us to succeed in the future. It is found only in the present moment, that time we are actually living and experiencing. Nothing less, nothing more. This opportunity to experience happiness has always been with us and there has never been a need to look for it anywhere else. Each one of us has the capacity to experience happiness, through inner peace in the present moment. If we are truly living in the present moment, it is a time when we are here and now, just experiencing what is occurring moment by moment. There is no grasping or craving at that time.

The real source of our happiness is therefore **inner peace**. If we want to be happy then that is the place we need to be, or should I say that is the state of mind we need to be in. Whenever we are happy, our mind is peaceful.

How do we get to this source? The nature of the mind is peaceful. According to Buddhist science that is its natural state. The problem is that our mind is often clouded with multitudes of agitating thoughts that constantly distract us. We already hold the key to happiness, inside our mind. What each one of us spends their entire lives searching for is a source of happiness. We have just been looking in places where happiness is not found. We need to understand and internalize that happiness is with us all the time. It is our natural state of being. It is just hidden under an enormous layer of mental constructs that we have created in our minds. We need to train the mind to let go of these agitating thoughts and to transform habitual mental patterns. To realize the highest reaches of happiness, we need to only become aware of our essential nature by loosening the grip of the ego and letting go of cravings and attachments to desires.

What it comes down to is that happiness is not something to search for, neither is it something we need to create. I like to think of happiness as a state that just needs to be uncovered, because we already possess it. We just need to tap into it and train the mind to experience inner peace to its fullest extent. Remember it is our nature to be peaceful.

AWAKENING TO OUR BUDDHA NATURE

> Our true nature is like a precious jewel: although
> it may be temporarily buried in mud, it remains
> completely brilliant and unaffected. We simply
> have to uncover it.
>
> – Pema Chodron

There was a Buddha statue, called Phra Phuttha Maha Suwanna Patimakon, made sometime during the period of the 1200-1400s, according to historians, in the ancient kingdom of Ayutthaha, Siam, which is known as present day Thailand. Its outer layer was covered with a thick plaster; it was painted and inlaid with pieces of colored glass. By 1767, during the Burmese-Siamese war, Burmese invaders destroyed the Ayutthaha kingdom, removed and looted everything of value but left this seemingly worthless ordinary Buddha statue standing amongst the ruins undisturbed for many years.

In the early 1800s, after the capital in Bangkok was established for the new kingdom, the king commissioned the construction of many temples there and ordered the relocation of old statues around the country. This Buddha statue was finally moved and found its place in the main temple building of Wat Chotanaram in Bangkok. Eventually the temple fell into disrepair and closed down, so in 1935 the statue was once again moved, this time to Chinatown's Wat Traimit, a temple of minor significance at that time. Since there was no building there large enough to house the statue, it was kept under an ordinary tin roof for 20 years. By now the true identity of the statue had basically been forgotten for two hundred years.

A new building was built to house the statue in 1954, and on May 25, 1955, the statue was moved to its new location in the building. During its relocation, there were several attempts to lift the statue and during one of the attempts the rope broke and the statue fell on the ground. What was revealed under a piece of plaster that accidently broke and chipped off was nothing less than astonishing. For under the thick layer of plaster, a solid gold Buddha statue was hidden, over three meters tall and weighing 5.5 tons. Its long forgotten secret, being hidden by layers of plaster to conceal it due to the threat of the Burmese-Siamese war, was finally discovered. Today, it is commonly known as the Golden Buddha, a major tourist attraction in Thailand, being the largest gold statue or object in the world, with a value estimated of more than 250 million US dollars.

In some Buddhist traditions, they speak of a Buddha nature, that all humans have the nature of the Buddha within them already. It is like a seed that has the potential to grow. This means that we all have the potential to become enlightened, to see reality as it really is, just as the Buddha did over 2500 years ago. In Buddhist philosophy, it is the fundamental nature of all beings. It is not just something that we hold inside, but it is something that we are. It stems from the idea of a true nature, a luminous mind of awareness that is always present, even if we are not aware of it. This Buddha nature is beyond our concept of thoughts or scientific explanations, and more like our intrinsic true nature. It is like our golden Buddha, uncovered beneath layers of disturbing thoughts waiting to be discovered. It is our natural inner state of happiness that we already possess.

Throughout the course of our lives, our attachments and ego have created layers analogous to plaster around this inner intrinsic golden core. We have forgotten that happiness is similar to that golden Buddha; it has always been within us. It is just that due to agitating thoughts, our mind often gets distracted and fails to take much notice. With mind training, we can chip away and gradually uncover the layers around our inner nature, through awareness and allow that golden Buddha within us to gradually emerge. This is the key to finding our source of inner peace and sustained happiness.

There is another popular parable about a beggar that had been sitting on an old box for years begging for spare change. A stranger arrives and tells him he has no money to give him but asks the beggar what is in the box he is sitting on. The beggar replies that he doesn't know and never cared to look inside. The stranger insists he look inside and when he does he discovers that it is a treasure chest full of gold. The old box can be equated to our mind that we choose to ignore and refuse to explore. Buddhist science likens this parable to the analogy that we are like hopeless beggars, because we are desperately searching outside for handouts of short-lived pleasure or fulfillment, while we hold a treasure inside that is infinitely greater than anything the external world can offer.

As you may have already seen, it is very common in yoga classes to use the ancient Indian greeting, *"Namaste"* while holding the hands in a prayer position and slightly bowing. This Sanskrit word can be translated to mean, "I bow to you", "I greet the light within you" or "The divine in me, bows to the divine in you." This common greeting communicates that each one of us holds within a divine state of inner peace, what we call our Buddha nature.

Buddhist science reminds us that we already hold all the potential for sustained happiness inside ourselves, inside our mind. This is what is meant by our Buddha nature, it is our natural state of inner peace and the true source of our happiness. The purpose of Middle Way Mind Training, as we will soon discover, is to train the mind to uncover and realize this untapped potential which we all possess.

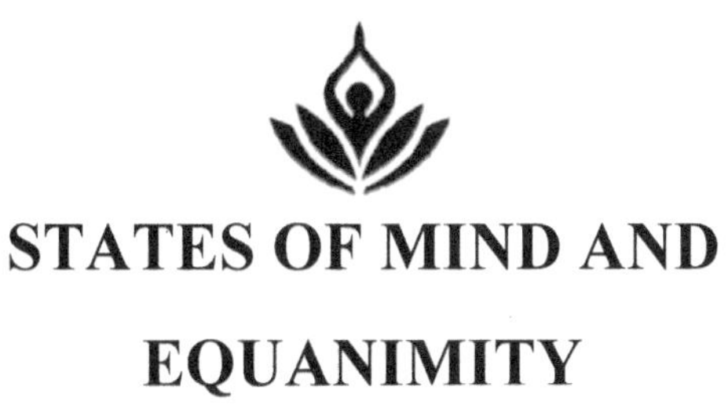

STATES OF MIND AND

EQUANIMITY

Happiness is determined more by one's state of
mind than by external events.

— His Holiness the 14th Dalai Lama

$\mathcal{I}$f the true inner nature of the mind is peaceful, and when we experience inner peace we are happy, then it is certainly important to uncover our inner nature if we want to achieve lasting and not just fleeting moments of happiness in our lives.

Have you ever noticed how many judgments we make every day? If we really take notice, we come to the realization that we make them all the time, minute by minute throughout our lives. When we see a person walking down the street, we immediately judge their appearance, perhaps we listen to them talk and we access our memory of any past experiences with similar people to help us in our judgments. We decide whether that person gives us a good, bad or neutral impression. We undergo this process in our mind with everything that enters through our sense organs. If we judge it to be good, we get a pleasant feeling, if we judge it to be bad, we get an unpleasant feeling, if it doesn't matter either way, a neutral feeling. We know that our mind is often distorted and frequently wrong in its judgments. I am sure you have been mistaken in many instances on first impressions. We are often surprised when the stranger that we met turns out to be someone completely different to what we thought initially. Being aware that this process is going on all the time is very important to our understanding of how the mind operates.

In Buddhist science, the words good and bad used conventionally in standard judgment are not preferred, because they are very subjective and prone to misuse. A suicide bomber with a distorted mindset may be truly convinced that the terrorist act they are planning to commit is really a good deed. Instead the words, beneficial and non-beneficial are better to be used. Buddhist philosophy teaches that instead of deciding if something is good, identify if it is beneficial to us and to others. Remember we are all inter-dependent and everything we do affects not just ourselves but everyone around us. Instead of judging that something is bad, it is better to assess whether it is non-beneficial to us or to others.

In this respect, nothing really good or bad ever happens in life, there are only beneficial or non-beneficial outcomes. By using these terms, we remove a lot of the subjective judgment from our interpretation of sensory information and biases encoded in the mind, because they are based on not just ourselves but also on others around us. In the example of the suicide bomber, their decision to perform a terrorist act is both non-beneficial to themselves and to any innocent bystanders who will all lose their lives in the process.

Cultivating beneficial states of mind, benefits us, as well as others with who we are in contact. Our state of inner peace is dependent on beneficial states of mind. These include unselfish love, joy, patience, compassion, generosity without expecting anything in return, and humor. When we experience any of these states of mind, we see that what is common to all of them is that they are peaceful. There is no intention to harm, no selfish motive behind any of them, no grasping, craving or obsessive attachment. They are all peaceful states of mind. When we experience any of them, our inner peaceful nature begins to shine through. When we exhibit patience we are not struggling against something that we don't want because we accept things the way they are. The same goes for when we demonstrate compassion or generosity as we are thinking about the benefits for others, not just for us. This frees us from any selfish behavior and brings us closer to our Buddha nature. Even humor in our lives, teaches us to not take things so seriously, that a lot of the external world is beyond our control. Cultivating these beneficial mind states alleviates our suffering in many ways and increases our happiness.

On the other hand, when non-beneficial or distorted mind states ensue such as hatred, impatience, self-centeredness, greed or jealousy, our mind is not in a peaceful state, it is agitated. It is therefore not possible to be happy when we are under the influence of these non-beneficial states of mind. When we are experiencing hatred or rage, we are certainly not at peace with ourselves as there is often an intention to harm. If we feel impatience, we are not accepting things as they really are and desire something to be different. This is certainly also not a peaceful state of mind. If we are self-centered, greedy or jealous, we have only our own self interests in mind, not those of others. We are attached to craving and selfish motives. These are all not states of inner peace so they will not lead to happiness.

The Buddhist Pali term *uppekha* refers to **equanimity**, a state of mental stability or composure in a mind that is not disturbed by any experience or by any emotion. Many meditation techniques, including those taught in Middle Way Mind Training are used to cultivate equanimity in the mind as they purify and counteract some of the non-beneficial states of mind. A state of equanimity means that no matter what happens in our life, whatever tragedy we may meet, or whatever heady successes we may achieve, we are able to face them with an unshakeable evenness or balance of mind. This is not to say we are indifferent or apathetic to the well-being of our self or others, but just free from the grasps of craving for pleasure and the demands of the ego. In a state of equanimity, our mind is unable to be upset by any fluctuations of fortune in our life. No matter what we gain or lose, no matter how much we are praised for our accomplishments or blamed for our failures, no matter how much pleasure we enjoy or pain we experience, we are still able to maintain a calm composure, and react to each experience in life with calm acceptance and infinite wisdom.

It is important to realize that any of the states of mind mentioned are transitory. All states of mind are impermanent, just like everything else. They arise in the mind and if we allow them, they then pass away. When we grasp or cling on to them with attachment and engage our ego, we suffer. Ultimately, we disrupt our inner peace and we cannot be happy in this way. In future chapters we will learn how to train our mind to cultivate beneficial states of mind, to counteract and dissolve non-beneficial states of mind and to maintain the highest levels of equanimity.

THE FIVE AGGREGATES

Wisdom tells me I am nothing. Love tells me I am everything. And between the two my life flows.

— Nisargadatta Maharaj

We have mentioned several times that according to Buddhist science, what we think of as the self, in reality does not actually exist. The abstractness of this concept has even been demonstrated through the modern scientific method of quantum mechanics. In truth, we are more like a dependent process rather than a concrete entity. This makes sense when we can understand that the world around us is constantly changing and we ourselves being connected to it are constantly changing with it. Our existence is certainly not static but in a dynamic flux. However, having a sense of this concrete self has evolutionary advantages as it does help us to navigate safely through this world around us. Holding on to it for dear life, however, and not clearly seeing it as it is, is unfortunately responsible for a lot of our unhappiness. Therefore, it is valuable to us to dissect and closely analyze the human experience so that we do not fall victim to any of its shortcomings.

The Buddha often spoke of the five *khandhas*, a Pali word for the five aggregates. According to Buddhist science these aggregates, or in simpler terms bundles or groupings, are all the material and mental factors that contain everything about the human condition and human existence. They are responsible for the arising of our personality, our sense of self, and all that we experience as human beings. More specifically to our study of happiness, they also give rise to craving and clinging. Modern psychologists and psychotherapists are particularly interested in this topic as it uncovers a lot of secrets of the workings of the mind and an analysis of human experience. The Buddha said that each aggregate is impermanent and without an enduring self or essence,

116

so it contains *dukkha* or suffering but one whose unwholesome activities can be interrupted by training the mind. Everything that we see ourselves as being is embodied in these five aggregates. To understand them, is to understand who we are as well as the psychology of our unhappiness. The five aggregates include form, feeling, perception, mental formations and consciousness. Each one is discussed separately below.

The Aggregate of Form (*rupa* in Pali)

The Buddhist texts state that the aggregate of form refers to all material objects, including the physical structure of ourselves and all objects in the material world. It includes all matter that is made up of the basic elements or forces of earth, water, fire and wind and their derivatives. The Buddha especially emphasized that the aggregate of form includes our sense organs (eyes, ears, nose, tongue, body) and all the sensory objects that they are in contact with (visible forms, sounds, odors, tastes, tangible things we can feel) He used the body as a foundation for discovering the other aggregates.

For us, the body holds elements of certainty, confidence, integrity, and place in life. The body gives us a sense of where we belong. According to Buddhist science this is again just an illusion. Although our body seems dense and compacted, science tells us that all of matter is mostly space and probably wave-like in nature. In actual fact there is no real solidity to our material world. Science also tells us that we are interconnected with the world around us and we are not separated from it. We are also reminded of the effects of impermanence when our physical body ages. The fact is that eventually this physical form or body is going to die and pass away. Just like all physical form, it is not permanent.

When our sense organs come in contact with material objects, we become aware of their existence. The illusory appearance of concrete solid objects outside us in the world, as interpreted by our mind, leads to the illusion that a concrete self must be aware of the object. Our mind interprets objects we see outside ourselves as ones with clear well-defined boundaries which reinforce our illusion of our self and our separation from objects around us. What this means is that the external world comes into solidness as the sense of I, me and mine comes into existence. This object is *mine, I* own this object, give it to *me*. The world appears concrete when our sense of I is strong. During deep meditation states, our boundaries become more relaxed, and as we begin to see reality as it really is, we begin to loosen the hold on our identity and objects lose their concrete definition or boundaries. This is what is meant in Buddhist science as seeing the oneness of things.

You can see how we are all prone to suffering because of the illusion of a concrete self and the view of a concrete material world outside. Our clinging and strong attachment to these objects and to ourselves as well as the inability to accept the reality that they are impermanent is a constant source of disappointment and dissatisfaction in our lives.

The Aggregate of Consciousness (*Vinnana* in Pali)

The aggregate of consciousness is often listed as the fifth aggregate but we will discuss it next as it ties in very closely with the human experience of form as well as being an integral part of all the other aggregates. According to Buddhist science, physical elements by themselves are not enough to produce a human experience. The simple contact between the eyes for example with visible objects or the ears with audible sounds cannot result in experience without the aggregate of consciousness. Consciousness must be present along with the contact of our sensory organs and the sense object in order to lead to experience. Consciousness is also required to unite the mind with its thoughts and ideas to formulate experience.

However, consciousness is mere awareness, not recognition; it is still not enough to produce human experience. Consciousness is the bare awareness of the object, but it is not experience as we do not have any feeling about it, no recognition of what the object is, or any formulated ideas about it. To complete our human experience, we further need the other aggregates of feeling, perception and mental formations.

The aggregate of consciousness only arises when a sense door is stimulated by the appropriate object, then that type of consciousness arises. For example, when a smell strikes the nose, the olfactory consciousness will arise and we become aware of smell. When a visual object strikes the eye, the visual consciousness arises. Each of the senses has its own consciousness. This consciousness arises and passes away in a split second.

Modern science has not found the seat of consciousness. Scientists have tried to locate it in the brain but to no avail. It is the subject of much debate and still remains a mystery. Consciousness gives life to the other aggregates of our existence. In Buddhist science it is defined as the knowing quality of the mind, not the cognitive part but the immediate knowing that an event has occurred. For example, the mere knowing that a sound has occurred is consciousness. With consciousness, we have the capacity or potential for human experience. Bare consciousness or pure objective awareness is that which is there before any feeling is sensed from it, before it is recognized or named and before any idea, opinion or emotional attachment about it is constructed in our minds.

The Aggregate of Feeling or Sensation (*Vedana* in Pali)

Buddhist science describes the aggregate of feeling as a physical or mental sensation that we experience through contact of the six sensory facilities with the external world. Every time we have contact of the eye with visible form, the ear with sound, the nose with odor, the tongue with taste, the body with tangible things and the mind with ideas or thoughts, and we become conscious of it, we experience a feeling that is either pleasant, unpleasant or neutral. Each human experience takes on one of these three basic feeling tones. Either we find the experience as something we like, something we don't like or we are just indifferent to it and don't care either way. This is how a human experience begins to come to fruition and this aggregate is also the root base of our conditioning of that experience. If it has a pleasant quality to it, we run towards it, if unpleasant we flee from it and if it is neutral we do not give it much notice and dismiss it as irrelevant. Because the aggregate of feeling is an experience of pleasure or pain, it conditions craving as either we wish more of it, or we wish to avoid it.

The feeling tone is not inherent to the object, but it resides only in us. We have a tendency to place the feeling tone on the object of our senses and chase after it with all our effort when what we are really chasing is the feeling tone that we feel in ourselves. For example we may get a pleasant feeling tone when we see an attractive person, an unpleasant feeling tone when we see someone we find unattractive and a neutral feeling tone when we don't care either way. We tend to place that feeling tone on the person when it is really only in our mind. Modern advertising and marketing is unfortunately a sad example of how our feeling tone can be manipulated and conditioned. Some examples include focus advertising directed at very young children associating a feeling tone with a certain toy or product or negative advertising often used in political campaigns to condition feeling tones in voters. Try to notice the feeling tones that are evoked as you are shopping.

As we increase our ability to be more aware with the training of the mind, we will be able to notice the feeling tone and prevent it from becoming embellished or habitual. As the feeling tone is conditioned, we should question it and not trust it. We have a tendency to avoid anything unpleasant and crave for anything pleasant. When a feeling tone gets embellished with thoughts, past experiences or past memories then emotions can arise such as greed, anger or fear. In most cases we are not aware of the simple feeling tone, because it can rapidly turn into a full blown emotion. Again by training our mind, we can observe what is happening and prevent negative reactions. When we look at the feeling tones we are really looking at the foundation of how all problems arise in our lives. When we initiate contact with an object and our sense doors, there will always be a feeling tone, and then there will be a grasping to it, aversion to it or a neutral reaction where we won't notice it at all. As we bring thoughts into the feeling tone, its briefness gets extended and prolonged and becomes corrupted by desire or aversion. Under this agitated state we do not have inner peace, which as we know affects our happiness. Feelings like everything else are impermanent and subject to change. The goal is to deal with the feeling tones as they really are without attaching to them, and letting go of habitual grasping to I, me or mine.

We tend to blame the outside world or people for our unpleasant feeling tones. We often fail to realize that the person does not contain them, we contain them. Our anger can be the reaction to our feeling tone; it is not inherent to something or someone outside us. No one is pleasant or unpleasant in themselves; it is only our conditioned response in our minds. The sober realization is that we need to take responsibility for our emotions. We cannot depend on the other person to bring pleasant feeling tones to us. We need to become more aware of them before they lead to non-beneficial conditioned reactions. We also need to realize that our happiness cannot be dependent on our feeling tones. Feelings are unreliable and are not permanent. They arise in the mind, not in the object. A sense of equanimity or acceptance without judgment is needed so that we can not only be aware of feeling tones that arise but be able to let them go and see them just as passing clouds in the sky. They are not permanent, so there is no need to attach to them.

Whether the experience is pleasant or not pleasant, we need to allow ourselves to experience whatever feeling tone arises. I am not saying to not enjoy a pleasant experience but we should not let it lead to wanting more and more as in craving or in the case of an unpleasant experience, to aversion by pushing it away. The less we depend on feeling, the more clarity we will have and the easier it will be to see reality as it really is, not the way we want it to be or have been conditioned to see it.

The Aggregate of Perception (*Sanna in Pali*)

When we speak of the aggregate of perception, we have in mind the faculty of recognition or identification. It is the process of attaching a name to the object of experience. For example, we perceive a tree, or a mountain or a color. When the object, after contact with our sense door, is brought into awareness through consciousness and a feeling tone is evoked, then along with that process, there is identification and recognition of that object. This is perception. We introduce a conceptual element or definite idea about the object of our experience, through recognition in memory. For example, we recognize a tree as a tree because we associate it with our previous experience with trees.

Perception is the minds way of making sense of things by putting the world into categories or naming objects. It allows us to navigate the world, to feel safe and to function. Perception governs how we view the world, what choices we make and allows a platform for habits to form. Our perceptions are conditioned by what we have perceived before and in this way they are rigid and make it difficult for us to explore other possibilities. We tend to stick to what is safe and familiar and what has worked before. Training the mind through meditative training techniques allows the analysis and observation of perceptions so that more possibilities can arise. We tend to distort reality with our minds perception. When we perceive the world through depressed states, we feel absolutely convinced that everything is hopeless and bad. Then when depression passes, our world is perceived in a completely different way. This is because perception was colored or clouded by the mood. We can see that perception is also not permanent.

We tend to also have a distorted perception of separation, as we hold on to the illusion of a self. This is only an assumption and based on the story we give to our self. What is important is bare attention, which is awareness without adding anything else like desires or fears to perception, which creates a separation of the world and our self. If there is no fear or desire, then there is no separation. In this way we are able to see beyond the perception. Bare attention in meditation is when we can observe the grasping, the feeling tones and perceptions. The Buddha said "in the seeing there is just the seeing, in the hearing there is just the hearing." This is bare awareness without all the clutter and confusion that comes with our feelings and perceptions.

The Aggregate of Mental Formations (*Sankhara in Pali*)

Finally, there is the aggregate of mental formation or volition. It can be described as our conditioned response or reaction to an object of experience. It includes any mental imprints or any conditioning that is triggered by an object. It also includes any process that makes a person initiate action.

The Buddha described 51 mental formations, some of which include hatred, fear, greed, envy, compassion and wisdom. In Buddhist philosophy, these mental formations are habitual patterns in the mind that are said to have arisen both from past lives and during the present life. They are called volitional formations because they result from volition and are the causes of the arising of future volitional actions. Remember everything begins in the mind. Once mental formations develop, they have the potential to produce volitional actions of body, speech and mind. They are also referred to as karmic formations because they have a moral dimension in that they have moral consequences.

Mental formations can be likened to mental baggage that we carry around with us throughout our life. It includes all our thoughts, our beliefs, our opinions, prejudices and all our stories. The mental formations also include the habitual responses that get triggered by the interaction of the other aggregates.

Over time, certain reactivity is nurtured to a particular object. This process originates from our initial feeling tone of being pleasant or unpleasant and then perception comes into view which draws on any memories or similar experiences of the past. As we bring it up and repeat it in our mind, assumptions are formed and thoughts and opinions proliferate which we attach to strongly. Thoughts convince us that our moods are an accurate depiction of the world. Emotions tend to color our perception of reality. Moods and attitudes develop that evoke good or bad reactions every time that object enters our sense doors. These are mental formations. With time, they form what we call our character or personality. They can be so habitual and deeply ingrained in our minds that we believe that they characterize who we really are.

We need to understand how mental formations arise because they determine our future human experiences. If we allow any negative reactions to spring from them uncontrollably, then we are bound to hurt ourselves and others around us. Remember our responses do not arise from the external environment; we do not react to the person because of them. We react to our mental formations that are constructed from our feeling tones, perceptions and thoughts. We blame things outside of ourselves, when in fact they originate only in our mind. This is how, according to Buddhist science, our concept of self is developed. Once we resist something in life as it arises, there has to be a resistor to life or an "I", and outside of that "I", is a world outside that is causing this feeling. The Buddha saw how we all have this tendency because we do not see reality as it really is. We do not accept the feeling tone with equanimity, and this leads to the mental formations and the illusion of the self. We develop negative attitudes that assume that the world outside is doing this to us, or that person is causing us this pain, that is why we feel this way. We do not want to take responsibility and realize that our problem is just a construct of the mind and not stemming from the external world.

Putting it all together – the Five Aggregates

From our discussion of each of the five aggregates, Buddhist science has revealed to us how human experience works inside our mind. We can now see how the physical and mental factors which make up these aggregates work together to produce personal experience. Let's look at a concrete example. Say for instance that you are walking outside in a garden. Your eyes come in contact with a visible object or form. As your attention focuses on the object, the aggregate of your visual consciousness arises and you become aware of a visual object but as yet you do not know what it is. Your aggregate of feeling arises with an unpleasant feeling while the aggregate of perception identifies through the memory of past experiences and names the object as a snake. Your aggregate of mental formation arises and you immediately react with a conditioned response to the snake with intense fear and with the volitional action of running away or picking up a stone to defend yourself. This entire process occurs in a tiny fraction of time. Here we can see how in our daily activities, all five aggregates work together to produce personal experience.

We can only reach the conclusion that the human being is actually only a closed system because we cannot make direct contact with reality; we can only make contact with an image of reality. Everything we experience is neurological. The problem arises when we take our internal experience in the mind as an objective fact of reality. We are convinced that reality is doing something to us, when actually we are doing it to our self. The making of human experience, which starts out as contact between our sense doors and an object, and from it initiates a feeling tone, allows consciousness to arise, perception and mental formations, is all just an internal experience. The hope is that with training and self awareness, we can see the truth of the reality beneath human experience and be able to intercept the process before any unwanted conditioned reactions occur.

The nature of the five aggregates, are that they are in constant change. The elements that constitute the aggregate of form, including all material objects and our bodies are impermanent and are in a state of constant change. We know this because the body grows old, weak, sick and eventually dies and all things around us are also impermanent and change constantly. Feelings too are constantly changing. We may respond today to a particular situation with a feeling of pleasure but the next day we may respond to that same situation with the feeling of displeasure. We may perceive an object in a particular way and then later, under different circumstances, our perception changes. In dim light we may perceive a rope on the sidewalk to be a snake, but when we shine a light on it, we perceive it to be only a piece of rope. Our perceptions, like our feelings and all the material objects of our experience, are ever changing and impermanent. The same applies to our mental formations, which too are impermanent and constantly changing. We can alter our habits. We can learn to be fearless, instead of fearful. Consciousness too is impermanent and constantly changing as it is dependent upon an object and a sense organ. It cannot exist independently. So, every one of these aggregates are constantly changing and impermanent. They are processes, not things and are dynamic, not static.

Why do we even bother to analyze our personal experience in terms of the five aggregates? Why is it necessary to break it down into the various elements of form, feeling, perception, mental formation and consciousness? What does this have to do with happiness? The purpose of this analysis is really to cultivate the wisdom of non-self and understand impermanence. Analyzing the five aggregates allows us to discern objectively whether there is an entity we call "I" that is actually there. What we want to achieve is to arrive at a way of experiencing the world that is not constructed upon and around the illusion of a self. We want to see personal experience in terms of processes, in terms of impersonal functions rather than in terms of a self and what affects a self. This allows us to create an attitude of equanimity, an accepting non-judgmental attitude that will help us overcome any emotional disturbances and impulsive non-beneficial reactions. We understand pleasure and pain in terms of the self. We understand them as personal pleasure and pain. Once we understand them in terms of impersonal processes and we get rid of the idea of the self, we can overcome these emotional disturbances.

Buddhist science teaches us the importance in understanding that the five aggregates are not us; they are only temporary, conditioned phenomena and empty of any permanent self. While the component parts of the five aggregates appear to work together so seamlessly that they create the sense of a single self or an "I," understanding their true reality is helpful to see through this illusion.

What is important is not to grasp at or cling to the forms, sounds, odors, flavors, tactile sensations, and mental properties which are brought into awareness, felt, perceived and formulated in the mind as a result of the input from the six sense organs. The insight, that the aggregates are not self, aids in letting go of this grasping. The Buddha taught that the aggregates were *dukkha* or suffering. By releasing our hold onto them, we release our suffering and become much happier in our lives.

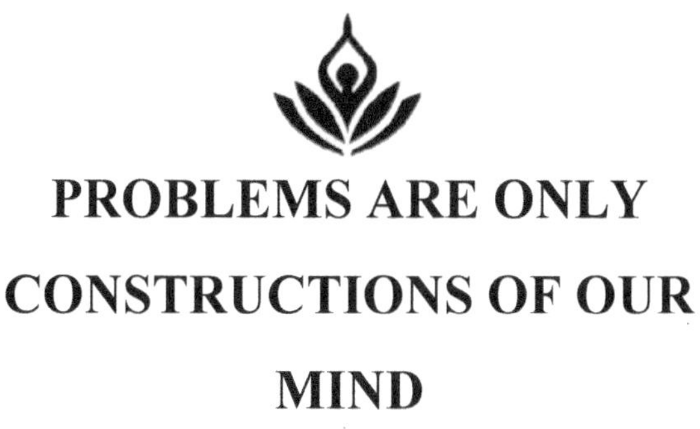

PROBLEMS ARE ONLY CONSTRUCTIONS OF OUR MIND

I am an old man and have known a great many
troubles, but most of them never happened.

— Mark Twain

Now that we have described the Buddhist view of human experience, we are better equipped to tackle problems that arise in our lives. The word *"problem"* is a Greek word meaning an obstacle or something that gets in our way, a source of trouble or worry. I am sure you can appreciate how we tend to view problems in our lives as being generally unwelcome, possibly harmful to us and something that we try to overcome or deal with. A problem can be likened to a dark, endless tunnel that has no exit, one that leads most of us to a lot of stress, frustration, anger and often hopelessness. Very few of us can honestly say that we are currently not dealing with any problems in our lives. Common problems include those related to our relationships with friends and family, our financial situation and those found in the workplace.

When we are faced with a problem, with it comes a sense of uncertainty as the resolution of the problem is immediately not clear. Usually problems are perceived as negative, as they represent a situation where we are not happy with the current situation as it is, and this creates a sense of tension, anxiety, often anger and even fear.

If we analyze the human experience of a problem according to the five aggregates that we discussed in the last chapter, we can see that once a problem is brought to our consciousness, usually an unpleasant feeling will initially arise. Our perception will then analyze and identify the problem and look back at our past memory to see if we have been faced with anything similar before. If there is no immediate resolution after it is perceived, then our mind tends to bring in more negative thoughts and emotions, which embellish the problem even further, often exaggerating its threat to us and its negative consequences. We tend to blow it out of proportion and make it much worse than it actually is. If we continue to worry about the problem it grows more and thoughts invade our minds and we grasp at them and become attached. Our imagination gets out of control and we play out the worst case scenarios and formulate the most negative outcomes for the future if the problem is not solved. These are all mental formations which lead to strong emotional reactions such as anger, anxiety and fear.

When we have a difficult problem, we are not at peace with ourselves nor with anyone around us. We are difficult to be with as our mind becomes obsessed with the problem at hand. We are unable to see it objectively and we can explode with anger and panic with the onset of this experience. The mind as we know can distort reality, so what may in reality be a minor obstacle, may turn into something we see as insurmountable or even life-threatening. Someone on the outside, who is able to see things objectively without emotion, will often see our problem as easily manageable.

It is important to be able to observe the mind as it goes through this process. Often our reactions to problems are habitual and ingrained in our minds. We often react uncontrollably and later regret our impulsive and erratic behavior.

Buddhist science views problems very differently. First of all, the problem is only a problem if you allow it to be one. Remember, we have that tendency to throw the blame on the external world and onto people outside of ourselves. The problem exists only in our minds. The cause of the problem is also not in the external environment, it is in our mind as well. If we choose to not accept the situation as it is without staying calm or refraining from judgment, meaning without equanimity, then the situation develops into a problem in our mind. After there is contact between our mind sense door with a thought or idea, and we receive an unpleasant feeling tone and act on it, we begin the processes of the five aggregates that lead to mental formations and reactions. When we accept that the world is constantly changing and that the external environment is beyond our total control, then we must accept that things will often not go as we planned. This is the law of impermanence. Everything is always changing. Being able to internalize this realization and accepting whatever comes our way will eliminate our resistance to anything that we experience that is different than what we desire. Developing equanimity and acceptance before we react is easier said than done. It takes considerable awareness but mind training can certainly cultivate this ability.

Buddhist science teaches that nothing that we experience is inherently good or bad. We are the ones that perceive it, name it and identify with it that way. Objectively an experience is just an experience. Take for example the grieving process after someone close to us has passed away. There is certainly a sense of shock and sadness when it happens, and we experience very unpleasant feelings, but as we know feelings are not permanent, they arise in the mind and they pass away. When we add much more to these initial feelings, for example grasp onto memories of the past or bring in negative thoughts and ideas into our mind, we aggravate and prolong the problem. We develop mental formations such as guilt or depression. We feel guilty that we should have spent more time with them, or told them that we loved them. We allow the initial feeling tone to grow and perpetuate into mental formations that may stay with us for the rest of our lives. Some people never can accept or get over the loss of a loved one. Intellectually, we all understand that we will die one day, and we see examples of death every day on the news and around us, whether it is by accident, murder, terminal illness or natural causes. The reality of the human condition is that we cannot be certain when death will arrive. An intellectual understanding of our impermanence though is often not enough. The mind needs to internalize these concepts so that the inevitable aggregates of the human experience can be observed, brought into our awareness and then they can be accepted with equanimity and wisdom.

The other delusion, according to Buddhist science, is that in the process of formulating problems that are blamed on things outside ourselves in the external environment, we further strengthen the construct of our self. We complain that <u>our</u> life is full of problems or that everyone is doing this to <u>me</u>, or <u>I</u> wish I could be free of all <u>my</u>

problems. In this way we separate ourselves from the outside world, when in reality we are all interconnected.

The Buddhist views of impermanence, *dukkha* or suffering and non-self are very important concepts that teach us to view reality and the problems we face with a completely different perspective. We begin to realize that we are not the center of the universe or the only one suffering in the world but that every one of us is in the same boat. No one gets a free pass in life, no matter how wealthy, famous, or successful one becomes. When we accept that everything is impermanent, we let go of our grasp and attachment to our feelings and mental formations. We come to realize that with human life comes uncertainty and discontent and that we no longer see ourselves as a concrete entity with a "me against the world" mentality. As our attachment to an illusory self dissolves, we become an interdependent process connected to the world around us. The Buddha taught us that when we can grasp these concepts not just intellectually but experientially, we will relieve the burden of all the problems we carry on our shoulders, and uncover lasting happiness.

TRANSFORMING PROBLEMS
INTO OPPORTUNITIES

Every problem is an opportunity in disguise.

— John Adams

*W*e learned that it is possible to look at problems in a different way through Buddhist science and that the entire concept of a problem is something that in reality is only constructed in the mind and does not come from the external environment itself. We can save ourselves a lot of unnecessary suffering from this profound realization. In this chapter we will not only see that problems can be diffused in the mind but they can also be used to be transformed into opportunities.

This seems like an unusual premise. How can a problem be turned into an opportunity? Just think though, about the many times that a problem has presented itself in our life initially and later in retrospect we realize that it was the best thing that could have happened to us. There are so many times this happens to us but most of us are not aware of it. We usually do not put the pieces together. Perhaps it was the job we didn't get, only to open the door to a much better job opportunity later, or the job that we got fired from which finally motivated us to open the business we have always dreamed about starting. There are just so many situations that happen to us in life like this but all of them have one thing in common. Initially they are perceived as negative and we allow them to cause us an immense amount of pain and suffering.

Since this book is about being able to maximize the amount of happiness we have in our lives, and since it is inevitable that we will encounter problems innumerable times, it certainly seems reasonable that we should learn how to deal with them in a positive way. First and foremost we will learn in later sections the practical ways of training the inner awareness of our mind to observe the aggregates before emotion gets blown out of proportion. But there is also a way to welcome problems in our life, yes welcome them and view them as opportunities instead of the usual burden on our shoulders that they invariably become.

Often a major tragedy or catastrophe is needed in our life that leads to a paradigm shift in our mind. Take the situation for example when someone we love is diagnosed with a terminal disease like cancer. As we see them slowly dying in front of our eyes, we are reminded that life is not permanent and also that most problems that we encounter in life are superficial and inconsequential. Even the sickness of a loved one, can show us that nothing that happens to us in life is inherently bad. From out of these types of helpless situations full of suffering, we often develop qualities that we may have not tapped into so much before. We learn to be much more compassionate and less self-centered. Feelings of love, kindness and generosity are enhanced especially when we know that we will lose someone. Remember, these are all beneficial states of mind that lead to peaceful mind states and happiness. We tend to look at life differently. It is like a wakeup call to start living life to the fullest and to really value the time we have. This is a great example of how our own worst difficulties can be transformed into opportunities.

We can think about our demanding boss at work that drives us crazy or a difficult colleague that consistently tests our patience. These problems may occupy our mind so much that they start to take away from our work. How can we turn this experience into something positive? When we feel impatient or resentful it is certainly unsettling and stressful. Our mind refuses to accept the situation as it is, and for this battle we suffer immensely. Training our mind to be patient, tolerant and accepting are beneficial mind states that maintain our inner peace and happiness. Our aversion or inability to accept the situation creates those unwanted negative feelings. Letting go of our expectations transforms the problem into just an opportunity to practice patience. Patience is a virtue that says that we accept the present moment as it is, calmly and without anger or judgment. It is interesting to note that several scientific studies reveal that patient people have more friends, are happier and have less health problems than those that are not (Umberson and Montez, 2010).

A lot depends on how we perceive our problematic situation to be. The old saying, "every cloud has a silver lining" is very applicable to this discussion. Intuitively we know this to be true but at the moment when we have to deal with the experience, we are usually not prepared to think that way. We become more miserable when we confront difficult experiences especially when we react with impatience, anger or sadness. We point the blame on the outside and this even perpetuates our suffering.

We need to remind ourselves that our future is uncertain, and negative feelings that arise now will always pass away. The reality is that we just don't know what lies around the corner or what will unfold. It helps to not dwell on things and see the world with a bit of humor and with the wonder of a child's eyes, a beginner's mind that is open to any possibilities. If we can cultivate equanimity, and accept things calmly as they are, whether good or bad, we can reduce a lot of our suffering and be much happier.

It also helps to internalize the fact that we are not the only one in the world with problems. The "poor me" or "why is this happening to me" syndrome that we often get caught up in, does not apply. Everyone experiences problems in their lives. No one has a problem-free life. There are no exceptions. We may say to ourselves, when I am rich or when I find my ideal partner, life will be free of problems but that will never happen. This is the nature of life. The Buddha stated this is the First Noble Truth. Pleasant experiences and unpleasant experiences are also impermanent so they don't last forever. How many problems that you had last year are still problems right now? I am sure many of them have been resolved or lost their significance since then and new ones have long replaced them.

When things do not go as we planned or we fail at something or get into trouble financially, we learn to realize that we cannot control all outcomes in our external environment. The positive side to this is that we are forced to let go of non-beneficial mind states such as greed, arrogance, pride and self-centeredness, which agitate the mind and overshadow its peaceful nature. Humility allows us to be more flexible and realistic in dealing with problems. We become more understanding of others who have faced the same problems. As we are forced to let go of some of our self importance and pride we become more generous and we release the grip of the self, that illusory construct which we know from Buddhist science is a major cause of our unhappiness.

Unfortunately, we will continue to encounter problems and react with them negatively until we change our mind set. Non-beneficial or distorted mind states will always distort the mind and lead to agitation. If the mind is not peaceful, then we cannot be happy because they cover up or cloud over the potential that is beneath. At the same time, attempting to make our external environment perfect so that no problems will arise is futile. The change has to come from within. No problem is ever as big as it initially appears and like all things, it will pass. Problems as we have seen can be transformed. The mind alone creates happiness and our life will continue to be unsatisfactory and we will react negatively to problems until we train our minds. Hopefully with insight and wisdom, we can come to the conclusion that nothing we encounter in life is ever a problem that cannot be solved with a calm and accepting mind.

FINDING HUMOR IN THE
HUMAN CONDITION

Life is a tragedy to those who feel and a comedy
to those who think.

— Molière

$\mathcal{L}$aughter and humor have often been considered a healing process, that which brings people together to share a common experience and provides a release from the tensions that come from human existence. The Buddha diagnosed the root cause of human suffering as our own obsessive tendency to cling to unreal ideas about ourselves and the world we live in. Humor offers a kind of disruptive therapy for the anxiety we often feel about life when the way we think the world should be, is not in agreement with the way the world actually is. Humor often makes us realize the absurdities that constitute the human condition. It often arises from the real tragedy of our ego-bound existence, where we seem stuck in our old habits of thought and behavior.

Humor provides us with a wonderful opportunity to challenge the assumed authority of the ego and over-ride its sense of control over us. It gives us a chance to transcend or step out of our conventional roles in life. It can help us to go beyond the constructed images of ourselves and to see through our egocentric view of life. Humor offers us a light-hearted approach to life and a taste of real freedom from our conditioned mind. Once we have an opportunity to be aware of this freedom, we see the humor in our inability to realize and sustain it in our daily lives. The realization that our plans and ambitions are subject to change and the external environment is beyond our control means we cannot count on things always working out the way we want. Instead of suffering from every disappointment that arises, bringing a little humor into the situation is certainly needed.

When people are asked what is important in their lives, they often mention humor. Couples listing the traits they prize in their spouses usually place a sense of humor at or near the top of their list. It is often valued very highly in friendships and social organizations. Humor, in many ways is a magical experience as it brings with it a much needed positive state of mind that diverts us from our focus on negativity or the tragedy that often dominates the human condition. We are very much social animals and humor is a highly social experience. According to one estimate, we are more likely to laugh with other people than when we are alone (Provine, 2000).

Some scientific studies have demonstrated the healing effects of humor not only on our state of mind but also on our physical body (Mora-Ripoll, 2010).

In response to laughter, our bodies produce pain-killing hormones called endorphins. Laughter stimulates the immune system and significantly reduces stress by lowering cortisol levels which return the body to a more relaxed state. There is extensive clinical evidence, including randomized controlled clinical trials which validate the therapeutic efficacy of laughter, particularly in the fields of geriatrics and oncology as well as palliative, hospice and terminal care (Rosner, 2002).

Humor also has a positive impact on our emotions, changing the perspective we have of life's trials and tribulations by making them seem less significant. It also helps in overcoming our fears and allows us to take ourselves less seriously. When we can laugh at the human condition and at ourselves, life become less complicated and we can accept things the way they are with equanimity. The humorous view on life helps us to take a gentler and softer look at things. It frees us of the roles we have been conditioned to play. We certainly notice how we tend to hide and protect our precious egos when someone ridicules us or makes a joke about us. The Buddhist wisdom we should take from this experience is that when it comes down to it, there really is no one there or no self to be embarrassed or humiliated so we can let others laugh all they want.

In some ways, humor is a kind of child play. Cultivating humor teaches us to be more playful and less serious about life. We often admire innocent children who have the natural ability to express themselves without any barriers by laughing, smiling and giggling at the silliest occurrences. As they get older and mature however, and the worries and stresses of life take hold, they tend to lose this spontaneous ability. The Dalai Lama is a perfect example of how he is able to inspire and show wisdom through his laughter and humor, while still projecting authority. Even though he lost his entire country, suffered invasion and endured the death of his fellow monks as he fled Tibet, he is the first person to laugh and smile. Whenever he laughs, people cannot help but laugh as well. If we can find humor in the face of sadness, we transform our grief and if we can laugh at your own stupidity we gain wisdom. The Dalai Lama has long realized that laughter connects us to the universe at the deepest level. He often shuns the formal pomp and circumstance that the public endows on him and his humor tends to break down the barriers between himself and his audience. In the end he is able to show he is only human, just like we are. His light-hearted humorous approach resonates very well with people who are even more encouraged to listen to his teachings.

We all know that painful things happen in life, and that ultimately we are going to age, get sick and die. But we don't have to take our human predicament so personally. Being able to laugh about all the many painful attachments we fall prey to is a great relief. In some ways, laughter and humor are a meditation that forces us to be in the present moment that stops our ruminating thoughts and worrying about our future or our past, at least for a short while. They go a long way to reduce our suffering, particularly when we are reminded that things aren't happening to us, they are just situations and events that are just happening. The benefit of our liberation from the notion of an enduring, independent self is that it makes it much easier for us to laugh at ourselves. Once we begin to question the notion of an independent ego, we are likely to stop taking the "self" so seriously. Bringing a sense of humor and curiosity to our fear and anxiety is liberating.

We are certainly missing out on a lot of happiness if we choose to take life too seriously. We have the opportunity to transform our minds and to soften each unpleasant experience with humor and laughter. Perhaps we will see that life does not have to be the tragedy we perceive it to be but more like a realistic comedy of human errors.

THE THIRD NOBLE TRUTH

The third noble truth says that the cessation of
suffering is letting go of holding on to ourselves.

– Pema Chodron

The First Noble Truth handed down by the Buddha as we know was the **truth of suffering**; the Second Noble Truth was the **truth of the cause of suffering**. Referring back to our physician analogy, since we have already identified the disease or the suffering that exists (the First Noble Truth) and diagnosed the cause as being craving (the Second Noble Truth), the Third Noble Truth can be likened to the prognosis. A comparable medical example would be predicting after diagnosing Stage 1 cancer, that it is treatable and has a good chance of recovery. The Third Noble Truth then, the **truth of the cessation of suffering**, was actually the Buddha's prognosis that suffering can be cured or extinguished. For the first time, the Buddha was revealing more than just doom and gloom for mankind that which Buddhism is often criticized as proclaiming. With his Third Noble Truth, he was now offering the real hope or prediction that the outcome of lasting happiness is possible to attain. In other words, he forecasted that the eradication of thirst or craving will eliminate all of our suffering.

The Buddha stated that there are three root causes of our suffering, which manifest themselves as greed, hatred and delusion. These require the elimination in our mind of any craving, aversion or ignorance of our true reality. As the first two noble truths showed us, we needed to first look deeply at the nature of our suffering, at the dynamic of craving in our lives and how these three root causes manifest in us and in human society. Now that we have done that, what is inferred from the Third Noble Truth is the logical conclusion that if we can remove the causes we can achieve our goal. In Buddhist philosophy, the final stage, after we eliminate all the impurities in the mind and totally let go of all our attachments is *nirvana*, the ultimate goal of enlightenment. It is often considered the ultimate happiness, one that can only be experienced to really describe and one that is beyond the conditioned states of *samsara* or our wandering state of human existence.

The Third Noble Truth changes everything. It transcends the teachings of Buddhist science from being just an exercise in analysis of the human condition to an invitation to transform our minds. Unhappiness and discontent does not have to be this endless dark tunnel but there is a way out. It is possible if we are willing to do the practical work needed, to really make that journey from *dukkha* (suffering) to its liberation. The Third Noble truth ends all intellectual exercise and gives new meaning to practicing what we preach. It gives a practical starting point for contemplative mind training practice to unfold and develop.

Our mind needs to be open and receptive in order to realize the profound insights taken from the noble truths. There is no room for any blind beliefs, so a contemplative approach is needed. By focusing inwards, we are able to continue our investigation and get beyond the gross and the obvious. There needs to be a willingness to actually look at our own reactions internally and to be able to see the attachments we have, contemplate what kind of feelings we get from them and analyze what behaviors they evoke in us. We need to ask ourselves whether we feel peaceful when we are being attached to a desire, or if we feel anxious or fearful. As we progress in our ability to discern our desires and aversions more closely in our minds, we will also be able to experience the consequences of our attachments to them. We can ask our self if attaching to material pleasures really offers the happiness we are craving for, or if it only brings suffering and disappointment in the long run. Do we really benefit being fixed to our ideas, attitudes or opinions, when they are subject to change or do they lead us to more isolation and separation from others? We need to reflect on whether our mind is being influenced by the external world or if we are really making your own unbiased decisions, free of judgment, free of past experiences, and whether any thoughts and reactions around them really reflect the true reality of every experience.

The noble truths are there to be deeply contemplated and internalized. Each of the four truths interconnects with the subsequent one. From their insights arises a true understanding unclouded by any of our sense doors or the external environment. This means they reflect a clear vision or view of reality. So far, we have only prepared our minds for this paradigm shift in thinking with an intellectual understanding of how to experience happiness. Now, in the final parts of this book, it is time to perform the internal surgery of our minds by introducing a practical method that can transform our suffering into sustained and genuine happiness. This practical method is of course Middle Way Mind Training and we will soon become familiarized with its foundational principles along with all its practical applications.

PART IV

FOUNDATIONS OF MIDDLE WAY
MIND TRAINING

We are shaped by our thoughts; we become what
we think. When the mind is pure, joy follows like
a shadow that never leaves.

— The Buddha

WHY DO WE NEED TO TRAIN OUR MIND?

We need a repeated discipline, a genuine training,
in order to let go of our old habits of mind and to
find and sustain a new way of seeing.

— Jack Kornfield

*I*t is easy to fall into the trap that it is enough to just interpret the nature of the mind through an intellectual understanding. Up to this point in the book, that is what we have presented, but our study of how to be happy remains only theoretical until we can actually put it into practice and evaluate the results ourselves. The problem exists, that no matter how much we intellectually comprehend all the concepts about how we can attain happiness, comprehension itself is unfortunately limited. It is just not that easy to change our minds. Our intellect, though very useful in navigating us through the external world, is not enough. Our cognition is still subject to manipulation by our ego and our five aggregates play a role in all of our experiences in our lives. Training the mind gives us the ability and resources to view reality with bare awareness, that which has not be distorted or polluted with emotion, perception and mental formations. We can then learn to stop reacting dramatically to all of our ups and downs that we go through in our lives and see them with true wisdom and with evenness of mind or equanimity.

Initially our untrained mind can be likened to the surface of a turbulent ocean full of crashing waves and blowing winds. As we train the mind and sink deeper internally, we learn to remain in the same ocean but now we are submerged to a certain depth beneath, where it is always calm and peaceful and in a place that is no longer affected by the situation on the external surface. So an intellectual understanding will not be effective unless we can internalize what we have learned. In order to be truly happy we need to train our mind.

The primary reasons why mind training is absolutely essential in our quest for happiness as extrapolated from Buddhist science, is threefold: to see the true reality of our existence, to let go of our clinging to our desires and to cultivate and maintain wholesome states of mind. Each of these three reasons are very much interrelated and discussed below.

Mind training is needed to see the true reality of our existence

One of the reasons we are not happy is because we are not living in harmony with reality. If Buddhist science teaches us that the true reality of our existence is impermanence and that we do not really have a self the way we think we do, then we are way off the track when it comes to seeing reality the way it is really playing out. Clinging to our external environment when it is impermanent and being selfish with material possessions with a self that we think is concrete and unchanging only exacerbates our unhappiness. According to Buddhist science, we fail to see reality in three major ways and that is a great source of our unhappiness and discontent.

The first is our failure to understand the nature of suffering (*dukkha*). We learned from the First Noble Truth that suffering or discontent is inherent in the human condition. We experience physical and mental pain when we are born, when we age and when we eventually get sick and die. There is no getting away from this reality. We also experience *dukkha* when we have contact with unpleasant experiences, when we are separated from pleasant experiences, when we do not get what we want and when we are unable to accept that pleasant experiences never last forever.

The second way we fail to see reality is in our inability to accept the law of impermanence (*anicca*). Because we see ourselves and our external world as fixed entities, we grasp onto them. Everything in our external world and internal world, including our thoughts, ideas and emotions is impermanent and subject to arising and passing away. Our inability to fully internalize this concept leads us to unnecessary suffering as we grasp and hold onto things, ideas and people as if they are permanent and unchanging. Mind training helps to internalize this concept, which will free us from our hold on things that will eventually change and pass away.

The third way we fail to see reality is through the concept of non-self (*anatta*). We see our self as an unchanging concrete entity and create separation by grasping onto the constructs of I, me and mine. We fail to see that we are all interconnected with others and the world around us and that we are a dynamic process that is always changing.

Mind training is needed to let go of craving to desires

The Second Noble Truth states that the cause of our suffering is craving. We know already how important it is to keep a close watch on our sense doors when they come in contact with a sense object. Reality can be easily distorted. As the aggregate of consciousness arises and the aggregate of feeling determines if we see the object as pleasant or unpleasant, mind training is needed to allow us to observe this process with bare unbiased awareness. It prevents perceptions that are based on past experiences and emotions to distort what is truly being observed, which often leads to craving and attachment. Usually if we allow this behavior to continue without observation, it leads to negative mental formations that can be very difficult to transform. Remember our ego will strengthen our tendency to search for happiness in places where it cannot be found, i.e. - our external environment. Hopefully you can see how time and time again we strive to grasp on to material possessions and people and external experiences to bring us the sustained happiness we desire, but this is not sustainable.

Mind training is needed to cultivate and maintain beneficial states of mind

It is easy to say in hindsight that we should stop reacting with anger every time we are in a certain situation because we know we just end up suffering and hurting others around us. However, in the heat of the moment, when we are gripped with intense anger, we all know that our reactions are often impossible to control.

It is very difficult to break out of these egoistic and habitual mental patterns. Someone may say something trivial that hits a sensitive chord within us somewhere in our mind, and we are immediately triggered to react negatively. With time, these habitual patterns get so engrained that they become our natural reactions when faced with similar situations. They occur so fast and unconsciously that we sometimes do not even know why we reacted the way we did.

Hence, initially there is a need to first slow down our wild thoughts and clear our minds of all the distractions that prevent us from seeing things the way they really are. This can only be done through mind training and contemplative practice. With contemplative science, which means the science of meditation and mindfulness, we can learn to use and cultivate antidotes to our negative states of mind. Most of us obviously do feel moments of love and compassion but these beneficial mind states need to be cultivated so that they are not just fleeting occasional states. The art and science of meditation and mind training is about cultivation, to become familiar with something and see it grow and expand to our benefit.

There are four ways that mind training can assist our mental states of mind. First of all it can transform existing states of mind that are unwholesome, such as mental formations of hatred, fear, greed or jealousy into wholesome states like, love, compassion and generosity. Secondly, it can be used to prevent unwholesome states of mind to ever arise in the mind. Thirdly it can be used to cultivate brand new wholesome states of mind and finally to maintain the wholesome states that already exist in the mind.

States of mind are mental formations or constructs. By applying mind training in the form of meditation and mindfulness, we can modify the causes and conditions of mental constructs. We allow our bare unbiased awareness to observe and monitor the five aggregates to ensure that unwholesome mind states are transformed and never get a chance to become engrained in the mind, while allowing wholesome mind states to arise and flourish.

In future parts of this book we will explain what we really mean by Middle Way Mind Training. We will also discover how this practical method can address each one of the above three primary reasons and why mind training is essential in our quest to uncovering and experiencing the happiness we have within.

THE FOURTH NOBLE TRUTH

Now I plant my thoughts
being mindful of their ways
let them grow from loving hearts
to tender words and wholesome deeds.

— Frank Navratil

s we move closer towards the actual training of the mind, it is fitting to bring up once again the fourth and final truth that the Buddha revealed to us. He taught it in nearly all of his discourses, showing it was one of his most important instructions. In fact, practically his entire teaching, which he devoted himself to during forty-five years, dealt with it in some form or another. He explained it in different ways and through different methods to a variety of people, according to the stage of their development and their capacity to understand. But you can find the essence of it in all the thousands of discourses recorded in the Buddhist scriptures.

The Fourth Noble Truth is of course the truth of the path leading to the cessation of suffering. In our physician analogy it is the treatment, prescription or cure to our disease. In Buddhist philosophy this is called the Noble Eightfold Path, often referred to as the Middle Way. It is the Buddha's eight practical elements that lead to the extinction of suffering or *nirvana*. Within the profound wisdom of the Fourth Noble Truth, we are equipped with everything we need to finally get on the path that leads us to happiness.

We can think of reality and the human experience as a flowing river. Remember the old saying, "You cannot step into the same river twice." As we know, we and our world around us are constantly changing. This is the nature of reality. When we try to go against it, we go against the current, we feel resistance and movement is more difficult. When we let go of all our desires, all our cravings and clinging to aspects of life that are impermanent, there is a sense of lightness, release and ease. When we accept the reality the way it really is, and do not fight it but accept it and go with the flow, immediately everything becomes easier and we experience less suffering. As we release all that we hold onto in our mind, our experience in life becomes like a flowing river, constantly moving and changing as we move with it, not against its current. As we let go of our self, and see it as only a construct of the ego, we start to lose the distinction or the distance between ourselves and the external world, we become one with all. We no longer just see ourselves as a separate being floating down a river, we become interconnected with the river and become the river itself.

The noble eightfold path, is a way of life to be followed, practiced and developed by each individual. It teaches us to accept the natural flow of that river, the true reality of our existence, and the futility of all our attachments and efforts to swim against it. It is a holistic journey of self-development, self-discipline and self-purification in all aspects of the body, word, and mind. It has nothing to do with any blind belief or form of worship or ceremony or anything that you would call "religious." It is a path leading to the realization of the ultimate meaning of reality resulting in complete freedom, happiness, and peace through perfection in morality, concentration of the mind and wisdom.

In brief, the eight elements of the noble eightfold path are:

> (1) ***Right view,*** which means to have an accurate understanding of the nature of reality, specifically the Four Noble Truths.

> (2) ***Right intention,*** which means to have the intention to avoid thoughts of attachment, hatred and harmful intent.

> (3) ***Right speech,*** which means to refrain from harmful speech such as lying and harsh, abusive, divisive or senseless speech.

> (4) ***Right action*** which means to refrain from harmful actions such as killing, stealing, sexual misconduct and using intoxicants or any substances that alter the mind.

> (5) ***Right livelihood*** which means to avoid any work which directly or indirectly harms others, such as slavery and involvement with weapons, animals for slaughter, intoxicants or poisons.

(6) ***Right effort*** which means to abandon unwholesome states of mind already present, prevent potential unwholesome states, maintain present wholesome states of mind and cultivate wholesome states that are not present.

(7) ***Right mindfulness***, which means to cultivate bare awareness of the body, feelings, thoughts and phenomena.

(8) ***Right concentration*** which means to cultivate single-pointed focus and concentration.

The Noble Eightfold Path invites us to embark on a journey to know and understand the workings of our own mind, to become aware of our intentions and how to live peacefully and compassionately in the world. It is designed to uproot unwholesome and harmful states of mind and instead cultivate wholesome ones. By understanding the psychology of our mind we can start to see that we are really the creators of our own happiness. By practicing the Noble Eightfold Path we will find it is a road of self-purification of our minds, leading to realization, awakening, freedom, liberation and the extinction of suffering, *nirvana*. The Noble Eightfold Path or Middle Way could really be called Buddha's instruction manual for uncovering and experiencing happiness.

THE 3 HIGHER TRAININGS: MORALITY, CONCENTRATION AND WISDOM

Moral discipline provides the stability for us
to develop meditative concentration which
enables our innate wisdom to arise.

— Unknown

We briefly discussed the eight principles of the Noble Eightfold Path or Middle Way in the previous chapter. To better understand their role in happiness, it is useful to regroup them into what are called the three higher trainings:

Ethics (*sila*) – avoiding deeds that are non-virtuous

- Right speech
- Right action
- Right livelihood

Meditative concentration (*samadhi*) – training and concentrating the mind

- Right Effort
- Right Mindfulness
- Right Concentration

Wisdom (*panna*) – developing insight into the nature of reality

- Right view (Understanding)
- Right Intention

According to Buddhist science, all three higher trainings of the Middle Way, *sila*, *samadhi* and *panna*, translated to ethics, meditative concentration and wisdom are needed in order to cure or treat suffering in our lives. Like a three legged tripod, they are each inter-related and each cannot function independently of the other. Ethics are needed as a foundation to strengthen mental concentration which in turn is needed to cultivate wisdom. In the same way wisdom and mental concentration are also both needed to strengthen morality.

Wisdom helps to get rid of our clouded view of things and assists us to see the reality of human life pertaining to impermanence, suffering and non-self. Remember, it is our inability to see reality as it really is and our futile attempts to cling to things that are not what we think they are, that are causing our unhappiness and dissatisfaction in life. We will look at each of these groupings and each of the principles of the Middle Way they contain.

Ethics

Training in morality is simply a preparatory practice for the training of the mind, which enables us to live peacefully and helps us to purify and stabilize our mind. This is the most important benefit, according to Buddhist science. The Buddha regarded morality as primarily a means of developing meditative concentration. As long as things continue to disturb the mind, the mind can never become concentrated, therefore morality is imperative. A virtuous lifestyle that is disciplined and ethical, cultivates a positive and clear mind, free of the burden of negative conditioning. Ethics in Buddhist philosophy is not just being obedient and refraining from harmful immoral behavior but it also means to cultivate or perform ethical behaviors that will benefit us and others. To achieve this, three elements of the Noble Eightfold Path that pertain to ethics or morality are needed: right speech, right action and right livelihood.

Right Speech means to:
- refrain from lying
- refrain from abusive or harsh speech
- refrain from gossip or divisive speech
- refrain from senseless speech
- perform speech that will benefit us and others

Right Action means to:

- avoid killing all sentient beings (any beings that have a consciousness and can feel and perceive which includes animals, insects, people)
- avoid stealing
- avoid sexual misconduct
- avoid intoxicants
- perform actions that will benefit us and others

Right Livelihood means to:

- avoid business with weapons
- avoid business in human beings (slavery, prostitution)
- avoid business in meat (butcher, slaughterhouse)
- avoid business in intoxicants (alcohol, illicit drugs)
- avoid business in poisons (manufacturing or selling poisons that kill sentient beings)
- avoid any business that directly or indirectly harms others
- perform work that benefits us and others
- balance our expenditures and earnings in a way to not spend more than we can afford and not hold on to more than we really need

Meditative Concentration

The second higher training is meditative concentration which means practicing the actual contemplative methods needed to concentrate the mind. Once we have a firm foundation of ethics, it is easier for us to move inwards to train the mind. This training requires the appropriate effort in purifying the mind of any unwholesome states, the development of single-pointed concentration as well as practice in mindfulness of the body, feelings, thoughts and phenomena.

Right Effort means developing:

- effort to prevent unwholesome mental states from arising in our minds
- effort to abandon any unwholesome mental states that have already arisen
- effort to cultivate any wholesome mental states not yet arisen

- effort to maintain the wholesome mental states that have already arisen

Right Mindfulness means:

- training the mind to be mindful of the body
- training the mind to be mindful of our feelings (pleasant, unpleasant, neutral)
- training the mind to be mindful of our thoughts
- training the mind to be mindful of phenomena

Right Concentration means:

- training the mind in meditation to achieve a concentrated one-pointed state and sharp focus
- achieving calmness and stability, which leads to states of meditative absorption

Wisdom

The cultivation of proper ethical behavior as well as training the mind through concentrated effort, as with meditation and mindfulness leads to the final higher training, the cultivation of wisdom. Hopefully, with a clear mind that is free of any distractions and trained in meditation, we can bring enough clarity that allows us to develop realizations about the true nature of our reality. This is what it meant by wisdom, which is the opposite of ignorance. Being able to discern aspects of our reality like impermanence, non-self and the nature and cause of suffering along with a deep understanding of the four noble truths is really our ultimate goal in Middle Way Mind Training. With this wisdom, comes inner peace and sustained happiness. In order to attain wisdom, we need to have right view or understanding along with the right intention. This in turn also benefits our contemplative meditation practice and strengthens our moral development.

Right View (Right Understanding):

- guides all the other seven principles of the Middle Way
- ensures that our behavior , speech and thoughts are born from a mind infused with wisdom and compassion
- means an understanding and view of the true nature of reality

- means an understanding of the relevance of all the 4 noble truths, that all phenomena are impermanent and unsatisfactory with no inherent existence and cannot provide sustainable satisfaction
- means understanding the actions of karma and that all actions have karmic consequences

Right Intention means:

- the intention of renunciation – to let go of selfish pursuits such as greed, jealousy, pride and other harmful emotions and loosen the grasp on external things and the belief that happiness is found in the external world.
- the intention of goodwill – to act with an attitude of goodwill and a wish to help others and all actions of the body, speech and mind should resonate to make others happy.
- the intention of harmlessness – to be motivated by compassion and not harming our self or others, through body, speech and mind.

In summary, the three higher trainings of ethics, meditative concentration and wisdom and all of their elements represent Buddha's required path for extinguishing all suffering in life and developing sustained happiness. In the next chapter, we will introduce Middle Way Mind Training and how through its many practical applications focuses on the development of all three of these important areas.

WHAT IS MIDDLE WAY MIND TRAINING?

There is no way to happiness, happiness is the
way.

— Thich Nhat Hanh

Each of the elements of the Noble Eightfold Path lead us away from the two opposite extremes of sensual indulgence and self-denial and in the process place us on a path of firm middle ground or what is often called the Middle Way. As we already know, if we seek happiness purely through indulgence, we are not free and if we fight against ourselves and reject the world, we are also not free.

The Middle Way teaches us how to live in the present, not in the opposite poles of the future and the past. When we practice the Middle Way we do not remove ourselves from the world, nor do we remain lost in it. This does not mean we have to live an emotionless life with no excitement; we just learn to enjoy life no matter what happens and not become attached to any desired outcomes. We learn to embrace every human experience as it presents itself in our lives. It is the Middle Way that brings freedom, liberation from suffering, inner peace and sustained happiness. Training the mind in order to learn to rest in the equilibrium of the Middle Way is what Middle Way Mind Training is all about. All eight principles are meant to be developed and cultivated simultaneously, not in any particular order. We will go through each of them and how they can be practically applied in much more detail in future chapters of this book. As we will soon discover, they are also all interrelated, each being essential in helping the development of the others.

Middle Way Mind Training (MWMT) was developed as a practical interpretation of Buddha's most important teaching so that the average layperson could easily understand and cultivate each element of the Noble Eightfold Path. In reality, MWMT is not a brand new innovation, just a rediscovery and modern application. Buddha even stated himself that he just re-discovered an ancient path that has always been there and available to each one of us. I sincerely believe that an easier-to-follow method for regular working people is needed in modern western society, one that is not just designed for monks who decide to devote their entire lives in a monastery to Buddhist practice.

Middle Way Mind Training incorporates practical scientifically-proven training methods that transform existing non-beneficial mind patterns into beneficial ones. It includes several meditation and mindfulness techniques which reduce craving and aversion, improve bare awareness, cultivate compassion, patience and develop sound moral behavior. Practical training methods are used to be mindful of speech, actions and work that can directly or indirectly harm others. As one is able to concentrate and sharpen the awareness of the mind, it becomes easier to be mindful of all of the five aggregates and guard the sense doors, so that unwholesome habitual mental formations do not get ingrained. MWMT techniques develop the ability to remain calm under whatever tragedy in life presents itself, to respond with calm acceptance rather than just react wildly. It enables us to see reality the way it really is without thoughts being clouded by emotion and perception. Contemplative meditation exercises are used to develop acceptance of impermanence and non-self, as well as to internalize the nature of suffering. Other MWMT meditation exercises use wholesome beneficial antidotes such as compassion and patience to combat unwholesome mind states such as anger, hatred and impatience.

Middle Way Mind Training is an effective and long-lasting program that trains the mind to create a happy, satisfied and balanced outlook with meaning. It develops the mind to react favorably to whatever life hands out to us, whatever tragedy comes our way or whatever difficulties we may encounter in our daily life. It results in happier relationships, better satisfaction at work and clarifies aspirations and goals. It is a method that trains the mind out of its non-beneficial habitual thinking to see reality as it actually plays out, moment by moment, not the way we imagine it to be.

You can say MWMT spans a program with elements influenced by mindfulness-based cognitive therapy, compassion focused therapy, scientific-backed meditation and mindfulness techniques along with Buddhist psychology. Just as we need to train our physical body to maintain its health, we also need to learn to train our minds to achieve optimum psychological health and to resolve the variety of complex problems that we are often confronted with in modern society.

Middle Way Mind Training requires dedicated participation and effort in order to be effective. While MWMT is not intended to replace conventional psychotherapy and psychology, it has been shown to be very helpful in assisting a variety of psychological problems such as depression, stress, anxiety, mood disorders and substance abuse problems including alcohol and drugs and other addictions, eating disorders, marriage, family and relationship problems, sleep disorders, attention disorders, self-harm disorders, and many others. It has also proven very useful in anger management, poor motivation, loneliness, and dealing with terminal illness, cases of abuse, post traumatic stress, and mental and physical pain. What's more is that many of these problems of the mind are also responsible and related to physical health problems such as heart problems, digestive, liver, skin, respiratory and hormonal problems etc. Middle Way Mind Training goes beyond assisting psychological problems; it goes much farther than just that. It puts you on a path in life full of meaning and happiness, full of promise and hope. In the next chapter we begin our practical journey with the first of the eight foundational principles of Middle Way Mind Training.

MWMT PRINCIPLE 1: SPEAK AND LISTEN WITH WISDOM

When you talk you are only repeating what you
already know. But if you listen, you may learn
something new.

— His Holiness the 14th Dalai Lama

The first of the eight foundational principles of Middle Way Mind Training is – **Speak and Listen with Wisdom**. It relates to the first element, Right Speech, one of the higher trainings of ethics found in the Buddhist teaching of the Middle Way.

Almost all of us have been given the gift of speech and in our daily life we use it to communicate our feelings, thoughts and opinions to the external world. Speech has dire consequences and that is why the Buddha emphasized it very strongly in his teachings. The effects of speech can often be overlooked as they are not as evident as the obvious effects of bodily actions. If we look closer though, speech can have an enormous impact for good or for harm. For us who are constantly immersed in verbal communications, speech has the ability on one hand to heal, unite, create peace, and share wisdom, but on the other, to strongly divide, be destructive and even cause war.

Speech is reflected from our mind and when our mind is deluded, and influenced by unwholesome emotions and mental formations, it has the potential to inflict a lot of suffering. Being mindful of our speech at all times is critical to our happiness and the happiness of all those around us. We have often heard that there is a reason why we were given two ears and only one mouth. Being able to actively listen, not only speak with wisdom, can also greatly improve our communication with others and prevent common misunderstandings that can often lead to negative consequences. We also cannot forget our internal dialogue that we engage in inside our minds, a type of self-speech when we talk to or criticize ourselves. Depending on where this inner speech is coming from, it can also assist or take away our happiness.

The Buddha mentioned four main types of speech that we should abstain from: **lying**, **divisive speech**, **harsh speech** and **senseless speech**. Not only should we abstain from these, but we should endeavor to cultivate skillful and beneficial forms of speech that promote kindness, that unite and that empower both us and people around us. In our self-analysis of our spoken word, the most important question we should be asking ourselves is, "Is what I am about to say beneficial for me and also for others? If it is not, even modern science shows that our happiness will ultimately suffer for it.

In most religions and societies we see morality and ethics as something that we are obligated to do or we will get punished or penalized, either by society or by God. In Buddhist philosophy, ethics is different; it is not based on obedience as there is no punisher. The reason for cultivation of ethics is in the end to benefit our happiness and the happiness of others, and to not harm ourselves or others in the process. Ethics in Buddhism is a sign of compassion not obligation, and so speaking and listening correctly is a prerequisite necessary to develop meditative concentration and wisdom, and thus lasting happiness.

The ethics of speech is not a very popular subject. Not many of us want to be reminded of what we should or should not say especially when we are provoked or overcome with emotion. We do have what is called freedom of speech right? Although we do have this human right, more often than not, without mindfulness, it is not used very wisely and often gets us into a lot of trouble. If you can understand the science behind abiding by Buddha's doctrine of Right Speech, you will soon see that it plays an important role in our happiness.

It should also be mentioned that the offshoot of speech, written words, whether in email communication, SMS texts, or by interacting through social media or other forms, should also be carefully monitored in the same way to ascertain if it is beneficial to us and to others.

Being able to speak and listen with wisdom requires a very mindful approach in its analysis. We need to consider many factors, including what type or tone of speech to use in our communications, the timing of speech, the type of person we are speaking to, if anyone else is around, whether our speech is needed or not and whether it will be beneficial or not. According to Buddhist science, many types of speech that we commonly engage in, provide little or no benefit in our lives and only detract from our level of happiness. Each of these four forms of speech is discussed below including any relevant scientific research.

A recommended prescription of Middle Way Mind Training exercises is listed for this principle at the end of this chapter and for the rest of the principles as we progress through the following chapters. Each practical exercise will be explained in detail in the final parts of this book.

Lying

There are many staggering statistics with regards to lying. This form of deluded and destructive behavior is far more common in society than we probably realize. Several scientific studies have shown that people tell an enormous amount of lies through conversation and during their daily activities. One example is an American study at the University of Massachusetts by Robert S. Feldman a psychologist, published in the Journal of Basic and Applied Social Psychology (Feldman et al. 2002). It showed that 60 percent of the people studied lied an average of 2 to 3 times, just during a ten minute conversation. Other studies indicate that between 25 to 67 percent of people lie on their resumes (Prater and Kiser, 2002) and a large proportion lie in their profile when looking for a partner on a dating site (Sharabi, 2018). Women commonly tend to claim to weigh on average several kilograms less than they actually do and men try to convince potential partners that they are taller, richer and more educated than they actually are. While these seem at first to be humorous and relatively harmless lies, they do reflect that in general most of us are not satisfied with our own reality and we have a tendency to exaggerate or bend the truth in the hopes to gain some sort of advantage.

Lies come in various forms. Some of the well-known types include those that try to cover-up the truth, to deceive others, to exaggerate a situation or qualities about our self, to fabricate an event that did not happen, to commit fraud, to omit or leave certain truths out, or state a partial truth or half-truth. Lies are even spoken to avoid conflicts or prevent someone from getting physically or emotionally hurt. Most of us can be untruthful in our attempt to be polite or nice so that people will not be mad at us or so they will like us more. We often lie to impress and make ourselves appear better to others or to feel better about ourselves.

Unfortunately a lot of times we do not even realize that we are lying. Our minds can be under so much delusion that we can even be convinced that our lies actually depict the truth. Remember when we discussed memory and thoughts and how they are often altered by our perceptions and emotions. In general, this shows that for the majority of the population, lying has reached epidemic proportions and in some ways has become not just prevalent but almost an acceptable evil in society. It seems ironic that one of our greatest complaints or disappointments with people is when they lie to us, yet often unknowingly, we seem to be doing it all the time ourselves.

What does this tell us about the state of our minds? It means that more often than not, we do not want to accept or take responsibility for our reality the way it really is. We are also motivated to lie because of unwholesome emotions such as greed, jealousy, pride, hatred or resentment. We make up stories because of our desire to gain something different or better than what actually is available. We get locked in a cage of falsehoods and end up spinning a web of new lies to cover up our tracks as the whole event becomes much more complex, stressful and chaotic. We often eventually get sucked in by our own deceptions and end up the victim, while hurting many people in the process. According to Buddhist science, when we desire something in this way or reject the truth, we only experience more suffering because under these unwholesome states of mind we certainly do not experience any inner peace. The act of lying in reality is not beneficial to us or to others around us and ultimately makes us unhappy. Lying also shows us how strong our ego can be and how much it influences the bolstering or propping up of our "self." Speaking the truth puts us in a vulnerable situation, and our ego does not like this, as being a construct of our mind it wishes to strengthen our illusory sense of our self and will often convince us that lying is the better way to go. Remember, according to Buddhist science, one of the main reasons we suffer is because we hold on to what we believe is a permanent concrete self.

The detrimental effects to both our mental and physical health have also been documented in scientific research. A "Science of Honesty" study, made at the University of Notre Dame in the U.S by Anita Kelly a psychology professor, revealed that when people lie, they are more prone to feeling anxious or depressed, to experiencing frequent headaches, runny noses, bouts of diarrhea and back pain (Kelly, 2012).

Not only do we tell lies when we speak, but we often lie to ourselves in internal conversations or dialogue in our mind. We make excuses or criticize ourselves for our inadequacies and imperfections. We often convince ourselves with limiting beliefs such us "I was born this way" or "the world is out to get me," "it's too late to start doing this," or "I am going to look stupid if....." Being honest with others is essential for creating and maintaining healthy relationships, and being honest with our self is vital for personal development and growth, as well as self-acceptance and self-esteem. If we lie to others as well as to ourselves, then according to Buddhist science we are not seeing reality the way it is as we are blinded by our delusions and fantasies. We know that if we go against reality, against the flow of that river, we end up suffering.

So it seems that both Buddhist wisdom, as well as current scientific research show compelling evidence that the act of lying to others and to yourself is certainly not worth the effort if we want to be mentally or physically healthy and happy. In terms of Middle Way Mind Training we need to train our minds to be aware of this damaging behavior and to evaluate and reflect on the roots of our lying.

If our desire is based on the unwholesome mind state of greed and we are lying in order to gain some advantage, to acquire more material wealth or to gain better status, respect or admiration, we need to become aware of our sense doors and aggregates of feelings and perception. In this way unwholesome mental formations and emotions do not cause us to grasp onto these external objects of desire that we know intellectually will not bring us sustained happiness. If we are motivated by ill will, hatred or aversion and wish to hurt or damage others with our lies, then we need to cultivate compassion to transform those negative states of mind. If our minds are overcome with delusion and we have a desire to exaggerate the truth, then we need to train the mind to become mindful of our true reality.

Through mindfulness and compassion-based meditation, which we will examine in the final parts of this book, we can learn to train the mind to speak truthfully, in line with reality and without delusion. By meditating on impermanence we can release the hold of our greed and see that it is futile and we are then less motivated to lie for this reason. By cultivating compassion for others as well as self-compassion, we can gain the confidence and express ourselves the way we are, to be genuine and forthright, even though it may seem at first terrifying to expose our vulnerability. We can then foster an authentic connection in line with reality when we speak to others, which will really form the basis of our happiness.

Divisive speech

When we mention divisive speech, we are really referring to what we commonly call gossip. Talking about someone behind their back to others when they are not there, with the intention to separate or create divisions amongst people, generally leads to disruption of cohesiveness and harmony. Modern society seems to be incredibly attracted to gossip, as we tend to delight in rumors especially related to other people's misfortunes, inadequacies, or failures. This can be found in the numerous television channels, gossip magazines and internet news servers that flood our senses every day. People like to stay in the know about social events and the latest rumors. While some gossip is natural and often harmless, and can even have some positive benefits in social settings, a lot of it seems to be very damaging to others. The problem with gossip is that it often exaggerates the actual truth in its attempt to be more entertaining to those listening. In the process, it places the person who is the subject of the gossip in a very vulnerable and uncomfortable position. Feelings are often hurt in the process. A 2019 study on 467 people by Robbins and Karan at the Department of Psychology, University of California found that pretty much everyone gossips, and this is across all age groups, gender and class (Robbins and Karan, 2019). This makes this type of speech even more prevalent than lying. The Buddha taught that divisive speech should be avoided and for a good reason. It seems to be one of the factors, that is responsible for really deteriorating the unity and harmony of society by creating sharp divisions amongst people as people tend to take sides. Again, it strengthens the illusory construct of an individual self and ignores the reality that we are all interconnected with one another. By separating ourselves from others it goes against reality and according to Buddhist science, this leads to suffering.

The act of divisive speech or gossip has several negative consequences in society. It tends to erode trust and morale, and as rumors circulate without clear information, it causes anxiety as to what is fact and what is not. It hurts others feelings and often damages reputations. It is usually a waste of valuable time and reduces productivity especially in the workplace. Generally people who gossip about others tend to be less happy especially if their motivations to gossip are done out of anger, jealousy or attachment. Gossip is often used as a defense mechanism. It makes our ego feel better to show that another person is inferior to us, so we can temporarily forget about our own shortcomings and insecurities. Some scientific studies have shown that gossipers tend to have less self-esteem and are much more critical of themselves (Cole, 2013).

The benefits of abstaining from divisive speech are numerous. By avoiding gossip, more friends are made that will not let you down. People will feel that they can confide in you, without the feeling that what they share with you could be used in the future against them. By not engaging in divisive speech, you will be much more respected and become surrounded by wonderful people that will always be deeply supporting.

What is important is to discern whether the intention to gossip stems from wholesome or unwholesome roots. We should ask ourselves these questions: Is our speech dividing people or uniting them? Is it supportive or critical and judgmental? Are we engaging in divisive speech because of our own insecurities, jealousies? Is it coming from anger or resentment? If it is materializing from these negative states of mind, then it should be avoided as it will only create division and make us and others unhappy. Mindfulness training is needed so that we can be aware of any unwholesome behavior and compassion-based training is needed so that we can cultivate empathy and compassion towards others and ourselves. As our mind is transformed from unwholesome mental formations with antidotes like compassion and kindness, there will be far less need to gossip or engage in divisive speech. With training, what we utter from our mouths will become much more truthful, honest and compassionate.

Harsh speech

In most cases harsh speech is not necessary and should be avoided unless we are using it wisely to help others. An example would be to yell at someone in a harsh tone to warn them of an impending danger. In most cases though, with harsh speech, it usually involves an intention to hurt or harm. Some common types of harsh speech include **verbal abuse**, **insulting remarks** and **sarcasm**. Generally the root of harsh speech is ill will, anger, or aversion.

We tend to use abusive speech when we are not happy with or cannot accept the way things are. We are often under the strong influence of anger or rage. We vent our anger outward to the external environment and often use threats that are directed at a person. We blame the external environment for our problem but the reality is that our mind holds on to this aversion and we end up suffering much worse than the recipient of our anger. Anger is, as we already know, a form of delusion of an untrained mind.

When we insult people, we use ill-will with an intention to bring someone down, to belittle or demean them and exploit their weaknesses. We look for their faults and use them to humiliate them, often being rude, offensive and disrespectful in the process. Insults often inflict shame by mentioning unappealing human traits such as obesity, shortness, baldness, mental competence etc. When we insult someone we show no empathy or compassion, patience or kindness. We use insults in an attempt to reduce the status of the recipient, while raising our status. Insults are often motivated by anger about our own insecurity. Many insults can be reactive and stem from the concern of how we are perceived, which creates insecurity that can be relieved by lashing out at other people. Insults only lead to unnecessary destructive consequences such as anger, disputes and violence. We also cannot forget ourselves when it comes to harsh speech or insults as the person we are most harsh to or insulting to can often be ourselves. Thinking is really the speech of our mind and it is important to be mindful of what we say to ourselves and ensure that our inner dialogue is also kind and compassionate.

Sarcasm is another form of harsh speech. It is when we speak to someone in a way that on the surface praises them but can be taken another way that is not so positive. New research claims that sarcasm is merely thinly veiled meanness. In fact, people who use sarcastic remarks usually believe their words are less hurtful than the recipient thinks. Sarcasm is simply a way of covering contempt or hate and usually stems from insecurity. Some people use sarcasm as a way of avoiding confrontation because they are afraid of asking for what they really want. It is also used as a passive aggressive way to assert dominance. We also often use sarcasm as a disguise, when we are angry or upset but afraid to directly bring it up. In a way, the hidden effects of sarcasm are not only hurtful, but are also the least genuine mode of communication.

When we use any form of harsh speech, again we need to be mindful that it is not stemming from the root of anger as this will only lead to negative consequences. The goal is to speak kindly and praise others as much as possible. One of the greatest antidotes to anger is patience and compassion and these skills should be cultivated during mind training as much as possible. We need to respect differences in viewpoints and be reluctant to talk about negative qualities in others if at all possible. In the same way we should be reluctant to talk or brag about our good qualities, to exhibit humility but to be open about our negative qualities.

Senseless speech

Idle chatter, chit-chat or small talk as it is often called, is in many ways senseless speech. It lacks meaning and purpose. According to Buddhist science we should not engage too much in speech that is only for the sake of speaking and has no other real significance or value. This includes speech that we often use to just fill in time, or fill in the silence with no objective or reason. Communication through speech should be a medium that helps, inspires and empowers others.

For most people idle chatter seems the most innocent, yet the most difficult to get past. Its very nature is that it is talk that comes out of the mouth without much thought. No thought is given to the intention of what you are saying or what it is meant to accomplish. It is a bad habit which promotes thinking mindlessly, the polar opposite of mindfulness. Senseless speech can lead to saying the wrong things, or hurting someone because there is no contemplation of what is going to happen as a result of what you say or if anyone will be harmed by the words. The old saying, "silence is golden" is a good lesson to learn that if you are to open your mouth, you should have something to say that is more valuable than gold.

Active Listening

As we mentioned, not only do we need to speak with wisdom but active listening is needed when we communicate with others. Active listening means to be fully aware of the moment when someone is speaking to you. It means maintaining eye contact with that person during the conversation, giving them your full attention and removing any distractions that could interfere such as mobile phones. Listening with compassion means that we avoid the mistake of interrupting the person with our own judgments and opinions and allowing them to freely finish their conversation with us. Remember, one of the most basic human needs that each one of us has is the need to be heard. Our communication will be greatly enhanced if we repeat what we have heard or ask questions to clarify what someone says to us. This lets them know that we are actively listening. Not actively listening is probably the main reason for misunderstandings. Allowing this beneficial connection to happen, and actively listening, is essential for long-term happiness in relationships and friendships.

Our emotional response to speech

It is also important to be mindful of our emotional response to the various forms of harsh speech that can be inflicted on us. If we are the recipient, then we need to get to a place where we are not affected by speech, whether it is positive or negative. For example, if we are praised for something, we should not let it get to our head. If someone yells at us angrily or insults us, then we need to have the wisdom to not react, but respond in a calm and peaceful manner. We do not take things personally. Those harsh words that are being hurled upon us by that person are just coming from a deluded mind. Before we react in the same impulsive and habitual way, and expose ourselves to unnecessary suffering, it is very useful to use a method that I call the Pause of Wisdom. It can help us to learn to absorb and accept criticism and respect differences in viewpoints without needing to retaliate immediately.

PAUSE OF WISDOM

If someone verbally abuses you or insults you, before you do or say anything:

Take 3 deep breaths so you can respond instead of react habitually.

Ask yourself if what you want to say will really benefit yourself and the other person (Is it wise?)

If you feel compelled to speak, ask yourself these 4 questions about what you want to say:

- Is it true?
- Is it useful?
- Is it kind?
- Is it the right time?

PRACTICAL MIDDLE WAY MIND TRAINING PRESCRIPTION
MWMT FOUNDATIONAL PRINCIPLE 1 – Speak and Listen with Wisdom

- Meditation of Observing the Breath – designed to focus and concentrate the mind in preparation for the practice of mindfulness
- Mindfulness Meditation – trains the mind to observe and become aware of the body, feelings, and thoughts to improve the wisdom of your speech and the ability to listen
- Compassion Meditation – trains the mind to cultivate compassion, empathy and kindness as you speak internally to yourself and to others
- Pause of Wisdom – trains the mind to stop and respond wisely instead of reacting, especially to harsh speech or insults
- Antidotes – meditative contemplations on Patience and the Reality of Suffering, Impermanence and Non-self, all of

which improve the effectiveness of speech and reduce unnecessary suffering for yourself and for recipients

- Mantras – repetitive affirmations that settle the mind and improve meditation

Note: An explanation of MWMT methods can be found in Part V

MWMT PRINCIPLE 2: PERFORM ACTIONS THAT DO NO HARM

> Beings are the owners of their actions, the heirs of
> their actions; they spring from their actions, are
> bound to their actions, and are supported by their
> actions. Whatever deeds they do good or bad, of
> those they shall be heirs.
>
> — Bhikkhu Bodhi

The second of the eight foundational principles of Middle Way Mind Training is – **Perform Actions that do no harm.** This principle is based on the second element of ethical behavior or Right Action, taught by the Buddha. As we know, everything begins in the mind and if we leave thoughts unchecked, unwholesome emotions and mental formations can develop which can manifest in harmful physical actions. Performing actions that are morally correct or right according to an individual can also be very subjective. If people are under delusion, they can still be one hundred percent convinced that they are doing the right thing. Primarily, Buddha's doctrine of Right Action mainly emphasizes to avoid doing any actions that hurt us or others. In Buddhist philosophy, it is the intention that is more important than the actual result of any action. Take for example, it someone accidently kills a person and they did not intend for it to happen, it is considered unfortunate but not morally wrong.

The Buddha taught that we should particularly abstain from three main actions, killing, stealing and sexual misconduct. The doctrine however is also interpreted to include avoiding doing any actions that hurt us or others. This can extend to alcohol or drug abuse or failing to take care of our own physical health. What these harmful actions have in common is that they corrupt the mind and introduce unsettling thoughts that prevent us from concentrating our mind and attaining wisdom.

Abstain from killing

The act of killing in Buddhist philosophy means taking the life of any sentient being, which includes humans, animals and even insects. The Buddha felt that all life has value, not just human life and no one has the right to take another life. Most of us can understand that the act of killing another person is morally wrong but the definition becomes vague once we talk about animals or even insects for that matter. Most people, who are not vegetarians, consider fishing or hunting for food from animals as a necessity for life. However with animal rights activists, there is a thin line of what is acceptable and what is not. Again I believe we have to go back to our intentions, if we wish to kill an animal or insect without any need for it, then it certainly falls into this category and should be abstained from. As we hear about more and more problems with diseases and viruses passed on from animals, it may be logical and wise to not have them on our plates as there are plenty of vegetarian alternatives. Insects, such a pests and mosquitoes inevitably get killed accidently by us by stepping on them or finding them on our car windshields, but they are also considered sentient beings and should not be killed intentionally. The Buddha stressed that compassion can be cultivated to all living sentient beings and we should understand that each has a right to live, and each desires to live the same as we do.

It should be noted that those with deluded minds such as murderers, terrorists or even political leaders like Hitler, who have been responsible for horrific crimes, have often been convinced of the moral correctness of their actions. However, these actions obviously have more to do with the influence or delusion of non-beneficial habitual patterns rather than with behavior that is in the service of helping others and themselves.

Killing stems from unwholesome mental states such as anger, rage, jealousy, greed and all these are not peaceful states so it is impossible to feel real happiness. The act leads inevitably to suffering. Even guilt from killing someone can plague that person's mind sometimes for the rest of their lives.

Abstain from Stealing

Stealing is the practice of taking something from others that doesn't belong to you. It can come in the form of taking physical items, cheating to gain, or even stealing ideas, data or rights that someone else owns. Ultimately it damages or hurts others and any type of stealing should be avoided.

The non-beneficial action of stealing stems from unwholesome mind states such as greed, anger and jealousy. Stealing can even be an addiction or a compulsion such as in the psychological disorder of Kleptomania. It obviously has a negative impact on society as it reduces trust, order and increases fear amongst members. Not only does the act of stealing hurt others and society but what is often overlooked is the harmful effect on the person doing the act of stealing. Often they suffer with feelings of guilt, anxiety, tension, shame or remorse after the act of stealing. They may also feel a great amount of fear of getting caught and suffer because of this. People who steal will often have a mind filled with agitation. They will usually have difficulty in maintaining any sense of inner peace and thus happiness, even though they may have benefited or increased their wealth greatly by their act of stealing. In the end, any perceived benefit is only a delusion of the mind and will never bring sustained happiness.

According to Buddhist science, stealing is not a wise action as not only will it harm the recipient, but in the end, also the person who commits the theft. It focuses also on the negative intentions and mind states of the person committing the theft and how they will ultimately suffer from their actions. Also, we know from Buddhist science that in reality, there is really no self to steal from nor a concrete self to hold on to things that we take, so the concept of ownership is only a delusion and the act of stealing is quite pointless, as we are all ultimately interconnected.

Abstain from Sexual misconduct

Abstaining from sexual misconduct means to abstain from harmful actions such as rape or adultery and being mindful that your sexual behavior is not harmful to yourself or to others. In a modern perspective we should not be having sex in ways that are harmful to ourselves or to others. Again sexual misconduct stems from unwholesome mind states, such as uncontrolled desire, jealousy, addiction, anger etc. According to Buddhist science, these mind states do not lead to a peaceful inner state of mind and thus they will disrupt the potential of achieving happiness.

Abstain from any Actions that harm

Buddhism basically considers right actions as those that do not harm us or harm others. The major actions that are morally wrong are of course killing, stealing and sexual misconduct, but there are other actions that can also harm. Examples include addictions such as alcohol or drug abuse, gambling or living an unhealthy lifestyle which can mean poor nutrition, excessive work, over indulging in food, lack of exercise or not enough relaxation. If we wish to be able to focus and control our mind so that we can see with wisdom the truth of reality and be happy, we need to ensure that we abstain from any of these morally wrong actions as well as any other actions that reduce our mind's ability to achieve focus and clarity. In many Buddhist practices, precepts are introduced that include complete abstinence of alcohol because even though small amounts are generally not damaging, any intake can lead to addictions, dependency, bad decision making and lack of clarity of thought which can ultimately result in a greater chance of killing, stealing, sexual misconduct or harm.

PRACTICAL MIDDLE WAY MIND TRAINING PRESCRIPTION
MWMT FOUNDATIONAL PRINCIPLE 2 – Perform Actions that do no harm

- Meditation of Observing the Breath – designed to focus and concentrate the mind in preparation for the practice of mindfulness
- Mindfulness Meditation – trains the mind to observe and become aware of the body, feelings, and thoughts to improve the wisdom of your actions

- Compassion Meditation – trains the mind to cultivate compassion, empathy and kindness in all the actions you perform to yourself and to others
- Antidotes – meditative contemplations on Generosity, Patience, Gratitude, and Reality of Suffering, Impermanence and Non-self all of which improve beneficial actions and reduce unnecessary suffering for yourself and for recipients
- Mantras – repetitive affirmations that settle the mind and improve meditation

Note: An explanation of MWMT methods can be found in Part V

MWMT PRINCIPLE 3: ENGAGE IN WORK THAT BENEFITS ALL

If the intention is to play a useful role in society in
order to support oneself and to help others, then
the work one does is right livelihood.

— S.N. Goenka

The third of the eight foundational principles of Middle Way Mind Training is – **Engage in work that benefits all.** This principle is based on the third and last element of ethical behavior or Right Livelihood, taught by the Buddha. In essence it means that we should perform work in our lives that is ethical, peaceful, kind and honest and which does not harm us or others. Primarily, the work that we do, no matter what it is, whether we are a waitress, janitor, businessman or lawyer, should in some way help and bring joy and happiness to others, not only to ourselves. If we do not engage in this kind of work which abides to this principle, then we should find work that does.

Our work represents for a lot of us a third of our lives in the time we spend, so it is important that it is in line with ethical principles. It stands to reason that engaging in immoral work activities only corrupts the mind, and allows it to be controlled by non-beneficial states such as greed or hatred. We know from Buddhist science that a mind occupied by these states is not at peace and thus devoid of sustainable happiness.

The Buddha specifically mentioned five businesses that should be avoided, **engaging in business with weapons, business that exploits human beings, business with meat, business with intoxicants** and **business with poisons**. He also mentioned that we should employ the Middle Way in our work life and balance our income with expenditures, ensuring that we don't spend too little and become miserly or that we don't spend too much and get into debt.

Avoid engaging in business with weapons

As weapons are used to kill human beings and other sentient beings, any kind of work that involves their design, manufacture, distribution, use or sale, should be avoided. We can see how progressive the Buddha was when we see for example how lax gun laws especially in the United States, have lead to countless unnecessary shootings and deaths every year. The sale and distribution of weapons around the world has only lead to more war and suffering. In the hands of those with untrained minds, which are the majority of the world's population, weapons have created a very dangerous environment with heightened levels of fear and violence.

Avoid engaging in business that exploits human beings

There are many ways that human beings are exploited. They include human trafficking, slavery, child labor, sexual exploitation such as prostitution, forced marriage, and pornography, domestic abuse, forced criminality, kidnapping, extortion, misleading advertising and many other illegal business practices that deceive or take advantage of human beings. These crimes are happening every day in every corner of the world and can include any person, regardless of age, socio-economic background or location. Any kind of work that involves these practices should be avoided for obvious reasons. All of them are not in line with ethical principles that promote kindness, peace, freedom or honesty and will only create suffering.

Avoid engaging in business with meat

As any business with meat involves the killing of animals, this goes against what the Buddha considered as Right Livelihood. This involves butchers or those that have a direct hand in slaughtering animals, hunting or fishing businesses, the selling of meat etc. Again, it is the intention that is most important with Buddhist philosophy. If one must kill for meat or do business with meat and there are no other options available and it will help others, then it probably would not be unethical. Although our western culture consumes a lot of meat products, we should also be aware that many diseases have arisen because of this. Infections like salmonella, E. coli or mad cows disease, are just a few of the common ones associated with the consumption of meat. The raising of cattle is also very destructive for the environment as every cow needs a huge amount of land. A vegetarian diet is generally seen as being much healthier, more ecological and more ethical. Perhaps in the future, meat production will no longer be sustainable, and we will have no other option but to consider a vegetarian diet. Engaging in the business of killing animals for meat is not in line with the ethical principles taught by the Buddha as we should show compassion for all living creatures.

Avoid engaging in business with intoxicants

Intoxicants include any substances that cloud or distort the mind, including alcohol and drugs. While most people engage in some light form of alcohol consumption without any major problems that harm others or themselves, the Buddha was quite a teetotaler when it came to any types of intoxicants. We are certainly aware that alcohol does cause extensive problems in society including being a major cause of driving accidents, arguments, divorces, addictions, violence, rape and sexual abuse. It is no wonder that Buddhist philosophy recommends we stay away from any work that involves business with intoxicants.

Realizing the harmful potential of alcohol, drugs or any intoxicant for that matter, the Buddha could see that it was not the way to achieve the goal of sustained happiness. When the mind is influenced by intoxicants, we are more prone to say the wrongs things that can hurt others, engage in sexual misconduct, or even kill or harm someone. I am sure that most of us can remember at least one incident that we regret when engaging in too much alcohol. We can all attest to witnessing these harmful types of actions when we see individuals under the influence of intoxicants. If we feel we really need alcohol or any drug in our lives, then we should ask ourselves why. Most of us will justify our need and say we are under tremendous stress, have relationship problems, conflicts at work or don't feel good about ourselves. Alcohol and drugs will certainly not provide a solution to these common problems in life, but will only numb our senses for a while and distort reality. The real solution to ending our suffering as we know, is only found in the mind, but the mind needs to be alert, aware and not clouded if we are to make any progress.

Dealing with drugs is certainly obvious to most of us why we should avoid that kind of work activity, as it is clearly responsible for destroying countless lives. Work around alcohol, including working in bars, selling alcohol or producing alcohol is unfortunately not as clear-cut. However, even though its consumption is socially acceptable in most societies and most of us enjoy a drink now and then, we should definitely not underestimate its damaging potential and be mindful of any harmful effects it can cause to ourselves and to others around us.

Avoid engaging in business with poisons

Since most poisons are developed to kill or inflict harm to humans, animals or insects, any business dealing with them, violates the principle of Right Livelihood and we should not be engaged in work that involves them. The Buddha saw all sentient beings as deserving to live just as we all want to, so work related with poisons should be avoided. We all know that they are also responsible for many deaths by children or animals that accidently ingest them. They have spilled into rivers and oceans and killed fish and wildlife. They have contaminated drinking water sources. They have been used in wars and in murders with harmful intentions that are usually corrupted by deluded mind states of anger, jealousy, hatred or greed. Unless they are used to assist crops and produce more food, they are usually not needed. Our work should always be based on doing no harm and promoting peace, kindness, and happiness for others.

Balancing our income and expenditures

The principle of engaging in work that benefits all, means not to steer towards the extremes and as the Buddha taught, choosing the middle way instead. This applies even to our spending and saving habits. If we succumb to extreme greed and we do nothing but hoard our money and become miserly, we lose sight of what reality really is, and we fall to one extreme. If we excessively spend more money than we earn and find ourselves immersed in debt, we fall to the other extreme. Being able to balance our income and expenditures wisely is another form of the Middle Way. We avoid both harmful extremes by letting go of our clinging to material wealth and sharing with others what we don't need for ourselves. We don't let our desires get out of control so that we only live within our means.

Buddhist science forces us to remember that everything is impermanent, and that clinging to things is futile and only makes us suffer. Ownership is really only an illusion as there is no real concrete self. In the end it is certain that we will lose everything that we have worked for, all our material wealth, our home and everything we have achieved. Understanding and internalizing this, we should endeavor to engage in meaningful work that has a purpose in the short time that we have, not just in making us wealthy but in helping others and making them happy as well. We are after all, interconnected and what benefits we share with others with the work that we do, ultimately will benefit us as well.

PRACTICAL MIDDLE WAY MIND TRAINING PRESCRIPTION
MWMT FOUNDATIONAL PRINCIPLE 3– Engage in work that benefits all

- Meditation of Observing the Breath – designed to focus and concentrate the mind in preparation for mindfulness
- Mindfulness Meditation – trains the mind to observe and become aware of the body, feelings, and thoughts to improve your wisdom when choosing what work you do
- Compassion Meditation – trains the mind to cultivate compassion, empathy and kindness for all sentient beings through your work to benefit not just yourself but others
- Antidotes – meditative contemplations on Kindness, Generosity, Gratitude, Patience, and Reality of Suffering, Impermanence and Non-self all of which transform your mind to provide work that will not harm yourself or others
- Mantras – repetitive affirmations that settle the mind and improve meditation

Note: An explanation of MWMT methods can be found in Part V

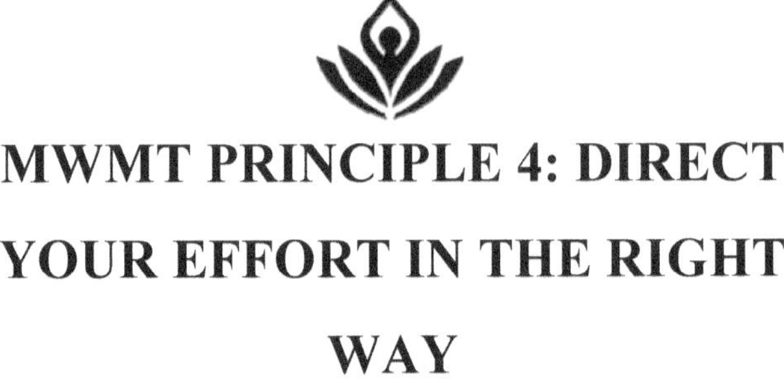

MWMT PRINCIPLE 4: DIRECT YOUR EFFORT IN THE RIGHT WAY

Your mind is your garden, your thoughts are the seeds, the harvest can either be flowers or weeds.

— William Wordsworth

The fourth of the eight foundational principles of Middle Way Mind Training is – **Direct your effort in the right way.** This principle is based on the first element of meditative concentration or Right Effort, taught by the Buddha. Cultivating effort in the right way can be compared to cultivating a flower garden. As with every garden, we initially start with an unkempt wild garden that is full of weeds. We must first make the effort to get rid of what we do not want in our garden, which are the weeds. We also want to put effort into preventing any new weeds from arising. Then we want to keep and maintain what flowers already exist in the garden, and finally cultivate or plant some new flowers that are needed.

The garden is our mind. Unwholesome mental states are the weeds. First we want to **direct our effort to eliminate those unwholesome mental states that already exist** in the garden of our mind. Next, we need to **direct our effort to prevent any unwholesome mental states form arising in our mind**. Once we have eliminated those weeds in our garden and prevented them from arising, we can **direct our effort to cultivate wholesome mental states that have already arisen in our mind.** These are the flowers that already grow in the garden in our mind. Finally we **direct our effort to cultivate any wholesome mental states that have not yet arisen**. These are the new flowers that we wish to plant in our garden. The result is that we end up with a pure cultivated mind free of any impurities, composed of only wholesome states, which will allow our inner nature, the beauty or source of our happiness to be uncovered.

Being able to direct our effort in the right way in order to purify the mind, teaches us to be diligent, persistent and to stay motivated. It is the willingness and determination to move away from our habitual ways of doing things and actively engage in transforming our mind. Directing effort in the right way is the necessary ingredient to produce the wholesome energy needed to develop meditative concentration and mindfulness which will be discussed in the next two chapters.

Direct effort to eliminate unwholesome mental states that already exist in our mind

Unwholesome mental states include those states of mind that are responsible for our suffering and unhappiness. These primarily include greed, hatred and ignorance or delusion. Most of us already have some form of these mental formations (weeds) already engrained in our minds and they tend to rear their ugly faces whenever we are provoked or triggered. We know already that if we do not guard our sense doors, when our sensory organs come in contact with a sense object, non-beneficial feelings, perceptions and mental formations can arise that are often difficult to eliminate. What are needed are meditative concentration and mindfulness techniques as well as antidotes to tackle and transform these engrained unwholesome mental states so that we do not react in harmful or non-beneficial ways. Directing our effort in the right way here means to be aware of their existence in our minds, understand their causes and direct effort to eliminate them by replacing them with antidotes, such as compassion, generosity, and wisdom.

Direct effort to prevent any unwholesome mental states form arising in our mind

The unwholesome states of greed, hatred and ignorance can corrupt the mind if the sense doors are not guarded. In order to prevent these weeds from arising in the garden of our mind, not only do we have to direct our efforts to be mindful of our sense doors, but we also need to cultivate wholesome mental states. These include developing generosity, compassion and wisdom so that there is no room for unwholesome mental states to take hold. Just like preventing weeds in a garden, they require us to be on constant watch ensuring that that they are removed and prevented from growing out of control, otherwise they take over our mind's garden and predominate. Mindful attention to our encounter with sense objects will over time, become more sensitive to this process and be able to catch it before it can develop. Mindfulness calms these unwholesome mental states by helping to keep our mind consciousness at the level of what is sensed or at the level of bare awareness of experience. It helps us to prevent our mind from embellishing the experience with perceptions and mental formations that arise out of greed, hatred, or delusion.

Direct effort to cultivate wholesome mental states that have already arisen in our mind

Most of us have a mind or a garden with some flowers or some degree of wholesome mental states such as generosity, compassion and wisdom, but usually it is limited to perhaps our loved ones and those closest to us. Having the capacity to extend these wholesome mental states to all sentient beings, including our enemies or those who have hurt us is certainly a challenge for most of us. This requires cultivation by recognizing those flowers in our garden and cultivating them to grow even bigger.The Buddha mentioned compassion, loving-kindness and equanimity as mental states that have no limits, they are immeasurable, and so we should direct our efforts to cultivate them as much as we can so they flourish in our mind.

Direct effort to cultivate any wholesome mental states that have not yet arisen

Finally, the garden of our mind may not contain some flowers or wholesome mental states that will be favorable, so we should direct effort in planting or cultivating any new beneficial states of mind that are based on compassion, generosity and wisdom. The seeds that we plant in the garden of our mind determine who we will become, how we will react with the people around us and to all our experiences that we encounter. Putting the right energy into this endeavor will certainly pay dividends. It will ensure that our mind is pure and it will allow our inner nature, the sustained happiness that we all possess already within us, to be uncovered and experienced to the fullest.

PRACTICAL MIDDLE WAY MIND TRAINING PRESCRIPTION
MWMT FOUNDATIONAL PRINCIPLE 4 – Direct your effort in the right way

- Meditation of Observing the Breath – designed to focus and concentrate the mind in preparation for the practice of mindfulness
- Mindfulness Meditation – trains the mind to observe and become aware of the body, feelings, and thoughts so that we can guard the sense doors and recognize the development of wholesome and unwholesome states of mind
- Compassion Meditation – trains the mind to cultivate compassion, empathy and kindness for all sentient beings in order to cultivate and maintain wholesome states of mind
- Antidotes – meditative contemplations on Kindness, Generosity, Gratitude, Patience, Sympathetic joy, Forgiveness and Reality of Suffering, Impermanence and Non-Self all of which transform your mind to counteract unwholesome states of mind and prevent them from arising as well as maintaining and developing wholesome states of mind
- Mantras – repetitive affirmations that settle the mind and improve meditation

Note: An explanation of MWMT methods can be found in Part V

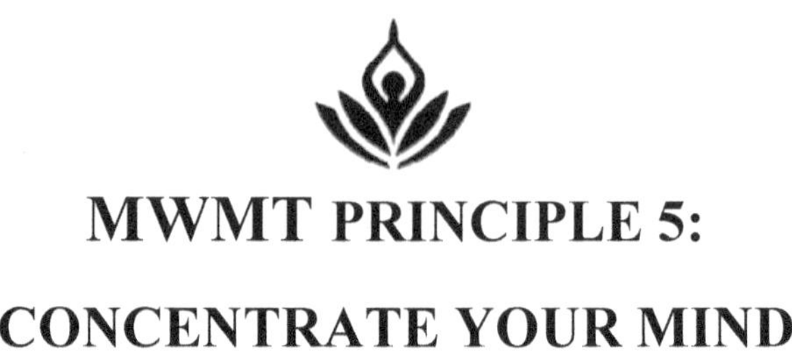

MWMT PRINCIPLE 5:

CONCENTRATE YOUR MIND

Listen to silence; it has so much to say

— Rumi

The fifth of the eight foundational principles of Middle Way Mind Training is – **Concentrate your mind.** This principle is based on the second element of meditative concentration or Right Concentration, taught by the Buddha. As we have discussed in the past few chapters, a solid foundation in ethics is needed, otherwise it is very difficult to progress in meditation. Initially our mind is a jungle of distracting thoughts that constantly arise and pass away. If we have a sound moral basis, our mind is already free from a lot of negative thoughts. These thoughts often distract us from reality, cause us to react in non-beneficial ways, distort our judgment and create a lot of unhappiness for us. When we concentrate the mind, we train it to bring it into sharp focus. This means training the mind in meditation to achieve a concentrated one-pointed state. When we do this long enough, we can achieve calmness, peace and stability, which lead to deep states of meditative absorption. Concentrating your mind really means the core of our contemplative meditation practice.

The Pali word for concentration is *samadhi,* which literally means to collect, bring together or integrate. Samadhi represents a deepening of a mental factor that is present in every state of our consciousness. We achieve *samadhi* by concentrating or meditating on a single object. When we center the mind on an object of our attention, it collects together or unifies our scattered streams of consciousness into one single stream. Achieving a level of *samadhi* is deeply restful and satisfying but it is not easy and takes a lot of mental training. The results of a concentrated mind are an unbroken attentiveness to an object and a calming or stilling of all the mental functions of our mind. With time and in combination with good ethics, our meditative practice can eventually achieve oneness with the object of our concentration.

The Buddha likened *samadhi* to a clear and fresh pool of water in the mountains that has no rivers running into it. How is it possible to maintain a clear fresh pool without having any rivers drawing into it? The Buddha said, that like *samadhi*, the source for the pool of fresh and clear water, is a spring that bubbles out from within the earth, not from any external rivers above. Our mind cannot achieve clarity, purity or sustained happiness from our external environment or the sensory world of sights, sounds, smells, tastes, touch or thoughts. It can only come within, beginning with right concentration.

In this book we utilize the most common meditative object that was very much encouraged by the Buddha, our breath. As we refine our concentration with meditation on the breath, distracting thoughts begin to lose their hold on us and we gain more control of our mind, as our senses become removed from sights, sounds, smells, touches, tastes and ideas. The breath is one of the greatest objects of meditation because it is with us all the time, whether we are conscious of it or not. What better way to observe the actual present moment, then when we observe our breath. Another method to concentrate the mind is reciting mantras which as we will learn in a future chapter can also be very beneficial.

The four *jhanas* are often mentioned in Buddhist philosophy in reference to *samadhi* as they are progressive stages of meditative absorption that result from concentrating the mind through this kind of meditation. During this process, we pass through stages of intense bliss when entering the *jhanas* as we slowly let go of our desires and worries in life and reach higher and higher states of equanimity and awareness.

It has even been documented by Buddhists that when one achieves certain higher levels of mental absorption as in the *jhanas*, the mind gets more and more focused and refined and gains remarkable abilities. These can even include supernormal powers such as being able to read minds, see previous lives, achieve powers of miraculous healing, experience enhanced sensory perception, or achieve abilities of levitation or teleportation. In ancient Buddhist texts it is written that the Buddha exhibited some of these above mentioned supernormal powers. Other

Buddhists have also been known to exhibit these powers such as Dipa Ma, an Indian Buddhist master, who taught at the Insight Meditation Society in Massachusetts, USA in the early eighties and died in 1989 (Schmidt, 2005). As this level of mental concentration is certainly not easy to achieve and can take many years, many of us with no doubt may find these powers far-fetched and very difficult to believe. However, whether these stories of supernormal abilities are true or not, we have all heard about instances when someone has lifted a car in order to save their loved one who is trapped underneath. These extraordinary feats are often perceived as miraculous or impossible under normal conditions but in a life or death situation with a concentrated mind, they undoubtedly demonstrate the potential strength of mind over matter.

Concentrating the mind through breath meditation will prepare us for what is next; to learn to be in the present moment and to see reality the way it really is, through the ancient art and science of mindfulness.

PRACTICAL MIDDLE WAY MIND TRAINING PRESCRIPTION

MWMT FOUNDATIONAL PRINCIPLE 5– Concentrate your mind

- Meditation of Observing the Breath – designed to focus and concentrate the mind in preparation for the practice of mindfulness
- Mindfulness meditation – to recognize and overcome hindrances to meditation and to be aware of all aspects of the breath
- Antidotes – meditative contemplations on Patience, Gratitude, Generosity, Compassion, Forgiveness, Sympathetic joy and Reality of Suffering, Impermanence and Non-self, to counteract the obstacles or hindrances to our meditation
- Mantras – repetitive affirmations that settle the mind

Note: An explanation of MWMT methods can be found in Part V

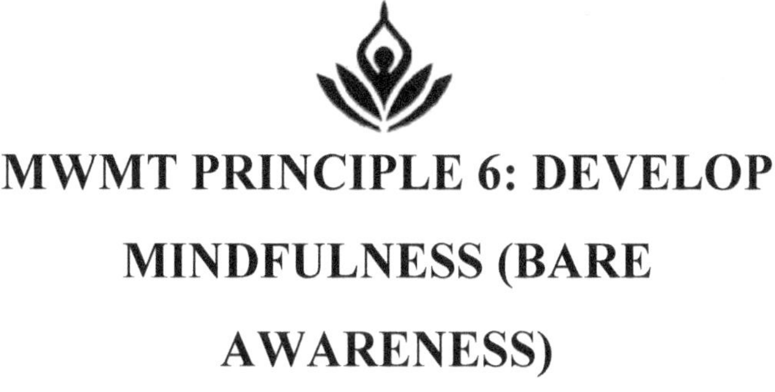

MWMT PRINCIPLE 6: DEVELOP MINDFULNESS (BARE AWARENESS)

My grandfather of mindfulness must watch
constantly after this spoiled child of deluded
mind, to save him from disaster.

— Milarepa

The sixth of the eight foundational principles of Middle Way Mind Training is – **Develop Mindfulness (Bare Awareness).** This principle is based on the third and last element of meditative concentration or Right Mindfulness, taught by the Buddha. As we have learned previously, it is important for us to direct our effort in the right way, as well as focus and concentrate our mind through meditation on the breath, so we can calm our thoughts. That forms a foundation for cultivating a state where we can view reality with bare awareness, unhindered by distracting and distorted thoughts and perceptions. We also saw how cultivating good ethical behavior is also conducive to calming the mind. In fact, all the principles mentioned so far, work together to ultimately achieve what this book is all about, uncovering and experiencing the happiness we already hold within and eliminating suffering.

Mindfulness can be likened to bare awareness because when we cultivate mindfulness we are living and observing everything that is happening in the present moment. Often the experience of reality that people have is different from the actual present-moment awareness of thoughts and emotions of the mind. Many people experience a reality that is unfortunately dominated by distressing imagery, rumination and negative emotions driven by harsh and inaccurate judgments about the self, the world and the future. With mindfulness training, we can learn to observe our body, feelings and mind as experiences arise, without adding any extra layers of judgments, opinions or ideas about them. When we practice right mindfulness, we really strip our awareness down to the bare reality, you might say. Mindfulness teaches us to respond wisely instead of reacting impulsively without any thought. It frees the mind from its habitual influences as we introduce new patterns of behavior. There has been a lot of research made on mindfulness in recent years proving its therapeutic benefits and modern methods such as Mindfulness-Based Stress Reduction (Kabat-Zinn, 1990) and Mindfulness-Based Cognitive Therapy (Segal, Williams and Teasdale, 2001) are now becoming some of the primary treatments for depression, anxiety and stress.

Mindfulness originates from Buddhist philosophy and comes from the Pali word *"sati"* or awareness. It means to bring ones attention to whatever is happening in the present moment. This includes being aware of sensations in the body, feelings, thoughts and laws that govern reality (*dharmas*), without judgment and with acceptance or equanimity. According to Buddhist science, right mindfulness means to cultivate the appropriate attention, that which leads to insight, wisdom and ultimately *nirvana.*

Mindfulness is not only a technique, but a path of recognizing and transforming our way of thinking, imagining and perceiving, by examining and recognizing their roots in the mind as they arise and pass away. In a way, it acts like a surgical operation of the mind that leads to a paradigm shift in our thinking. If we cultivate right mindfulness, all fundamental principles of Middle Way Mind Training will develop along with it. This means, not only will our ability to concentrate our mind improve, but our ethical development will be strengthened and wisdom of true reality will be cultivated. When we practice mindfulness, we develop an ability to feel and experience life without getting lost in it. This means being aware of the body as it is, aware of our bare feelings without adding any associated secondary feelings to them. It also means being aware of bare thoughts and states of mind, without all the stories, elaborations, judgments, perceptions or comparisons to the past that we often add to them. We also learn with mindfulness to be aware of any hindrances or obstacles that impede our meditation practice and how they arise. Finally as we advance in mindfulness, we learn to be aware and to fully understand the laws that govern our reality, or in Buddhist science, the *dharmas*. This consists of being objectively mindful of and internalizing primarily the Five Aggregates, the Four Noble Truths, and the Three Marks of our Existence (suffering, impermanence and non-self) and accepting them with equanimity. It is one thing to intellectually understand these laws but only with mindfulness training can we can actually digest them and internalize them into our being, so that transformation occurs.

We tend to maintain our view of the world with our inner dialogue of our mind. Our mind often completes the story without living in the reality of how it really is. Mindfulness creates a sense of presence and freedom in the moment and opens up a space for being aware to allow thoughts to come and go. With mindfulness, we don't fight, distort or suppress our thoughts; we see them as they really are. The power of mindfulness is to know what is so, and see it for what it is, whether it is a thought, a picture, a feeling or an imagination. We learn that moods and feelings last maybe ten or twenty seconds at the most, if nothing is added to them, and then change to another mood. We learn that thoughts appear and disappear even quicker, and sensations in the body when observed, can last longer but can also move and change within us.

As we explore mindfulness, we know how our thoughts and feelings arise and then dissolve and we begin to see the repeated mental patterns and how we attach or identify to them. The more we cultivate mindfulness, the more we see that our sense of self is only a story that we tell ourselves and that it is only a construct in our mind. We begin to understand our futile attempts of grasping to I, me and mine and realize that there is really no concrete self we can find, only a sequence of processes or experiences. We begin to see the potential for happiness if we release these habitual mental patterns that we grasp onto so strongly, those which cause us a lot of suffering. Mindfulness of each moment brings us to freedom, as we are not caught up with feelings or thoughts at that time. The heart becomes calm and still, and more capable of expressing compassion. When mindfulness becomes established, we really rest in our true inner nature and this in turn results in inner peace and an abundance of happiness. We will learn several practical applications of mindfulness training in the final parts of this book.

Let's look briefly at each of the four foundations of mindfulness that are mentioned in Buddhist science. Each is important to develop in order to achieve our ultimate goal of seeing each experience with bare awareness, to see the true reality behind every thought and experience as it arises and passes away in the present moment. Ultimately, the cultivation of the four foundations of mindfulness is the key to dissolving all the layers that encase our inner nature and the path to uncovering our inherent inner peace and happiness.

Mindfulness of the Body

When we practice mindfulness of the body, Buddhist science reminds us to see "the body in the body." This means we should recognize that the body is not a solid or concrete entity, but only a collection of parts. Each part, whether the bones, heart, liver, skin and others is in reality a small body in itself, part of a larger entity or process that we just call a body. Being able to be mindful of each part, helps us to view the body as just a body, not "my body" or "myself" but just a physical form, like all other physical forms. It teaches us that like all forms, it comes into being, is present for a certain time and then passes away. We learn to objectify the body and move away from I, me and mine. Mindfulness of the body teaches us that we should not cling to it as a source of happiness because it will eventually succumb to injury, illness and death. It helps us to recognize the impermanence of the body, how it is unsatisfactory or contains *dukkha*, and how in reality, it contains no concrete self.

There are many ways to practice mindfulness of the body. They include mindfulness of breathing or as it is called in the Buddhist tradition, "*anapanasati* ", mindfulness of postures and activities (such as walking, moving, eating, drinking, and talking) and mindfulness of the anatomical parts of the body and interior organs and components as performed during mindful body scans. The point of all these techniques is to objectify the body, and move away from I, me, and mine. When we see the reality of the body as being made up of many elements, none of which have a concrete self, we loosen the hold of the ego and of the self.

This, as we already know, leads to a reduction of unnecessary suffering and much greater gains in happiness.

The Buddha also taught mindfulness of impurities of the body, such as contemplations on blood, pus, urine, feces, sweat, and discharge along with many other unpleasant human constituents. This mindfulness practice is designed to loosen our hold on sensory desires and our fixation on the beauty of the body. We often admire or even envy people who have beautiful hair or beautiful nails, but are quickly reminded of the impurities of the body and look with disgust when we find that same hair in our food or a piece of that same nail somewhere other than on the finger. In this way we can see the impermanence of the body as it arises and decays, not that the body is ugly, but it is not perfect and it will eventually change and not be so beautiful anymore. Therefore, we should not get attached or cling to it, as there is nothing we can do about it, it will pass away one day.

Finally, the Buddha also taught what are known as charnel ground contemplations or mindfulness on death and decay of the body. In ancient India, it was common to dispose of a corpse by two methods, either burn it or dispose of it in what was called a charnel ground. There the corpse would be left to rot away, exposed to the elements and eaten by insects, rats or vultures and would go back to its natural state of earth and ground. In Buddha's day, the monks were instructed to actually frequent these charnel grounds, to see this process firsthand and contemplate on human death and decay. If there were no charnel grounds, contemplations would be made on the decaying stages of the human body. The point of this kind of mindfulness training was again to internalize that this body that we have is impermanent and the process of death and decay happens to everyone, and will eventually but surely even happen to our bodies.

For most of us in Western society, such mindfulness techniques are usually considered morbid and very disturbing, and many would certainly never consider them. This general attitude reveals however a deeper problem; our aversion to the mere subject of talking about death or terminal disease, not to mention seeing death firsthand. These subjects are generally considered taboo in our society. We often don't know what to really say when someone mentions death or cancer. The Buddha had a very good reason to teach this kind of mindfulness of the body and he did it for the sole purpose that we could reduce the suffering in our own lives, by accepting the inevitability of our death. The result of this practice leads us to fully appreciate the time we have left on this earth while we are alive and to live the happiest lives possible. The reality is that our life can end at any time. Deep down we all know this, but we certainly don't act like it. Some of us cannot get over the death of a loved one for our entire lives. The point is to come to terms with our own mortality, to see reality as it really is and not to shun it away or hide it under a rug. We need to let go of our fear of death, and learn to approach it as a natural process of the human condition and accept it with peace and equanimity. This type of mindfulness of the body is one of the most profound and deepest contemplations, teaching the wisdom of impermanence, *dukkha* and non-self.

Mindfulness of Feelings

Similarly, when we practice mindfulness of feelings, Buddhist science reminds us to contemplate "the feeling in the feelings." Like the body, feelings can also be broken down into components. Here we are not talking about emotions but the bare beginnings of their development. As we know there are only three basic types, pleasant, unpleasant, and neutral feelings. We also know that when there is contact between our sense organs (eyes, ears, nose, tongue, body, and mind) and sense objects (sights, sounds, smells, tastes, tactile objects, thoughts), one of these types of feelings arises. At any given moment we are able to notice only one type. When a pleasant feeling is present, neither a painful feeling nor a neutral feeling is present. The same is true of an unpleasant or neutral feeling. If these feelings are not kept in check, pleasant feelings can lead to craving, desires, jealousy and greed or unpleasant feelings can lead to aversion, anger and hatred. Even neutral feelings can lead to a sense of ignorance as there is no motivation to investigate them due to our indifference.

With mindfulness of feelings, we become less identified with the pleasant and unpleasant. We are even able to investigate the nature of our indifference with neutral feelings. We learn to put a space between the arising of craving and aversion as we cultivate this mindfulness, which allows time to prevent them into turning into non-beneficial states of mind. As we see these feelings as impermanent and not perfect, we stop our tendency to cling and crave.

Being able to regard feelings in this way through mindfulness, helps us develop a simple nonjudgmental awareness of what we are experiencing. We do not let our experiences get clouded or distorted. We learn to see a particular feeling as one of many feelings, rather than just seeing it as <u>our</u> feeling or something that is a part of <u>us</u>. As we observe each feeling as it arises, remains present for a while, and passes away, we learn that feelings are also impermanent. We begin to internalize that feelings are quite unsatisfactory and subject to *dukkha* as pleasant feelings never last and leave us wanting more, and unpleasant feelings are often painful and we want to push them away. Since feelings come and go, we realize that they are not us, they have no-self. Just as the body, there is no reason to cling to our feelings. Mindfulness of feelings trains our mind to not get caught up with the feelings we experience or to let them get out of control and turn into non-beneficial mind states that can distort our reality.

Mindfulness of Mind or Mental Phenomena

The same applies when we practice mindfulness of mind, where Buddhist science reminds us also to contemplate "the mind in mind." Consciousness arises from moment to moment on the basis of information coming to us from the senses in what we see, hear, smell, taste, and touch and from internal mental states, such as thoughts and memories from the past. Even though we think of the mind as a single entity, it too is a succession of instances. When we look at the mind, we are not looking at just consciousness. The mind alone cannot exist, only specific states of mind appear depending on external or internal conditions.

When we pay attention to how each thought in the mind arises, is present, and then passes away, we learn to stop the domino effect of one unsatisfactory thought leading to another until non-beneficial habitual mental formations become engrained. We become detached and begin to understand that we are also not our thoughts and that there is also no need to cling to them. Ultimately, we see the reality of the mind as it really is. We can identify and observe ordinary states of the mind such as when we are greedy, angry, and full of desire, distracted, focused or tired. As we progress in mindfulness of the mind, we can also observe higher states of mind such as whether our mind is concentrated or liberated from suffering, what *jhana* or stage of absorption it resides in, or whether our mind is compassionate, kind, empathetic or in a state of equanimity.

It is important to be mindful of our states of mind because ordinarily we have a tendency to ignore or overlook bad states of mind and suffer from delusion as to the character of our mind. With mindfulness of our mind, we can see our mind objectively without any clinging to any mental formations. It gives us space to respond wisely and ethically to any challenging situation.

Mindfulness of Dharmas (laws or phenomena that govern the mind and the body)

The practice of mindfulness of *dharmas*, or natural laws or truths of our existence that govern the body and the mind is the fourth and final foundation of mindfulness. The Buddha said that we should develop mindfulness first of all, of states of mind that hinder or create obstacles in our meditation practice, such as sensory desire, anger, restlessness and worry, laziness and doubt. These are called the Five Hindrances and will be discussed in more detail later in this book. We should be aware when they are present, when they are absent, when they pass away, aware that they are temporary or impermanent and should be aware under what conditions they arise and how they can be prevented from arising.

Mindfulness of natural laws also includes being mindful of our sense doors in order to prevent the arising of craving or aversion. This means we need to be mindful of the Five Aggregates (form, feeling, perception, mental formations, and consciousness) and their arising and passing. They create our personality or the mental construct of the self, and if left unguarded can lead to ingrained ideas, opinions and mind states that may not be beneficial to us or others.

Mindfulness of the *dharmas* also means deep contemplations on the three marks of our existence, impermanence, *dukkha* or suffering and non-self and accepting them with wisdom and equanimity. We should also develop mindfulness of the 4 Noble Truths directly and experientially. This means knowing and experiencing the truth of *dukkha* or suffering, knowing and experiencing the arising of *dukkha*, knowing and experiencing the cessation of *dukkha* and knowing and experiencing the path leading to cessation of *dukkha*. We have discussed all these natural laws of Buddhist science in past chapters, so mindfulness of the *dharmas* means we need to develop a deep awareness or internalization of all of them.

In the Pali Canon of Theraveda Buddhism, the Buddha mentions two qualities of mind that should be developed in meditation, *calm abiding*, which can be achieved through breath meditation as we have discussed in the fundamental principle of concentration of the mind, and *insight* or *vipassana*, which we can gain through cultivating an awareness of each of the four foundations of mindfulness. *Vipassana* is a Pali word which translates to "seeing clearly" or "insight" and it denotes a mental quality that allows one to be able to perceive the fundamental reality of our existence with clarity and precision. It has led to development of *vipassana* or insight meditation techniques which cultivate similar elements of mindfulness of the laws that govern the mind and the body. As we progress in mindfulness meditation, we gain more and more insight into our fundamental nature of our reality and through this, gain wisdom.

Ultimately, all the fundamental principles of Middle Way Mind Training we have discussed so far lead us to developing what is the main theme of the last two fundamental principles, wisdom. These will be discussed in the next two chapters.

PRACTICAL MIDDLE WAY MIND TRAINING PRESCRIPTION
MWMT FOUNDATIONAL PRINCIPLE 6– Develop Mindfulness (Bare Awareness)

- Meditation of Observing the Breath – mindfulness of the breath
- Mindfulness meditation – mindfulness of the body (mindfulness while walking, mindfulness while eating, mindfulness while speaking), mindfulness of feelings, mind, and the *dharmas*

- Antidotes – meditative contemplations on Hindrances or Obstacles to Meditation
- Mantras – repetitive affirmations that settle the mind and improve meditation

Note: An explanation of MWMT methods can be found in Part V

198

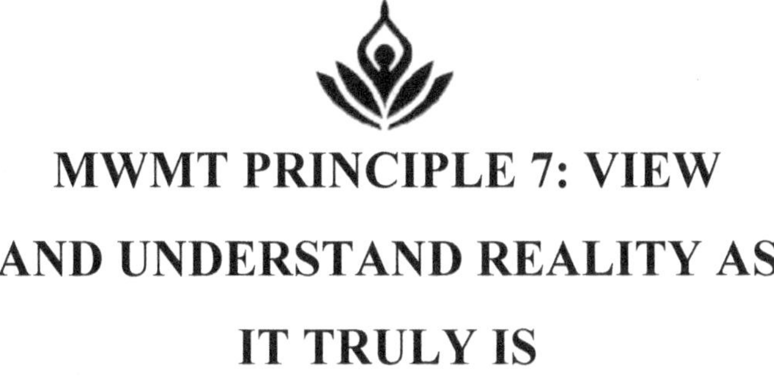

MWMT PRINCIPLE 7: VIEW AND UNDERSTAND REALITY AS IT TRULY IS

To see the mind, you must look and probe with
the eye of wisdom.

— Milarepa

The seventh of the eight foundational principles of Middle Way Mind Training is – **View and understand reality as it truly is.** This principle is based on the first element of wisdom or Right View, taught by the Buddha. In some ways this principle is certainly needed at the beginning of our journey in Middle Way Mind Training and at the same time it is developed as a result of our training. It is very important as it guides all the seven other fundamental principles. It ensures that our behavior, speech and thoughts are born from a mind infused with wisdom and compassion. Having the right view can be likened to looking into a still pool of water and being able to see the bottom with absolute clarity.

The first six principles so far have been based on establishing the firm foundations of morality and mental concentration. Both of these are needed to establish wisdom. It should also be emphasized again that all the fundamental principles of Middle Way Mind Training overlap and complement each other. Therefore, they should be developed simultaneously and not in any specific order.

If we search for definitions of wisdom, we find that it generally means having <u>knowledge</u> that is gained by experience, having <u>insight</u> or the ability to discern inner qualities and relationships, and possessing a good sense or <u>judgment</u>. It also means to be able to challenge conventional accepted beliefs and views, and that is certainly what we are endeavoring to do throughout this book.

Wisdom is developed from directly observing the truth of our experience. We cultivate wisdom as we become able to live fully in the present moment, rather than being lost in our memories of the past, our dreams and plans, and all the commentaries of the thinking mind. It is only in the timeless present moment that we can really come to that silent knowing of the truth. This becomes the wisdom that is able to liberate us. Insight is developed by seeing the phenomena of experiences arising and passing away and how we relate to them. Through our open and mindful inquiry into the workings of the body and the mind, we see how it relates to the whole world around us. To foster this insight we need observation, deep questioning and contemplation. We need to collect and quiet the mind so we can observe and examine its ways and understand the natural laws of reality that we are governed by. Wisdom is an ongoing process of discovery that unfolds with the full awareness of each moment. It is cultivated out of our genuine openness and it leads us to a new world of freedom.

The Buddha said that in order for us to see clearly and understand reality as it really is, we must have the right view. Before we talk about right view, we need to look at what we mean by a view itself. When we hold a view, we have a belief or what we perceive something to be. The Buddha however, made quite a distinction between just having a belief and seeing things clearly as they are. He was quite against the reliance on beliefs. He encouraged his followers to become independent of any beliefs that they had and arrive at the right view of reality for themselves by firsthand personal experience.

For example, there was a time when people believed that the world was flat. Even though this belief for them was a true statement because they believed it, it still had nothing to do with viewing reality as it really is. We also know our mind is often subject to delusion because it is influenced strongly by our emotions, perceptions and past experiences. This means that our beliefs often stem from a mind that is deluded and not from a mind that sees reality clearly. If we believe something and we say it is true, then we need evidence to support it. Otherwise, we simply open ourselves up to being wrong, or having a wrong view, when our beliefs turn out to be out of line with reality. Beliefs have to be in line with reality, not just because our mind says they believe in something. The problem arises when we depend on our beliefs and do not bother finding out if they are true or not. In this way, we close ourselves off from the investigation of the truth.

We tend to be less concerned about whether our beliefs are actually in line with reality then simply whether we believe in them. An example is, you believe in God. How do you know that God exists? Do you have proof? or you believe in Buddha's teachings? How do you know that they accomplish what they say they do? If you believe in the Buddha's teachings, then you have a view or belief but this, according to Buddhist science, is not Right View according to the Eightfold Path. To gain the Right View, you need to experience it yourself through contemplative meditation. Only through this way can you really see or experience the truth of reality. To cultivate Right view is to relinquish all of your previous views. If you remember at the beginning of this book, when we discussed developing a beginner's mind, I encouraged you to let go of your expert views to be open to infinite possibilities. The Buddha taught to give up all views in favor of a direct experiential view of reality. Instead of only intellectualizing our view on reality, we need to penetrate it and experience it internally. It involves moving away from "I believe" to seeing things how they actually are.

As we practice mindfulness and meditation to cultivate insight and wisdom, we are trying to understand or see reality as it truly is. As we observe our thoughts, emotions, feelings and movements of the body we start to see that the things that we initially thought were stable, controllable and satisfying turn out to be impermanent, unsatisfying, unpredictable and unmanageable. We come closer to seeing the real truth of suffering, and then after some time, we can see that things are unsatisfying, impermanent and contain no-self. In Buddhist philosophy, right view also means an understanding of the actions of karma and realizing that all actions have karmic consequences.

The Four noble truths are not that hard to understand intellectually and at this point as a reader, we may feel that we already know them quite well, and may even ask why we need to meditate to find out what we already know already. But it is only during meditation that we come to realize what we didn't really know, and that what we had prior to training the mind was only a mundane view of reality, not the right or absolute view. In Buddhist science, enlightenment and freedom from suffering comes from not just a belief in the Four Noble Truths but seeing and experiencing them with the right view.

This brings us to what is meant by the two truths in Buddhist Science, relative truth and absolute truth. <u>Relative truth</u> includes all the dualistic phenomena- ourselves, other beings, material objects, thoughts, emotions, concepts-that make up the relative reality of our world. According to Buddhist science, this truth is only an illusion, because we mistakenly believe they are solid, separate, and independent realities. The problem is not the relative truth itself because we need it to navigate in our world, but our misunderstanding of its nature. <u>Absolute truth</u> is the reality beyond dualism of any kind. It is the true nature of relative phenomena.

Our happiness depends a lot on how we view and understand the way reality really is. When we can internalize the understanding of our true reality, we can liberate ourselves from all the suffering that is created from not viewing reality the way it truly is. Insight into this important principle, offers us deep understanding, inner peace and true lasting happiness.

PRACTICAL MIDDLE WAY MIND TRAINING PRESCRIPTION
MWMT FOUNDATIONAL PRINCIPLE 7 – View and understand reality as it truly is

- Meditation of Observing the Breath – mindfulness of the breath
- Mindfulness meditation – mindfulness of the body (mindfulness while walking, mindfulness while eating, mindfulness while speaking) mindfulness of feelings, mind, and *dharmas*
- Compassion meditation
- Antidotes – meditative contemplations on Hindrances, Patience, Gratitude, Reality of Suffering, Impermanence and Non-self
- Mantras – repetitive affirmations that settle the mind and improve meditation

Note: An explanation of MWMT methods can be found in Part V

MWMT PRINCIPLE 8:
MAINTAIN THE RIGHT INTENTIONS

Intention leads to behaviors which lead to habits
which lead to personality development which
leads to destiny.

— Jack Kornfield

The eighth and last of the eight foundational principles of Middle Way Mind Training is – **Maintain the right intentions.** This principle is based on the second and last element of wisdom or Right Intention, taught by the Buddha. In the last chapter we learned that in order to develop wisdom we need the right view or strong understanding of the Four Noble Truths so that we can progress along the path of ending our suffering and achieving sustained happiness. However even a strong deep understanding is not enough. What are also needed are the right intentions.

Take the example of a drug addict or alcoholic. He knows that taking the drugs or alcohol is ruining his life. He knows through experience what he has personally lost and what he will lose if he continues with his addiction. This means he has the right view and understanding of the grim reality of the consequences. However, he continues taking the drugs or alcohol nevertheless. He does not have the conviction, persistence or determination to stop his bad habit, which are central to right intention. Another example is when we are tired and stay up late at night watching a television program that captures our attention. We understand that in the morning we are going to be very tired as we have to go to work, but we still watch until the late hours. We need to develop the conviction so that we let go of all the desires that delude us and veer us towards the extremes instead of keeping us on the middle path. This is what is meant by maintaining the right intentions.

The same can be applied to our pursuit for eliminating suffering in our lives and gaining happiness. Along with the right view of the way reality truly is, we also need the correct intentions to progress in our development of wisdom. Are we honestly ready to change our behavior to do what it takes to be happy? To maintain the right intentions, the Buddha stated that we need to make three vows. Each of these vows or intentions counteracts a strong negative tendency that we have in ourselves, namely greed or desire, ill will or anger and ignorance or delusion, the root causes of suffering.

The intention of renunciation

What we mean by the intention of renunciation is to make a vow to let go of selfish desires or pursuits such as greed, jealousy, pride or other non-beneficial and harmful emotions. This requires us to loosen our grasp on external things as well as the belief that happiness can be found in the external world. It does not mean we have to live like a monk and totally rid ourselves completely of our material possessions. It means though that we see behind their illusion, their empty qualities and their impermanence and do not hold onto them for dear life. We become disenchanted with the material world because we know that it can only provide short-lived gratification, not sustainable happiness. Because of this, sense objects become less alluring as we can see the trap or suffering that is embedded in the experience and we are able to renounce worldly things and pleasures much more easily and not cling to them when they pass through our awareness. We know that they never last. Developing the intention of renunciation counteracts one of the strongest causes of our suffering, that of desire and greed.

The intention of goodwill

When we develop the intention of goodwill, we make a vow to act with an attitude of goodwill for the benefit of others. All of our actions that we initiate through our body, speech and mind should resonate with the intention to help others. By strengthening this intention, we give up or let go of any angry reactions of revenge or punishment or any feelings of ill will towards any sentient beings, including humans, animals and insects. If any of these attitudes arise in our minds, we make a vow and resolve not to feed the anger or ill will or allow it to grow out of control. Developing the intention of goodwill counteracts anger or ill will, another major cause of our suffering.

The intention of harmlessness

The intention of harmlessness means to make a vow of not harming our self or others through any action of the body, speech or mind. It is developed and motivated by compassion. This is a broad and sincere determination of not causing any pain, loss, or destruction to any living being. This means that we also must have a good foundation of ethics, be mindful of harmful speech, actions or livelihood and business dealings that can directly or indirectly cause harm. Intention of harmlessness means also to avoid any intentional killing of humans, animals or insects. There is no way to avoid all harm to others in our life but we make a sincere vow to aspire towards harmlessness. Having the strength and conviction of this intention, is one of the most powerful ways to transform our lives and the lives of others. As a result we counteract our ignorance and delusion by respecting that we are interconnected with every living being and that each of us wishes to be happy, just as we do.

PRACTICAL MIDDLE WAY MIND TRAINING PRESCRIPTION
MWMT FOUNDATIONAL PRINCIPLE 8– Maintain the right intentions

- Meditation of Observing the Breath – mindfulness of the breath
- Mindfulness meditation – mindfulness of the body (mindfulness while walking, mindfulness while eating, mindfulness while speaking), mindfulness of feelings, mind, and *dharmas*
- Compassion meditation

- Antidotes – meditative contemplations on Hindrances, Generosity, Patience, Gratitude, Forgiveness, Sympathetic joy and Reality of Suffering, Impermanence and Non-self
- Mantras – repetitive affirmations that settle the mind and improve meditation

Note: An explanation of MWMT methods can be found in Part V

PART V

PRACTICAL EXERCISES FOR
MIDDLE WAY MIND TRAINING

If you want a difficult life, try to change others.
If you want an easy life, try to change yourself.

— Tulku Lama Lobsang

INTRODUCTION TO

MEDITATION

Meditation is not evasion; it is a serene encounter
with reality.

— Thich Nhat Hanh

*W*e have now gone through the necessary steps for uncovering and experiencing our happiness, through the eight fundamental principles of Middle Way Mind Training. It is now up to each one of us to take this intellectual understanding and put it to the test through practical experience. This importance is stressed once again and expressed profoundly in an interpretation of Buddha's words from the Kalama Sutta:

"Do not believe in anything simply because you have heard it. Do not believe in anything simply because it is spoken and rumored by many. Do not believe in anything simply because it is found written in your religious books. Do not believe in anything merely on the authority of your teachers and elders. Do not believe in traditions because they have been handed down for many generations. But after observation and analysis, when you find that anything agrees with reason and is conducive to the good and benefit of one and all, then accept it and live up to it."

The only true practical vehicle for transformation of the mind is meditation. This is how you can put your intellectual understanding into practice and internalize it, to make permanent positive and beneficial changes to your life and your experience of happiness.

Meditation is a very broad term, an English word that stems from the Latin term *meditatum*, which means to ponder. In the oldest texts of the Buddhist tradition, it comes from the word *dhyana* (Sanskrit) or *jhana*

(Pali), which means meditation or contemplation. Meditation was around long before the Buddha, as seen in some ancient art paintings from India that date back to 5000 BC - 3500 BC, that depict people sitting in postures, presumably in meditation. Documented texts have also been discovered from the Vedas from around 1500 BC that describe meditative practices that had been passed down orally for centuries. Meditation in its many forms, including contemplation and prayer, has a long history and is found across many cultures and religions.

In recent times, meditation has been the subject of much interest and now increasingly in numerous scientific studies. Meditation is being introduced to children and results show that their ability to focus and concentrate improves significantly. Meditation is being used for stress, depression and a variety of psychological disorders and even in pain management. While most of the studies focus on health and psychological benefits, few focus on transformation of the mind and ability to see reality as it really is. Many brain studies are being made on serious meditators such as Buddhist monks, and finding that meditation has an association with neuroplasticity or the ability of the brain to form new neural pathways and synaptic connections (Davidson, 2008). This means that meditation has the power to rewire the brain to function differently than it did before as in mind training (Hanson, 2009).

Types of Meditation

There are many types of meditations; the three primary ones in Buddhist science are calming or concentration meditation as in meditation of the breath, mindfulness meditation of the body, feelings, mind and *dharmas* and compassion meditation as in Metta meditation. These will each be explained as we journey further into this book.

There are many other contemplative meditations found in Buddhist practice that are used to reflect and focus on specific areas such as the concepts of impermanence, non-self and *dukkha*. There are also contemplative meditations (including patience, generosity, gratitude, forgiveness, compassion and sympathetic joy) that are used as antidotes to combat negative mind states such as impatience, greed, hatred, anger, rage, jealousy, pride and many others.

Even the chanting of *mantras* which is repeating a sound, word or phrase over and over, can be used as a meditation or method to prepare a restless or distracted mind for meditation practice.

A solid meditation practice should consist of a combination of the above mentioned meditation practices and contemplative meditations depending on the needs of the individual. Due to the fact that we all come from different backgrounds and have different mental formations constructed though our diverse experiences, we need to each cultivate those areas of weakness that are not beneficial to ourselves or to others. Through providing the needed meditations we can satisfy the requirements of each of the fundamental principles of Middle Way Mind Training.

Misconceptions about meditation

While meditation is quite a commonly known practice, it is interesting how it is often misinterpreted and there are a lot of misconceptions about its meaning. People often look at meditation as an escape from reality, which according to Buddhist science is the exact opposite in that it offers the possibility to really see reality as it really is.

Another misconception is that meditation is only for relaxation. Although some of the long-term effects of meditation certainly include relaxation and feelings of bliss, the initial stages can be the exact opposite. Meditation at the start is often not relaxing at all and it can allow suppressed feelings and thoughts to surface that may be initially very disturbing. Remember, the purpose of meditation is not to act as a method of relaxation but a way to calm our thoughts and purify the mind so that we can see and experience reality in the present moment. It is a method that trains the mind to respond favorably to every situation we experience. As our mind becomes transformed and we accept reality the way it is, inner peace is naturally uncovered leading to a deep sense of contentment, relaxation and happiness.

Some critics of meditation may at first glance find it to be a selfish practice as it involves spending so much time alone and absorbed in our own thoughts. Some may believe that it is a practice meant only for monks or people living a monastic life, as only they have the time and discipline to engage in hours of meditation. Again, nothing could be further from the truth. An untrained mind is almost always a predominantly selfish mind, in which the ego plays a large part in behavior and actions that only benefit the self. With meditation, we learn to calm and diminish the ego, dissolve the construct of the self, and perform actions that benefit not only us, but others. Practicing meditation correctly will certainly make us less selfish. While Buddhist monks do have the opportunity to train their minds to a very high level because of their dedication and commitment, the average lay person also has a wonderful chance to train the mind to at least reduce a lot of unnecessary suffering in life and greatly improve levels of happiness.

Another common misconception is that meditation can make all our problems go away. I would explain it better this way. Meditation trains the mind to see our problems differently than we have before. It teaches us to view the experiences that happen to us without any judgment and with only bare awareness, as they really are and as they present themselves. This does not mean that the problems or experiences disappear or go away, but with mind training we will perhaps no longer see them as problems at all.

Finally, it is often forgotten that meditation alone cannot result in enlightenment or the extinction of our suffering. Along with meditation we need to develop the other fundamental principles such as those that strengthen our foundation in ethical behavior as well as those that develop wisdom. All of the factors of the Noble Eightfold Path need to be cultivated in order to achieve this goal. These have all been incorporated into the Eight Fundamental Principles of Middle Way Mind Training.

Posture during Meditation

There are a number of different postures used in meditation. They include sitting with legs crossed in partial or full lotus positions, kneeling, or even sitting in a chair. Each of these can be very effective. What is most important is being in a comfortable, stable and alert position, where we feel grounded and where we can keep our back straight without dropping or hanging the head down. In a sitting position on the floor, it can be beneficial to sit on a cushion, with the hips slightly higher than the knees or while kneeling to have a cushion placed under the bottom. If sitting in a chair, the feet should be flat on the floor, there should not be any armrests and the back should not recline but remain straight. While meditation can be done even in a lying position, it is usually not recommended as it makes it harder to stay alert and a lot easier to fall asleep.

There are also a variety of positions to keep the hands, including resting on the lap or on the legs. Usually it is most comfortable during longer meditation sessions to have them rest in a relaxed position on the lap with one hand lying on the other.

It is recommended that our eyes are kept closed during the meditation session to reduce any external stimuli that could distract us from our practice. Alternatively, eyes can be kept half open but fixed on a place down and in front of us.

It usually takes several sessions for our body to get used to being in a meditation position, so we need to be patient during this adjustment period that may involve some pain in the body. With time and practice, pain is lessened dramatically along with our minds ability to focus and observe it and we will be able to extend the time of our meditation sessions.

Time and Duration of Meditation

The time and duration of a meditation session is personal and individual, and will depend on availability of time and determination. I would recommend devoting at least some time every day to a meditation practice. Perhaps start with five or ten minutes and gradually build it up to one hour, twice a day. Meditation is like physical exercise, it needs to be consistent, so practicing meditation requires a regular practice. With time it becomes a beneficial habit that we can incorporate into our daily life. Some people prefer meditating in the morning, others in the evening before bed. It does not matter. What is important is that we do it at the same or similar time every day and be consistent. Initially it will take a lot of effort to stay motivated and there may be times that we have an aversion to the practice. We will go over all the hindrances to meditation in the next chapter. It is important to not let them take us away from our practice. Learning to do our meditation under any conditions, whether we feel tired or restful, sad or happy, stressful or relaxed, is what matters.

Do not wait for an ideal time to practice meditation, because what often happens it that no ideal time ever comes. It is similar to a writer who has to sit down every day during some period of time to write a book. Some days the writer will experience writer's block and will not be able to write anything substantial, other days the creative ideas flow naturally. The important thing is to be there, with no expectations, on a regular basis, and meditate.

Where to Meditate

If possible it is nice to dedicate a room or part of a room to our meditation practice. There we can keep our meditation mat, cushions, blankets etc. Whether we decorate our meditation area like a Buddhist temple or if it is just a simple modest place on the floor, what is important is to feel relaxed and safe there, and that it is quiet and free from distractions like phones or computers or other people.

What to expect and setting goals for Meditation

We are so used to high expectations and setting goals for ourselves in our modern existence. The wonderful and refreshing thing about meditation is that we should not come in with any expectations at all. In fact, the more expectations we have of meditation, the less we will progress along the path. The same goes for setting any meditation goals. For example, "I want to achieve the first *jhana* in two weeks". It just will not work that way. The mind has its own way of progressing and it is different for every one of us. Taking the Middle Way is the best advice. Progressing in meditation is like tuning guitar strings. If we go in too strong and adjust them too tight, the strings break. If we come in too weak and allow the strings to be too loose, they will not have the right tone. There has to be a balance, a middle way, so that our meditation sounds or progresses the best. For some, progress will take longer, for others it comes faster. We need to be patient, release all our expectations and let go of any goals, and if we follow these guidelines, in S.N. Goenka's words, a past prominent Indian teacher of *Vipassana* meditation, "we are bound to be successful."

THE FIVE HINDRANCES

(OBSTACLES) TO MEDITATION

All of humanity's problems stem from man's
inability to sit quietly in a room alone.

— Blaise Pascal

*S*o now we have set up our meditation room, complete with the perfect atmosphere. It looks like a replica of a Buddhist temple, complete with statues, candles, beautiful colorful mandalas on the wall and incense sticks. We have our meditation mat and comfortable cushion set up perfectly waiting for us in a dedicated room that is free of any noise and absolutely void of external distractions. Our family has been told to keep quiet at least for the duration of our meditation session. Everything is ready and just perfect and there is absolutely nothing that can disturb us. We sit down expecting to put in a solid and effective meditation performance. We find however, that even in this perfect ideal meditation environment that we have set up so meticulously for ourselves, after only just a few minutes into our session, we are confronted with yet another battle in our minds. We find that we come across obstacles that we did not take into account. Our meditation practice seems destined to fail. It is impossible to continue, we become frustrated, forced to resign and to quit. This unfortunately is a very common meditation experience.

All kinds of things can hinder or obscure our sense of inner peace. It may be a serious matter like a conflict with a loved one, or a more minor incident like being late while stuck in rush-hour traffic. When things do not go our way, according to our plan, we just don't like it at all, and we suffer in the process. In Buddhist science, the concept of "The Five Hindrances" reveals what gets in the way of us feeling as peaceful as possible and what prevents us from making beneficial decisions. It sheds light on what we need to do to overcome any obstacles, regardless of the particular circumstances we face. The Five Hindrances – known as **sensory desire, anger and aversion, restlessness and worry, sloth and torpor, and doubt** – refer to the primary mental states that stir up in our mind, that lead to a variety of emotional or behavioral difficulties. They also prevent us from gaining insight through our meditation practice into the true nature of phenomena and existence. They tend to bend the truth and distort the way we see reality. For purposes of this book, these hindrances relate mainly to our meditation practice, but they can also be applied to everyday life. We already know that difficulties are unavoidable in life and come with the human condition, so the aim is not to minimize them or suppress them, but to work with them more effectively.

The Five Hindrances can be likened to five impurities found in gold. If we find iron, copper, silver, tin or lead, then the gold is not as radiant, malleable, is more fragile and is not suitable for processing. If it is free of these impurities, then it is much more radiant, pliable and suitable for making rings, gold chains or earrings. The same goes for a mind that is tainted by the Five Hindrances. It is no longer radiant; it is very fragile, and unable to uproot its impurities. A mind without the Five Hindrances radiates inner peace and happiness and is flexible to deal in a beneficial way to any difficult situation that arises.

The Buddha recommended a middle way approach when doing meditation and he compared the effort required to the tuning of a musical instrument, like a lute. As we know, if we tighten the strings too much, they will break. If we allow the strings to be too loose, then the tone will not be right. A middle way approach, not too tight, not too loose is needed. This analogy can be applied to our meditation practice. If we approach meditation with too much intensity, or energy or the opposite, too little intensity or too little energy, then our practice will not flourish. Mind training through meditation requires an approach that is somewhere in the middle of these two extremes.

Sensory desire (the wanting mind)

A very strong distraction or hindrance to our meditation practice is sensory desire. It is often referred to as the **"wanting mind."** Buddhist philosophy compares a mind that is in its natural untainted state of clarity to be like pure, clear water. When it is subject to the distraction of sensory desires it becomes more like a dye that discolors water. A "wanting mind" seeks pleasure through our senses and when overwhelmed by sensory desire, views the world through rose-colored glasses. The clarity or true nature of reality is often distorted, like colored water. Remember, the greater the desire, the greater the suffering and unease we can experience when our desire is not satisfied. The objects of our desire, the forms we see, the sounds we hear, the tastes we savor, the aromas we smell, the touch of sensations we feel or the thoughts we imagine are all subject to perception, judgment and past experiences. They can develop into cravings that lead to mental formations or non-beneficial mind states such as greed, envy, jealousy or addictions. These mind states can be very detrimental to our meditation practice as they disrupt our sense of inner peace.

In the initial stages of our meditation practice, we can be sure to encounter thoughts that relate to our sensory desires. Our mind may try to convince us that rather than meditate, we should check our mobile phone or surf the internet or reach for a snack or watch a movie instead. Thoughts permeate our mind such as, if only I had more money, or if only I could find that perfect job or perfect partner. These are examples of the many sensory desires that try to convince us that whatever we have is not enough. We get entangled in the belief that some other sensory desire will make us more complete or more satisfied. The wanting mind of greed blinds us and takes us out of the present moment, which means we are not able to concentrate during meditation and certainly unable to experience inner peace.

The list of sensory distractions is endless. This is the wanting mind. If we can learn to recognize it when it appears and understand it for what it is, we will be able to realize that it is only a thought or a feeling that arises in our mind and will pass away if we let it, like a cloud in the sky. When a sensory desire appears during our meditation session, it is best to give it a name or a label, and say to our self, "sensory desire, sensory desire" or "wanting, wanting" We should not try to ignore it, fight it or suppress it, this will only give it more energy and power to overwhelm us. Recognize it and peacefully accept it for what it is. By giving it a name, we objectify it; we create space between us and the feeling or thought. This allows us to investigate it without being taken over by it. Remember we are not our thoughts. Instead of saying, "I am hungry" say instead I have a thought about hunger, or I have a desirous thought. Instead of saying "I am bored" think instead that "I have a feeling of boredom" or "I have a desirous thought for excitement." In this way, we do not identify our self with the sensory desire. It does not become personal, but stays as just a transient objective state in our mind.

Being aware and recognizing our sensory desires for what they are and labeling their associated thoughts or feelings, will make it much easier for us to let them go. We know intellectually that sustained happiness is not found in the external environment, so cultivating healthy desires to be compassionate, generous and kind are much more beneficial and meditation will allow these qualities to be developed inside our mind, from within.

Anger and aversion (the not-wanting mind)

The second hindrance or obstacle to our meditation practice is anger and aversion. It is the opposite of sensory desire. This is the **"not wanting mind"** as it is often referred to in Buddhist science and it is likened to water that is frothing, bubbling or boiling. It represents ill will or a mental aversion towards another or towards an experience. It often exhibits itself as dissatisfaction, irritation, resentment, dislike, or even hatred, anger or rage. The mental pain felt with this hindrance is usually much more obvious than with sensory desires. We all know how anger feels, how quickly and dramatically it can arise in us and how difficult it is to concentrate when we are trapped within its hold. Often our mind is irritated and preoccupied with negative judgments, with thoughts of how unfair the situation is and can even be embroiled in plans for revenge.

Anger often appears when we take a situation personally, which adds fire to it and can make it much bigger than it actually is. This causes us a lot of unnecessary suffering. Some anger may be justified in cases where we have been really hurt or treated unfairly, but if we can learn to understand the impersonal nature of anger and how it is arises and develops in our mind then we can avoid adding a lot of unnecessary layers to it which usually makes it a lot worse.

If anger arises during our meditation practice, we can first be mindful of it, recognize it and accept it for what it is. Try to avoid suppressing it or pushing it away. Give it the room it needs. It is a powerful force. We can give it a name and identify it by saying to our self, "anger, anger," "aversion, aversion," "irritation, irritation" or "judgment, judgment." Again, we create space between the feeling or thought, so we can investigate it further. Often upon investigation, when we can see anger objectively, we find that the underlying causes of our anger are often fear, shame, loneliness or sadness. Just like all feelings or thoughts, they are impermanent and subject to arise and pass away. Listen to the story our mind is telling us, but remember we cannot believe our distorted, angry mind. If our investigation shows that fear is the cause, this means that the anger is coming from fear of what will come in the future, not what is happening now, so it is only our imagination creating this mind state.

Often there may be physical feelings that we feel in our body that are associated with anger and aversion. During our meditation, we can try to be aware if we feel any tension or physical pain anywhere in the body, notice the temperature in our body or any other physical manifestations. By being aware and investigating the causes of our anger, we gain space to diffuse the negative emotions and open the door to develop patience, compassion and forgiveness. *Metta* or Loving –Kindness Meditation, which we will discuss in detail in a future chapter, is especially effective as an antidote to anger and aversion.

Sloth and Torpor (the slow and drowsy mind)

The Buddha mentioned sloth and torpor as another significant hindrance to our concentration and meditation practice. It refers to low mental energy, laziness, dullness of mind, apathy, or drowsiness. It is often likened to a pool of water that is overgrown with moss or algae, which is sluggish and slow moving. This is the **"slow and drowsy mind."**

It may arise if we are deprived of sleep and in that case it is recommended to ensure we get regular, quality sleep. We may feel lethargic after a meal, so the time of our meditation session should also be taken into consideration. Intense stress can also induce apathy and drowsiness when it comes to meditation. Many of us who start a meditation practice are not used to being still for any amount of time as our daily lives are inundated with constant stimulation. Anything that does not enhance our self image or satisfy our cravings and desires can make it hard to stay motivated in our practice. The moment we close our eyes in meditation, our bodies may automatically react with drowsiness and mental dullness as if we are preparing to go to sleep. Finally, during times when we stop paying attention, become lazy and bored, lose touch with what is really important in our lives or lose our sense of purpose, this hindrance can often present itself.

To overcome a slow and drowsy mind, we need to redouble our effort, be persistent and strengthen our level of motivation and discipline. It is important during meditation to keep our back straight and not allow our heads to hang down so we can remain alert. When we encounter this hindrance, we can again recognize it with acceptance, identify it and give it a name such as "boredom, boredom," "laziness, laziness" or "drowsiness, drowsiness." We try not to shrug it away, but allow it room, while investigating what the possible causes can be. We should also be mindful and aware of how the body feels.

In this state of mind, it is important to remind ourselves of the benefits of meditation and that life is short so we should make us of every moment and not waste precious time. When we can see that every moment in our lives is brand new and just waiting to be experienced, our mind cannot become bored and will break out of this slow and drowsy mind state.

Restlessness and Worry (the restless mind)

While the previous hindrance has the characteristic of not having enough energy, **"the restless mind"** is the opposite and has too much energy. Remember the middle way, we should be somewhere in the middle of these extremes. In Buddhist science, this mental state is often called the "monkey mind"; it is likened to a pool of water stirred up by the wind into waves and ripples. Our mind tends to bounce from one thought to another like a monkey. It can be one of the most difficult hindrances to overcome in our meditation practice. Our untrained mind is constantly bombarded and disturbed with thoughts. It becomes easily bored, gets restless and becomes lost in thoughts. A lot of our restlessness is just our imagination. Overstimulation with sensory input in today's technological world can also make us feel restless and overwhelmed. Research has shown that the average mind has up to 60 thousand thoughts daily, that's 1 thought every second of every waking hour (Fermelia, 2017). The majority of these thoughts are like a top 10 song list that is played in our minds over and over again. These thoughts are primarily focused on what happened in the past or on fears or worries about the future as well as constantly searching for things to do. As we know, according to that Harvard study, our untrained mind wanders about 50 percent of the time. We certainly don't like to rest in the present very much, but that is where all the inner peace and happiness resides. Meditation forces us to focus and become aware of the present moment.

During our practice, especially in the beginning stages, it is normal to experience a restless mind state where we find that our mind is constantly wandering. This makes it very difficult to stay focused on our meditation object, such as our breath. We may feel like we are missing out on something while meditating and staying still becomes a challenge. Our mind has an insatiable craving for new experiences. Again, we need to recognize that this is all happening in our mind. It is not wise to resist it, as it often gets worse if we do. When our mind wanders, we try to just be aware of it, accept it calmly, take note of it and label it, "wandering, wandering" and return back to our meditation. We can investigate why we are bored and restless and what is causing it to happen. We can make a mental note or label our state of mind, "bored, bored" or "restless, restless." Often our mind may wander for several minutes or more before we even realize it. It is very easy to get caught up in our thoughts. Again, calmly with acceptance and without blaming ourselves for it or getting frustrated, we return back to our meditation. We can also be mindful of what sensations we feel in our body when we are feeling restless. With time and training, our mind becomes more and more focused and concentrated and less prone to wandering. Our mind gets transformed from a **constantly doing mind** to a mind that can **just be** in the present moment. This profound transformation has the potential to put us in a very peaceful state, a state that most of us have never ever experienced before.

Doubt (the doubting mind)

Human beings do not like uncertainty. When we are caught in a mind that is crowded with a lot of questions and indecision, the **"doubting mind"** can become a strong hindrance to our meditation practice. We may feel skeptical and uncertain about whether we should continue with our meditation practice. In Buddhist science, this hindrance is often likened to a pool of water that is murky or cloudy.

Doubts or questions that may arise can include, whether the teachings about meditation are really true, if the meditation instructor is qualified, if the method is right and if it will work, or if we will be able to understand the teachings. It is important to analyze all the questions we may have and investigate them rationally. Usually most doubt and confusion clears up on its own as the meditation practice progresses because we can see results for ourselves. It is healthy to be critical and have some doubt. Even the Buddha taught to not just believe what he says but to try it so we can experience it firsthand. With a beginner mind, as we discussed in the first part of this book, we keep our mind open to all the possibilities and not shut it down because of our beliefs, judgments and opinions. Most of us in the modern world are trained to believe that we should have control over everything we do, yet in reality life is full of uncertainty. We should all do thorough research as much as we can, but at the same time be able to let go of some of our control and find a sense of trust and balance in our approach.

How to work with the Five Hindrances

Our aim should be to work towards becoming free from all the five hindrances as much as possible. This is certainly not an easy task. The fact that we may come to our meditation with one or more of these hindrances does not mean we should stop our meditation. Some of the hindrances will always be there or arise, so we need to work with them, not fight against them, but approach them in an effective way. Our ability to become aware and mindful of everything that is happening is of utmost importance. If we lose our awareness, then the hindrance may overcome us and get out of our control. If we peacefully accept it with equanimity, and just observe it calmly, it can transform into just another cloud passing in the sky.

The Buddha taught that we should know when an obstacle or hindrance arises in the mind, and when it disappears and should also learn to be aware of its presence. We should be aware of any obstacle which has not arisen yet, but that is ready to arise, know how to let go and extinguish each hindrance and know how to prevent it from arising in the future. This kind of mind training will give us freedom even amidst the difficulties in life.

In regards to dealing with the Five Hindrances, it is helpful to follow these guidelines of Middle Way Mind Training:

1. Recognize the obstacle or hindrance that has arisen in the mind.
2. Do not push it away or suppress it.
3. Accept it with peace and equanimity and with the knowledge that it is impermanent.
4. Give it a name or label it to objectify it.
5. Give it the space it needs and just observe.
6. Do not identify with it and understand that the feeling or thought is not you.
7. Be aware of any sensations in the body that are related to the hindrance.
8. Investigate the hindrance objectively.
9. Ask the question, why is this hindrance really arising in your mind to uncover the cause.
10. If the hindrance persists and makes it impossible to continue your meditation, apply antidotes by using one or more of the Meditative Contemplations (explanations of these are found in later chapters of this book):
    - For a "wanting mind" - Suffering, Impermanence and Non-self, Generosity and Gratitude meditative contemplations
    - For a "not-wanting mind" - Metta and Forgiveness meditative contemplations

- For a "slow and drowsy mind" - Mindfulness meditation or walking meditation
- For a "restless mind" - Mantras and Mindfulness meditation
- For a "doubting mind" - Compassion meditation and Suffering, Impermanence and Non-self meditative contemplations

The importance of training the mind to be mindful of the five hindrances when they arise cannot be overemphasized. This chapter is very critical and should be referred back to often especially when you are starting to build a solid meditation practice. When you can learn to be aware and overcome these obstacles, your inner Buddha nature will soon naturally emerge and strengthen, negative mental formations will lose their hold and dissolve as you let go and happiness and inner peace will be uncovered, will shine through and be experienced.

THE MEDITATION OF
OBSERVING THE BREATH

Breathing in, I see myself as still as water.
Breathing out, I reflect things as they are.

— Thich Nhat Hanh

The meditation of observing the breath is the first practical meditation exercise to be described in detail in this book that we will incorporate into Middle Way Mind Training. It is also one of the best and most effective methods we can use to develop concentration as we discussed in the Fifth Fundamental Principle of MWMT. Since our breath is an integral part of our existence and with us at all times while we are alive, observing our breath always keeps our mind in the present moment. To observe our breath is to observe and to be aware of what is happening to us right now. In our normal life, we rarely take notice of the coming in and out of the breath. It is usually taken for granted or automatic and something we don't normally pay attention to. We also know from the five hindrances that it is not an easy task to maintain awareness on the breath, as our mind frequently wanders during our meditation session. Learning to use methods to deal with the hindrances helps us to cultivate an effective meditation practice and we should keep that in mind when we meditate on the breath or any other meditative technique.

Meditation on one specific object, the breath, cultivates our ability to develop single-pointed concentration for a prolonged period of time. This means the ability to stay focused on a single point or object of our concentration. The benefits of developing this ability are tremendous relaxation, freedom from distractions that can negatively influence the mind, and clarity and stability in thinking. With improved concentration, we will be able to strengthen our ethical and moral behavior and open our mind to states where we can access wisdom of the nature of our reality. Again we can see that all the fundamental principles of MWMT depend on each other. When the mind achieves a high level of concentration, only then does it have the ability to develop aspects of wisdom and insight. This goes far beyond just an intellectual understanding.

A concentrated mind is very powerful and has enhanced abilities that are needed to see and experience reality the way it really is. As we develop our meditation on the breath, we will be able to utilize our concentrated mind to progress along with other meditations, especially those that involve insight on what causes us to be unhappy. We can then become more aware of the world around us, the people around us, and the emotions inside of us that are arising in the present moment. Instead of being taken off guard during difficult situations and falling victim to fear, anxiety, confusion and stress, we are able to handle these experiences much better. Even our ability to deal with old age, sickness and death improves. We are able to see much more clearly how unwholesome mind states such as greed, fear or hatred have no real benefit, as they only create unhappiness and suffering for us.

Instructions on meditation on the breath usually come from the *Anapanasati Sutta*, a Buddhist discourse from the *Pali Canon*. The Buddha taught five preliminary instructions to meditation. First to find a secluded place, sit down, cross our legs, keep our body erect and establish mindfulness of the front. This is usually interpreted in most Buddhist traditions as the entrance where breath enters and exits, meaning the area above the upper lip to the area of the nostrils.

Initially, when we begin meditating on the breath, it may be difficult to feel our breath entering our nostrils or passing over above our upper lip. If it is not possible at first, start by noticing the chest and belly rising when we breathe in and falling when we exhale. Once our concentration becomes established in that technique, we can move to the face area and focus especially on the small triangular area from the upper lip to the nostrils. As we start to be aware of air moving anywhere in that area, we can gradually start to reduce the size of the area of focus. Eventually with practice, we will be able to feel air passing in an out on a very small point, such as a point inside the wall of the nostrils. The aim is to progress from gross awareness of the breath to finer and finer awareness, as our concentration develops into single-point concentration. Since it is much harder to feel the air passing over a specific fine point, meditation on the breath takes practice. With time, and as we overcome the hindrances, it will become more and more refined and our concentration will become sharper and sharper. Meditation on the breath can be likened to sharpening a dull pencil to attain a very fine point.

The Buddha's teachings also stressed to be aware of whether we are breathing in or whether we are breathing out and whether our breath is long or short. While we are breathing we should also be sensitive to the entire body, and should breathe in and out with a sense of calmness and letting go. As we meditate on the breath, we need to be aware of each and every breath, we observe as we inhale and exhale. We can even try to notice the gap or pause between each inhalation and exhalation. It is important to let go and to not interfere in any way with the natural flow of our breath. We avoid any attempt to control it or slow it down; just allow it to calm down by itself naturally. Remember we are just being an observer of the breath, not a controller of our breath. We just take note whether the breath is going in or out and whether it is long or short, it does not matter what quality it has. We just observe and let the breath be as it is.

Many people are also not aware that there is a nasal cycle that occurs in most of us which refers to the natural cycle of greater airflow through one nostril with periodic alternation between the nostrils. Therefore, we should also be aware in which nostril we feel the air is dominantly coming in, the left nostril, right nostril, or through both, as it often changes throughout the day.

After some time in practice and as we progress in meditation on the breath and reach single-pointed concentration, our breathing will become very slow, calm and almost indistinguishable. We may start to experience blissful feelings in the body and our meditation will change from being initially a burden to a very pleasant experience. Although not the topic of this book, advanced meditators can reach and pass through incredible meditative absorption states, called the jhanas that further deepen concentration and make it easier to access qualities that lead to greater insight of our reality (Brasington, 2015).

The meditation of observing the breath is backed by numerous scientific studies that have shown a wide range of benefits (Horowitz, 2010). Physical benefits include increases in immune cell count, better sleep, decreased pain and inflammation and many others. Mental benefits include an increase in positive emotional states as well as attention span and memory and a decrease in anxiety, stress and depression. Benefits to the brain include increases in development of grey matter, and increased volume found in areas of the brain that deal with emotional regulation, positive emotions, and self-control. Social benefits include increases in compassion in those who meditate regularly. Some studies of neuroplasticity of the brain point to the possibility that when you are exposed to meditation for enough time, there can be lasting changes in brain function and structure, in improved health of the immune system and in positive behavior (Goleman and Davidson, 2018). This requires meditation of certain regularity and some duration to make a significant difference.

How long should we practice meditation on the breath for? A good starting point is 15 to 20 minutes a day. Gradually, the time can be increased to one hour a day. Meditation on the breath is one of the three core meditations of Middle Way Mind Training that we should incorporate into our meditation practice every day. The other two are Mindfulness Meditation and Compassion Meditation, which will be discussed in the next chapters. It may seem at first like a simple pointless task to just sit down and observe the breath and difficult to see how it can really benefit. That is what our ego will try to tell us, but 2500 years of Buddhist science should convince us otherwise. The effects that meditation on the breath has on training the mind are so incredibly profound, that they have the power to really open our path to transformation. Our first practical MWMT exercise can be likened to a surgical operation of the mind, one of several that will be needed to cure our suffering and achieve lasting happiness.

PRACTICAL MIDDLE WAY MIND TRAINING PRESCRIPTION
MWMT MEDITATION SUMMARY – Meditation of Observing the Breath

- Find a secluded place to meditate, sit down, cross your legs
- Keep your head and back straight, close your eyes
- Breathe with your nose
- Observe the area above the upper lip to the nostrils if you are able
- If unable, start first with observing the rise and fall of the chest and belly
- Be aware of each inhalation and exhalation and whether it is long or short and through which nostril air is passing
- Notice the gap between breaths
- Be sensitive to how the breath is impacting the entire body
- Relax and let go, do not try to change the breath, just observe it as it is
- Gradually with time, decrease the area in focus until you can feel the air on a single small area such as a small point inside of the nostril
- Deal with any hindrances to your meditation and return to observing the breath
- Start with 15-20 minutes a day and increase gradually to one hour or more

INTRODUCTION TO
MINDFULNESS MEDITATION

Life is a dance.
Mindfulness is witnessing that dance.

— Amrit Rai

While the primary aim of meditation on the breath is to calm and concentrate the mind, the aim of mindfulness meditation is to gain insight, or *vipassana* as it is called in the ancient Pali language. This type of meditation trains us to see things as they really are with bare awareness. Mindfulness meditation is the second core meditation in Middle Way Mind Training. As we noted previously in the book, there are four foundations of mindfulness as presented in the *Sattipathana Sutta*, a discourse on mindfulness taken from the *Pali Canon*. They are mindfulness of the body, mindfulness of our feelings if pleasant, unpleasant or neutral, mindfulness of the mind and mental formations, and mindfulness of the natural laws or phenomena that govern the mind and the body. Our mindfulness meditation should therefore include developing our awareness of everything that is going on in and around our physical body as well as in our mind. This allows us to gain insight into understanding how non-beneficial mind states develop and how suffering is caused, as well as to develop a deep understanding of the impermanence of all things and our illusion of a concrete self. What mindfulness meditation does is objectify what we observe so that we stop clinging to our delusions and can let go. When we can let go and develop a mind that has this kind of clarity, it becomes peaceful and sustained happiness will inevitably arise.

When we practice mindfulness meditation we are trying to observe everything that is going on in the present moment with acceptance, without judgment and with the calm composure of equanimity. This is what we mean by seeing our world with bare awareness. In this way our experiences are not tainted, distorted or altered in any way by our thoughts, emotions, expectations, judgments or past experiences. We see them in the present moment as they really are.

The benefit of practicing mindfulness meditation is that we become better at reacting to situations no matter how difficult they are. We become more accepting of ourselves and of others, more patient and understanding. We stop holding on to our solid opinions and judgments and become more flexible. We let go of a lot of unnecessary suffering because we are more aware of the development of negative mind states and do not let them get to a point where they control our behavior. With mindfulness training we are much more in control of our life; we don't over-react or let our emotions take hold of us. Mindfulness training will also develop all the other MWMT Foundational Principles, especially cultivating our ethical behavior by improving our ability to speak and listen wisely, perform actions and engage in work that does not harm us and others. Mindfulness enables us to make wise choices in our lives so that we can be free of suffering.

An effective mindfulness meditation session should include observing our physical body, by doing a body scan where we can observe each anatomical part. The purpose is to break down the body into its components, so that we can objectify it and not identify with it or cling to it as a source of our happiness. This helps us to break away from our habit of seeing ourselves as a permanent self, which as we know is a great cause of our suffering. We can be mindful of any sensations we feel on each anatomical part of our body and take note of any sensations that we feel inside our body as well. Even though it appears to us as a solid entity, our body is really a process that is undergoing change all the time. Cells are replicating and passing away, chemical reactions are occurring and processes such as respiration, digestion and circulation are constantly in motion. There are changes in our skin temperature and pressure and tension inside our organs and muscles. We rarely take notice of these sensations as we usually take them for granted. There are many other sensations such as tension, pain, expansion, itching, heat, cold, tingling etc. that we often experience. Every reaction and process arises and passes away just like everything in life. Nothing is permanent. This is the law of impermanence. Mindfulness of the body according to Buddhist science means to see the body not as a solid entity but as a collection of parts, to be in tune with everything that is happening in the present moment and be aware of the impermanent nature of all things.

As we scan the body part by part from the top of our head to our toes, and notice any sensations, we can be mindful of what feelings they create, whether they are pleasant, unpleasant or neutral. When we come across a pleasant sensation in the body, we don't cling to it or crave for it, because we know that all feelings arise and pass away. The same goes if we come across a painful or unpleasant sensation. We don't try to push it away with aversion; we just accept it the way it is with equanimity. We will notice that all sensations will not last, they arise and then they pass away. Even painful sensations once observed with calmness will also pass away. With mindfulness, we put a space between the arising of craving and aversion, which allows time to prevent these basic pleasant or unpleasant feelings into turning into non-beneficial mental formations. We develop a non-judgmental awareness of our feelings.

We then observe any thoughts in our mind that are associated with the sensations or feelings. We should be aware if there are any negative or positive emotions or specific states of mind in the present moment. We can ask ourselves, what is our state of mind at this moment; do we feel any anger, greed, anxiety or aversion? At the same time we should also be aware if there is no anger, no greed, no anxiety or aversion. If we feel anger or anxiety, we can ask ourselves, how does a mind that is angry feel? How does an anxious mind feel? What is aware of anger is not anger, it is awareness. What is aware of anxiety is not anxiety, it is awareness. When we have cultivated a mind of mindfulness, our awareness is not distorted by the anger or anxiety. Bare awareness is like an illuminating light, it reveals and allows us to see things, but it does not get modified in the process. When we shine a light on a piece of mud, the light does not get dirty, if we shine it on a piece of gold, it does not become more expensive either. It just reveals what in reality is really there and allows us to see, the same as our awareness. As we maintain awareness of the anger and anxiety, it will lose its stability, dissolve and break down. By being mindful, we avoid the common mistakes of either suppressing anger or other negative emotions or venting them out, both of which do not help in training the mind.

Mindfulness of mental states has been compared to cradling a crying baby. When we hear a baby cry, we don't leave it alone and ignore it, we are aware and pick it up, embrace it and hold it in our arms and repeat the process over and over again. We accept it without judgment and with compassion. The repetition of mindfulness with equanimity will lessen these negative emotions and they will progressively lose their strength until they lead to a transformation of the mind.

As we develop mindfulness of our mind and mental states we can learn directly from the experience. We can learn how our mental constructs are formed or if they have any validity or benefit to us. We can ask ourselves questions like; "does this thought make me calm and happy or distressed and fearful? Do I want joy and contentment or misery and worry?" Being mindful gives us the opportunity to choose. We learn that we are not our thoughts, so we should not get attached to them.

As we observe these mental states and thoughts during our mindfulness meditation session, we just accept them all with equanimity and we do not introduce any craving or aversion to them. We don't judge them, form opinions on them or add any stories to them, we just let them be. Remember, mindfulness is simply just observing things without adding anything else to our observations. The mind always has the innate faculty to be aware of mental states and to be able to watch them, just like an observer on the outside. Mindfulness allows us to step back and look at our experience with the eye of the mind. When we are mindful of all that is truly present, we get released from the past and the future. This is a very liberating experience.

Our mindfulness practice will also uncover mind states that hinder our progress such as sensory desire, ill will, restlessness, laziness and doubt and we will be better equipped to deal with them. With every small step of mindfulness meditation, we will gain a small degree of insight. The practice should be done with patience and not rushed to allow the insights to slowly unfold. As we cultivate mindfulness, we will develop these insights, including our understanding of impermanence, suffering and non-self. We will be able to delve more deeply into how our mental constructs are formed through each of the five aggregates and be able to realize and experience the four noble truths.

Modern scientific research on mindfulness has identified a wide range of benefits in psychological health, such as decreasing stress, anxiety, depression, rumination, and emotional reactivity and increasing well-being and concentration (Kabat-Zinn, 1990) (Segal et al., 2001). It has also been found to help foster physical health by improving immune function, quality of sleep, chronic pain management and blood pressure. Structural and functional brain changes have been documented in areas dealing with attention, empathy and emotional regulation (Goleman and Davidson, 2018). In business and educational settings, mindfulness has shown improved communication and work performance, improved social and emotional skills, and decreases in work-related stress and burnout. Modern science is finally catching up to the importance of mindfulness training and its intimate connection with the mind and the body.

MWMT Mindfulness Meditation Instruction

There are many forms of mindfulness meditation techniques but for the purposes of this book and for Middle Way Mind Training, I suggest you use this method initially.

As you begin your meditation session, ensure that your head and back is straight and your body is stable. You can start first by taking a few moments to be aware of what is occurring outside of your body, through your 5 sense doors. Notice any sounds that you hear and be aware that you are using your sense of hearing. Notice any tastes in your mouth and that you are using your sense of taste or any aromas or odors that you smell and that you are using your sense of smell. Slightly open your eyes for a few brief seconds and be aware of what you see and that you are using your sense of sight. Be aware of your sense of touch and feel all the points of contact that your body is making with the floor, the point of contact where your hands and fingers are touching each other as well as your legs and any other part of your body.

Next, move your awareness to your breath and spend a few minutes being aware of your in-breath and out-breath. Breathing in you know this is your in-breath, breathing out you know this is your out-breath. Follow your entire breathing cycle, including noticing the gap between breaths and be aware whether your breath is long or short and what nostril the breath is passing through at the present moment. Breathe in and out being sensitive and aware of what the entire body is doing. Notice the rhythmic movement of the chest and belly as it rises and falls with each breath. Relax as you breathe in and when you breathe out, let go of any emotions, feelings, thoughts or worries. Remind yourself that your breath is your anchor, you can always return to the breath at any time if you mindfulness gets interrupted or hindered.

Next, start what is called a **Mindfulness Body Scan**. This means scanning the entire body, to be aware of any sensations on the surface of the body and inside the body. Sensations may present themselves in many forms, including a tingling, itching, pulsing, hot or cold sensation, or in the form of vibration, tension, pain or pressure or any other kind of sensation. Whatever sensation you notice, just become aware and take mental note. At first you may not be able to feel many sensations but with practice, you will be able to feel sensations all over the body. Begin at the top of the head and slowly move down the body part by part, the face, front of the neck, chest, right shoulder, upper arm, elbow, lower arm, wrist, fingers, then the left shoulder, upper arm, elbow, lower arm, wrist, fingers, then the abdomen, then move up to the back of the head, back of the neck, upper back, lower back, gluteals, right thigh, knee, lower leg, ankle, foot, toes, then left thigh, knee, lower leg, ankle, foot, and toes. There is no set sequence to follow, you can scan the body as suggested or any other way that you like, just ensure that you do not miss any body part.

You can repeat the Mindfulness Body Scan several times, and be mindful whether each sensation you encounter is pleasant, unpleasant or neutral. Whatever type of feeling a sensation has, accept it with peace and equanimity. Do not cling to it or get attached to any sensation you encounter. If the sensation is painful or unpleasant, do not suppress it or push it away. Just spend some time observing it as it is, with the calm understanding that no matter what sensation appears, it is subject to impermanence and will arise and pass away.

Next, move your attention to your mind and to any thoughts or emotions that present themselves in the present moment. Do not suppress them or push them away even if you have disturbing thoughts, just accept them with calmness and equanimity. Ask yourself, "What kind of mind state am I experiencing right now?" "Am I experiencing any mind states that are hindering my meditation practice?" Ask yourself, "Are my thoughts really true?" "Do they bring me peace and happiness or do they just bring me anger, fear and worry?" Notice how your thoughts and emotions are also impermanent, they constantly change and so you should not cling to them or get attached to them. Spend a few minutes contemplating about how your sensations, feelings, thoughts and emotions arise in your mind and then change and pass away. They are all impermanent. There is no need to hold on to any negative mental states because this only causes additional suffering and you are not your mental state, so you can let them go at any time. Notice how your mind feels when you let go of any negative mental states, thoughts or emotions.

Return back to observing your breath. Slowly bring your attention back to your surroundings, and slowly open your eyes. With mindfulness be aware of all the movements you make when you stretch out your arms and legs, and all the movements you make when you slowly stand up.

Bringing conscious awareness or Mindfulness to our daily activities

Mindfulness is not something that needs to be done just by formal meditation as in the Mindfulness Body Scan but it can also be incorporated into several of our daily activities. We can try to be aware of our posture, when we walk, when we eat, when we wash the dishes or any other physical activity that we are engaged in. The more we develop our skill of mindfulness, the more we will improve our awareness of the world around us. Long term mindfulness practitioners report that they are able to notice things that they never noticed before, food tastes better, colors are more vibrant and their experiences in life are dramatically improved and enhanced. When we do not pay attention to the present moment, so much that life has to offer just passes us by without us even noticing. Remember, the average person spends half their time thinking about the past or the future.

Walking meditation is another popular method of mindfulness. It involves walking very slowly as in slow motion and taking note of when each foot is lifted, moved forward and placed in front of us, being aware of our entire body and what it is doing in the process. After walking several meters we stop, and we are aware that we have stopped and slowly turn around and repeat the process.

Mindfulness of our speech is another important exercise to improve our relationship with others and prevent us from unnecessary suffering. The more we cultivate mindfulness, the more we will have control over our emotional state and to our reactions to what people say to us. We have already seen how lying and harsh, decisive and senseless forms of speech do not benefit us or others around us. Each time we need to say something, we can remind ourselves again of the Pause of Wisdom, which gives us some space for mindfulness.

PAUSE OF WISDOM

If someone verbally abuses you or insults you, before you do or say anything:

1. Take 3 deep breaths so you can respond instead of react habitually.

2. Ask yourself if what you want to say will really benefit yourself and the other person (Is it wise?).

3. If you feel compelled to speak, ask yourself these 4 questions about what you want to say:

- Is it true?
- Is it useful?
- Is it kind?
- Is it the right time?

PRACTICAL MIDDLE WAY MIND TRAINING PRESCRIPTION
MWMT MEDITATION SUMMARY – Mindfulness Meditation

- Find a secluded place to meditate, sit down, cross your legs, close your eyes
- Keep your head and back straight
- Focus your attention first on your surroundings and then be aware of all 5 of your sense doors (hearing, taste, smell, sight, and touch)
- Focus on being mindful of the breath for a few minutes

- Do a Mindfulness Body Scan- start with the top of your head and slowly move down the body part by part, being aware of any sensations
- When you experience a sensation, take notice if it causes a pleasant, unpleasant or neutral feeling
- Whatever the feeling, do not cling to it or get attached to it, just accept it with equanimity and let it be as it is
- Observe your thoughts and your mind state. Ask yourself if they are true and benefit you or not. Notice if there are any hindrances to your meditation.
- Contemplate the impermanence of sensations, feelings, thoughts and emotions
- Contemplate the suffering caused by holding on to negative mind states
- Contemplate that the body is made up of many components that are always changing, none of which we can really call a concrete self.
- Return your attention to being mindful of the breath
- Move your attention back to your surroundings and slowly open your eyes
- Stretch and stand up being aware of all movements that are required to do that.

COMPASSION: A FOUNDATION
FOR HAPPINESS

If you want others to be happy, practice
compassion. If you want to be happy, practice
compassion.

— His Holiness the 14th Dalai Lama

The Buddha taught that compassion or *karuna* in the Pali language should be radiated in all directions to every sentient being. Compassion knows no bounds; it is boundless so it should not be limited in any way. He also taught that in order to realize enlightenment or to be totally free of suffering, you need two qualities, wisdom and compassion. These qualities have been compared to two eyes that enable sight or two wings that are needed to fly. Compassion is one of the *Brahmaviharas*, a set of four Buddhist virtues that signify immeasurable strength and power and should be cultivated as much as possible to the best of one's ability.

There are many methods of compassion meditation in the various Buddhist traditions but what they all have in common is that they develop a state of mind of wanting others to be free of suffering. In Buddhist science, cultivation of compassion can be accomplished through *Metta*, a Pali word commonly translated to mean loving-kindness. The cultivation of loving-kindness is an essential component of Buddhist philosophy and can also be used to combat non-beneficial mind states, which disrupt our inner peace. For this reason we include it as one of the three core meditations in Middle Way Mind Training. In order to have genuine compassion we must have both wisdom and loving kindness. That is to say, first we need to understand the nature of the suffering from which we wish to free others or what is called wisdom, and secondly we must experience deep empathy with other sentient beings which is loving kindness. It also follows suit that in order to show compassion to others, we also have to have compassion for ourselves.

Compassion means a sense of "feeling with" which is a recognition that what you feel, I feel as well. Anything that hurts you hurts me, and anything that helps you, also helps me. It is a complete identification with others, and an active readiness to help them in any way. The well-being of others is the foundation of our own piece of mind, and therefore our happiness. If we are all inter-connected as Buddhist science and Quantum mechanics has revealed to us, then our own happiness must be interlinked with the happiness of others. In other words, we are all in this ocean of life together. One of the best methods to cultivate compassion is through loving-kindness meditation.

Metta meditation is a practice that recognizes that we all experience the same kinds of wants and needs. No matter who we are, or from what culture, race or country, we all want to be happy. We all have the desire to go about our life free of harm, free of disease and live in peace. With *Metta* meditation we send this message of intention first to ourselves, then to someone close to us, then to someone who we have neutral feelings for, then to someone we dislike, and then we further expand our wish to all sentient beings. According to Buddhist Science, loving-kindness meditation is the intention that all sentient beings and ourselves and even those that we do not like, can experience the same sense of joy, happiness, safety, freedom, health and peace that we aspire to fill. We begin with our self and gradually extend the wish for well-being and happiness to all beings.

In Buddhist science *Metta* is often used as an antidote to anger, hatred, selfishness and fear as it is said to soften the heart and leads to compassion, equanimity and empathy. At first it may seem to us that *Metta* is an overly simplified and non-effective practice and we may have doubt whether the practice of sending wishes of goodwill to others in our mind can actually benefit us. Numerous scientific studies on *Metta* meditation however, have shown dramatic and surprisingly positive benefits from the practice. They have shown that regular *Metta* meditation can increase activation in brain areas involved in emotional processing and can improve how well a person processes stress or extreme events. Some fascinating studies have found that *Metta* increases grey matter in the brain associated with emotional regulation (Leung et al. 2013) and as it decreases stress levels, it may also slow biological aging (Le Nguyen et al. 2019). Reports of long-term effects and changes in emotional regulation, demonstrate that *Metta* meditation may not be just a short-term remedy. Studies have demonstrated reduction of self-criticism and increased self-compassion (Stefan and Hofman, 2019). Self-criticism is a trait that has been shown to lead to numerous forms of psychopathology such as depression, anxiety, schizophrenia, stress, eating disorders, bipolar disorders etc. Other scientific studies have shown that it cultivates kindness, empathy and compassion as well as being integral in anger management and reducing fear (Kaur and Tee, 2017). It helps us feel more connected to ourselves and others and both positive thinking and happiness are improved with its use (Salzberg, 1995). Metta also helps cultivate peaceful and pro-social emotions (Luberto et al., 2018). Some interesting physical benefits are that it also often assists with migraines and chronic pain (Tonelli and Wachholz, 2014).

MWMT Metta (Loving-kindness) Meditation Instruction

To practice *Metta* meditation, sit in a comfortable and relaxed manner, with your back and head straight. Close your eyes. Allow your facial muscles to relax and adopt a slight smiling facial expression. Take a few deep breaths. Let go of any concerns or preoccupations. For a few minutes, observe the breath as it moves through the center of your chest into the area of the heart.

Please be aware that sometimes during loving-kindness meditation it is possible that opposite feelings such as anger, grief, or sadness may arise. It is important to take these as signs that your heart is softening, which can cause other emotions to be uncovered. Just try to be mindful of them, without any judgment and accept them with patience and kindness.

Metta is first practiced toward oneself, since we often have difficulty in being compassionate to others without first being compassionate to ourselves. Then subsequently, it is extended and directed to others.

As you sit quietly, mentally repeat, slowly and steadily, the following phrases:

May I be happy
May I be safe
May I be healthy
May I be peaceful

Let your heart slowly soften and open up to the meaning of the words. Allow yourself to accept this kind and compassionate wish and to feel that you deserve this unconditional kindness.

After a period of directing loving-kindness toward yourself, bring to mind someone close to you in your life, one who deeply cares for you. Then slowly repeat these phrases of *Metta* towards him or her:

May you be happy
May you be safe
May you be healthy
May you be peaceful

As you say these phrases, again contemplate their intention and heartfelt meaning. If any feelings of loving-kindness arise, connect the feelings with the phrases so that the feelings may become stronger as you repeat the words.

Next, as you continue the meditation, bring to mind an acquaintance or stranger that you have neutral feelings for and slowly repeat these phrases toward them:

May you be happy
May you be safe
May you be healthy
May you be peaceful

With every repetition, be aware that even people that we do not know very well or those who do not mean very much to us, also wish to be happy and deserve love and compassion.

Again, as you say the words to yourself contemplate their intention and feel their meaning.

Next, as you continue the meditation, bring to mind a person who you may dislike, hate or someone for whom you may have very negative feelings. It may be a person who has hurt you in the past. Even though it may feel difficult to do this, find the courage and understanding and remember that everyone deserves to be happy, even though they make mistakes and suffer from delusions of the mind, just like we often do. Slowly repeat these phrases toward them:

May you be happy
May you be safe
May you be healthy
May you be peaceful

With every repetition, be aware that even people that we do not like or have hurt us, no matter what they have done, they too, just like us, wish to be happy and deserve love and compassion. Again, as you say the words to yourself contemplate their intention and feel their meaning.

Next, bring to mind the person who is close to you, the person who is neutral and the person who you dislike and imagine that they are all in a room together with you. Slowly repeat these phrases toward them:

May we all be happy
May we all be safe
May we all be healthy
May we all be peaceful

Finally, expand your loving kindness and include all the people on this planet, including all animals and living creatures and send them this wish, silently repeating it to yourself for the next few minutes:

May you all be happy
May you all be safe
May you all be healthy
May you all be peaceful

With every repetition, be aware that all living beings in the world have a common wish and that is to be happy, to live safely with optimum health and in peace.

As you come to the close, take a few last breaths and with your exhalation, let the phrases of *Metta* go, along with all the images and feelings associated with them. Return to just observing your breath for a few minutes before you close your meditation session.

PRACTICAL MIDDLE WAY MIND TRAINING PRESCRIPTION
MWMT MEDITATION SUMMARY – Metta Meditation

- Find a secluded place to meditate, sit down, cross your legs, close your eyes
- Keep your head and back straight, relax your facial muscles and adopt a slight smile
- Observe your breath for a few minutes
- Direct the phrases of *Metta* first to yourself while contemplating their meaning
- Direct the phrases of *Metta* to someone close to you
- Direct the phrases of *Metta* to a neutral person
- Direct the phrases of *Metta* to a person you dislike
- Imagine the person close to you, the neutral person and the person you dislike all in a room together with you and direct the phrases of *Metta* to all of you
- Direct the phrases of *Metta* to all sentient beings, including people, animals and living creatures
- Take a few breaths and with the last breath release and let go of the phrases and all images and feelings along with them
- Return to observing your breath for the last few minutes

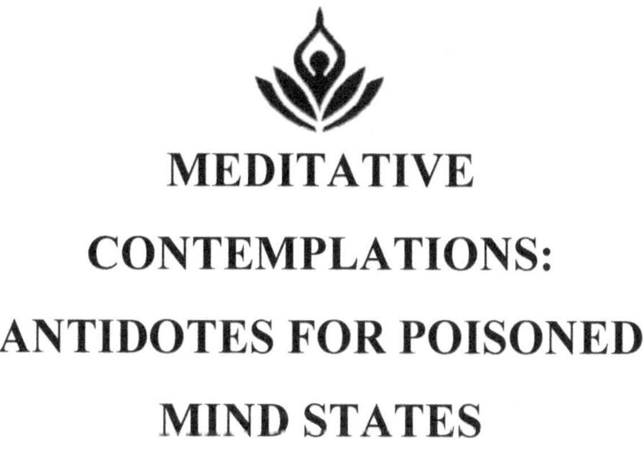

MEDITATIVE CONTEMPLATIONS: ANTIDOTES FOR POISONED MIND STATES

Meditation is the antidote to all the poisons of
your life. It is the nourishment of your authentic
nature.

– Osho

The core meditations in Middle Way Mind Training are the Meditation of observing the breath, Mindfulness meditation and Compassion meditation. These three techniques are so vital to our level of happiness that we should try to include them in our meditation practice every day. Each of them has a specific purpose, one creates a sharply focused and concentrated mind, the other cultivates our bare awareness so we can see reality the way it really is, and the final develops a deep connection with all beings to realize that we all experience suffering and share common desires and needs.

Despite these being paramount to our ability to uncover and experience the happiness that we have within, there are still many poisoned mind states that we hold as mental formations that often require specific and directed attention. When we speak of poisoned mind states we mean those that are non-beneficial or detrimental to our happiness and cause us to suffer. In Buddhist science these negative mind states are often called defilements, those that cloud the mind and manifest in unwholesome thoughts, emotions and actions. Throughout this book we have covered many of them; greed, hatred, jealousy to name just a few.

Just as someone who has been bitten by a poisonous snake and requires specific anti-venom treatment to eradicate that poison, a mind that is contaminated with a certain defilement or poisoned mind state, requires its own specific antidote in order to counteract its negative effect.

Our minds contain many deep-rooted defilements, ones that we have developed through our attachment or aversion to what we experience through our sense doors, and those according to Buddhist philosophy that we carry as a burden from past lives or our karma (if you believe in rebirth). These poisoned mind states are often responsible for our suffering or dissatisfaction in life. They manifest when our mind reacts uncontrollably or when we react unfavorably to other people and situations that present themselves. The First Noble Truth, as taught by the Buddha, revealed to us that this suffering or dissatisfaction is inherent to the human condition. It comes from our ignorance of craving for things in our external world that will not bring us sustained happiness. This is our constant desire for something in our lives to be different or better, no matter what level of success we achieve or material possessions we acquire. We should know by now that happiness cannot be found from external phenomena but comes from within our own minds. If we can purify our mind of the defilements, then the way we view the external world will be with pure happiness, without any feelings of suffering or dissatisfaction. Purifying our mind of defilements is easier said than done. It requires meditation, mindfulness as well as specific meditative contemplations.

The Buddha recognized sixteen defilements or poisoned states of the mind. This list includes: greed, ill will, anger or hatred, hostility, contempt, being domineering or disrespectful, envy, jealousy, hypocrisy or deceit, fraud, stubbornness, rivalry, conceit, arrogance, vanity or pride and negligence or lack of consideration. As many of these in the list are similar or related to each other, they are often grouped together to form the *Five Kleshas* or the five major defilements or poisons of the mind. These are craving, hatred, jealousy, pride and ignorance.

These five can be further reduced down to the three unwholesome root poisons, because all the multitude of negative thoughts that can arise from the mind originate from these three major mind states, which are:

- Greed (craving)
- Hatred (anger or aversion)

- Delusion (ignorance)

All the misery that we experience in the world is due to one of these three major states. Either our greed causes us to crave for future happiness, or our hatred or aversion causes us to be angry about something if our desires are not met, or our delusion or ignorance causes us to be blinded by the true reality of our existence. If our mind is poisoned by any one of these states, we will always be agitated, unhappy and unsatisfied.

The Buddha said we should follow the path of purification of the mind, to cleanse the mind of these defilements. All these defilements are not permanent, so they can be diminished and eliminated. The mind can be trained by using meditative contemplations that act as antidotes to each specific defilement. The defilements are like layers upon layers of plaster around our inner nature. As we combat these poisoned mind states with antidotes, our mind becomes more and more purified, and the natural tranquility and inner peace of our inner nature arises. As the layers dissolve, our true happiness is uncovered and can be experienced.

As we develop each of the fundamental principles of Middle Way Mind Training, our defilements will slowly lose their hold in our mind and will be replaced with beneficial mind states. It is impossible to be compassionate and to love if our mind is full of hate. It is also impossible to have inner peace or happiness with a mind full of hatred. As we train the mind with contemplative meditations which cultivate beneficial mind states such as compassion, we will develop a mind that is full of love, empathy and consideration, one that will be impossible to be hateful. This will result in a peaceful mind from which will radiate only happiness.

In the following chapters we will discuss various antidotes or specific meditative contemplations. We can then add them to our arsenal of peaceful weapons against any harmful states that can contaminate our mind or get in the way of experiencing the happiness that each one of us truly deserves.

GENEROSITY: RELEASING
YOUR GRASP

No one has ever become poor by giving.

– Anne Frank

The meaning of life is to find your gift. The
purpose of life is to give it away

– Pablo Picasso

*I*n the last chapter I mentioned that according to Buddhist science, greed, hatred and delusion are the root evils that prevent us from accessing our happiness that we have within. A very effective antidote to the first root evil, greed is its exact opposite, generosity. The Buddha often spoke of generosity or *dāna* as it is called in the Pali language. A foundation of the Buddhist path, generosity is known as the very first *parami*, or perfection, the most important virtue in Buddhism and the basis for all others.

Generosity is the act of giving, but there are three important factors involved in this process, before we can claim any real benefits of happiness. First we need to look at our intention when we give. Do we have feelings of regret or remorse when we give something to someone? If we do, that is indicating that we are still battling with our attachment and desire and have difficulty in letting go. Are we giving so that we can get something back in return? Again this kind of giving is only compounding our greed. Under these conditions, we cannot truly be happy. Our mind is not at peace and still full of wanting desire. If our generosity does not stem from good intentions, our mind remains deluded with non-beneficial states that only make us suffer.

The same goes for receiving a gift. In these times it is often very odd when someone gives us something and doesn't expect anything in return and we can even feel guilty about accepting a gift from someone under these circumstances. We tend to reciprocate by giving a gift back in return. While this is a nice gesture, our intention for giving may be to just even the score and not really an act of letting go of our attachments. This can in some way negate or diminish the antidote effect on our greed. Companies and individuals often give donations or charitable contributions for the wrong reasons, such as for tax purposes, status or advertising and promotion. It is rare in our society to see someone give just for the sake of giving and not expect anything in return. Most of us fail to realize that we get back far more than we can imagine, yet we are missing out on a lot of happiness by not doing so. The mantra, "Greed is good", so well characterized by Michael Douglas in his portrayal of Gordon Gekko in the movie Wall Street, unfortunately resounds strongly in our modern materialistic society. From a Buddhist science perspective however, there is nothing good or beneficial in greed as it is just a delusion of the mind, a defilement that can easily misguide us and lead us to destructive states that only take away our inner peace and happiness.

The second factor is what we decide to give. The process of giving or being generous does not have to mean just money or material gifts. It can mean giving time to someone or mental support or passing on wisdom or engaging in friendly conversation. It can be as simple as a smile that is shared or helping an elderly person cross the street. Generosity is not limited to just those who can afford it or those that are wealthy but the opportunity is available to each and every one of us, in every minute of every day.

Thirdly, the recipient of our generosity is also an important factor to take into account. This should be someone that truly needs our help or is worthy of our help. Helping someone that does not need our help may not be beneficial and may even cause negative feelings or reactions. This last factor requires some degree of wisdom. For example, giving money to a homeless alcoholic or drug addict who will just use it to foster their habit is not wise. So, in summary, taking a look at what our motivations or actual intentions are in giving, what we want to give and who should receive our gifts are all important factors we should take into consideration.

When we cultivate the right generosity with the right intentions, it can be a transformative experience as it has the power to change us. Not only does the act of giving lessen the suffering of others and improve their trust towards us, we also move the focus on the importance of our self to that of others. We diminish the hold that our ego has on the self, as we slowly realize that life is not just about us but that we are all one and interconnected. As we have learned from previous chapters and through Buddhist science, our concept of a concrete self is one of the main causes of our suffering and unhappiness.

Generosity also frees our mind from attachment and clinging, reducing our greed. The more we give, the more we are forced to let go. This is often not easy to do and may be a painful process at first, but through mindfulness and generosity training we can become aware of what our attachments are really saying. Statements such as "I will give this much and no more," or "I will give this gift only if I will be appreciated for it," are only telling us that we are still desperately holding onto the illusory concept of I, me and mine.

Only when we can let go of the negative mind states of greed and attachment, can we attain inner peace and allow happiness to arise. The incredible rewards are there for each one of us to benefit from; we just need to be able to see things with more clarity and wisdom.

As we move through this transformative process by cultivating generosity, we can see that our greed is like a tight fist. If we make a tight fist and then slowly open it, we experience relief. When the mind becomes filled with the feeling of generosity, it moves out of a rigid confinement into a less bounded space. Our world opens up because we are free of our attachments and we can let go. Through the joy of giving, our heart opens and we experience confidence; we grow in self-esteem, self-respect and happiness because we continually test our limits of generosity. We challenge our mind because we already know that it cannot always be trusted and it is not necessarily out for our best interests. Certainly our ego is not. We learn to see through our attachments and that they are transparent and have no solidity. They only hold us back from our happiness, so we need to free ourselves and go beyond them.

An interesting experiment on the neural link between generosity and happiness was done in 2017 in Switzerland (Park et al. 2017). Participants promised to spend money over the next four weeks either on others (the experimental group) or on themselves (the control group). Magnetic resonance was used to investigate the brain mechanisms that link generous behavior with increases in happiness at the neural level. They measured activity in areas of the brain that was associated with their happiness level. Results showed that the experimental group made more generous choices and showed stronger increases in self-reported happiness levels. It also didn't seem to matter how generous people were. The experiment showed that even thinking about or planning to give away just a little bit of money had the same effects on happiness as giving away a lot.

Just reading about how generosity can increase our happiness is often not enough for us to act accordingly, as greed and attachment are extremely strong mental forces or defilements in our mind. Generosity should be cultivated through meditative contemplation. Training the mind in generosity can be used to support and strengthen several of the fundamental principles of Middle Way Mind Training that affect our happiness. These include helping to guide us in performing the right actions and engaging in the right work to benefit ourselves and others as well as directing our efforts to cultivate and maintain beneficial mind states. Meditative contemplation on generosity also assists to weaken the ego, loosen the mental construct of the self and internalize the impermanence of things. We come to the realization that there is really no need to cling on to them, as we just suffer if we do.

MWMT Antidote 1: Meditative Contemplation on Generosity

To practice Meditative Contemplation on Generosity, sit in a comfortable and relaxed manner, with your back and head straight and your eyes closed. For a few minutes, observe the breath as you relax and inhale and exhale.

Allow your mind to step back and release yourself from the pursuit of status, wealth and power. Free your mind from any distractions, demands, desires and needs and create an oasis of tranquility inside your mind and in your heart. For a moment just stop your desire for doing, accomplishing, or attaining something. Realize that you cannot ever have everything, do everything or be everything. Just accept that you are just a part that is interconnected with the whole. You already have everything that you need.

Contemplate on the things you have amassed during your life: your home, your car, your furniture, your investments, and all the things that you own and call yours. Remind yourself that life is short and your material possessions are only with you for a short time after which you will have to let them all go. That is the law of impermanence. There is really no point in hoarding or clinging to possessions and amassing more wealth than you or your loved ones need as it will only slip through your fingers one day.

Spend the next few minutes repeating in your mind quietly:

All the material wealth that I have will one day be gone. There is no point in holding on to more than I need.

Contemplate on how every time you have desired something and purchased it, initially it brought you some form of happiness but it never really lasted. Observe and understand that all your sensory desires come from contact with an external object and your sense organs and if they are pleasant, they create a desire. This desire is created only in your mind and is also impermanent as well as any feelings and perceptions created from it. All desires arise and pass away, only to be replaced with new ones that undergo the same fate.

Spend the next few minutes repeating in your mind quietly:

All my desires are impermanent, they arise and then they pass away.

Contemplate that your desire can easily turn to greed if you are not careful. Remind yourself that greed is not a peaceful state of mind. Therefore it cannot bring you happiness. Clinging on to things with greed only makes you suffer.

Spend the next few minutes repeating in your mind quietly:

Greed is not a peaceful state of mind; it can never bring me lasting happiness.

Contemplate how your mind feels like a tight fist when it is overcome with greed. You are not in a relaxed state. Try to imagine that you release your grip and allow your mind to let go of all your desires. Be aware of how calm you feel when your mind lets go. When you practice generosity, it is like releasing a tight fist, there is a strong sense of relief.

Spend the next few minutes repeating in your mind quietly:

Being generous will allow me to let go of my hold of my desires.

Contemplate on the ways that you can express your generosity. Remind yourself that the things that you find the most difficult or painful to give are the ones that will release and free your mind the most from its attachments.

Ask yourself and ponder these questions:

If I have more money or material possessions than I really need, is there someone I can help right now that needs them more than me?

If I have time, can I donate my time to someone who needs some help or companionship?
Is there anything I can give that I have, that I find very difficult to let go of?

Contemplate on the benefits of generosity. Remind yourself that the process of letting go is not easy but results in an enormous relief or piece of mind. Remind yourself that your mind and your ego are not to be trusted. They are not out for your best interests. The more generous you are, the more you can let go and the happier you become.

Spend the next few minutes repeating in your mind quietly:

The more generous I am, the more I can let go and feel piece of mind and happiness.

Return back to just observing the breath for a few minutes, without contemplating any thoughts. Slowly become aware of your surroundings and open your eyes. Make a personal list of generous things you promise to give this week.

GRATITUDE: AN AWAKENED STATE OF BEING

Gratitude turns what we have into enough.

– Aesop

*I*t is very common in our modern world to see all the bad aspects of life and to constantly complain. We generally don't think too much about the things that we are grateful for in our lives. Expressing gratitude just does not seem to come natural to us. Our inability to understand where to really find happiness, leads us to focus entirely on our external world. We constantly compare ourselves to others. Our never-ending craving to match or be better than others, in levels of success, material wealth and status creates emotions of envy, jealousy, resentment and greed. It is very hard to feel gratitude when we are constantly craving for a reality that is different from what we have now. Gratitude is a way of embracing reality instead of fighting it.

Just as generosity invites us to let go of attachment to the "self," gratitude reminds us to treasure and be thankful for all present and past conditions that lead to the fruition of what we can enjoy in the present. This is what Buddhist science refers to as *dependent origination* or dependent arising, a concept that all things in the world arise and come into existence by causes and that everything is interconnected. We are all part of this dynamic system that everything affects everything else and what is happening now is part of what happened before and is part of what will happen next. For example, we can be mindful and grateful of all the wonderful conditions our parents have made possible for our very existence, our upbringing, and every success. By the same token, we can extend our gratitude to our friends, teachers, community, and even the environment that we live in. We can even be grateful for mundane things such as inventions and discoveries by the scientists of the past that have made our lives a lot easier with the advent of things like electricity, airplanes, automobiles and computers.

One of the main reasons why people are ungrateful is ignorance of this reality. People who are ungrateful do not see the wisdom of dependent origination. Their narrow-minded and egoistic points of view erroneously lead them to think of themselves as being special and the sole contributor of their success. They do not see the dependent nature of their relationships with others, the community, and with their environment, not to mention the close links with their predecessors and future generations. If we want to understand the importance of gratitude we need to internalize the principle of dependent origination and not take things for granted because many of the conditions we enjoy today are the results of many conscious decisions made by others in the past. Because their efforts have contributed to our success, we should be inspired to feel gratitude and repay the kindness that these deeds have provided for us, by practicing gratitude.

We tend to only be grateful when the circumstances are right, but gratitude is not about the circumstances. Real gratitude is also not about comparing our life to someone whose life is worse. These are two common misconceptions when we think of gratitude. Gratitude does not envy or compare and it is not dependent on what we have. Dependence on others to be worse off than we are, only feeds our ego. We can even find gratitude through our difficulties and suffering that we endure in our life. Sometimes it is through the hardest circumstances that our heart learns the most important lessons. Remember the Buddhist concept of inner nature; our source of happiness, compassion and inner peace. It is something we already hold within, and it is not found in the externals. This means we already have everything we need to be happy and to feel gratitude. We just need to awaken to this understanding. We need to learn to let go of all the identities we construct in our mind that we closely cling to; especially those that constantly seek to improve and better our external situation. There is a comfort and deep feeling of inner peace that comes with the realization that we already possess that which we spend so much time desperately searching for.

When we are grateful, we are not craving anything, we are in peaceful acceptance and appreciation of what we have now. It is for this reason that gratitude is a mind state that is cultivated as an antidote to craving and greed, jealousy, resentment and envy. Being grateful does not allow our desires to get out of control. The more we are able to experience and practice gratitude, the more happiness we have. In many ways it is a form of mindfulness, as we take notice or become mindful of how fortunate we are so we don't take anything for granted.

Gratitude is also an antidote to anger, one of the other root evils. When our mind is in a state of anger, we are dissatisfied and not appreciative or grateful for life. Practicing gratitude forces us to understand that we are lucky to even be alive. It also helps us with jealousy. If we are satisfied and appreciative there is no need to compare ourselves with others or to be jealous of anyone. Practicing gratitude removes the focus on our self, which reduces our self-cherishing and conceit. People who have a strong sense of gratitude, are generally more patient, compassionate and understanding because they are appreciative of the situation that they are experiencing in the present moment. Take the example of something simple such as traffic lights. We often lose our patience waiting at an intersection for a green light, but as we develop gratitude we learn that we should be grateful even for red lights because they actually protect us from dangerous collisions and without them there would be chaos on the streets.

If you find that you are constantly rushing in life, struggling to keep up with deadlines and barely managing, there is often little time to even think about gratitude. Try to do what Vietnamese Buddhist monk Thich Nhat Hanh recommends: *When we walk like [we are rushing], we print anxiety and sorrow on the earth. We have to walk in a way that we only print peace and serenity on the earth. Walk as if you are kissing the earth with your feet.* These words of wisdom teach us that if we want to really be happy, we need to slow down. After all, we are all doing what we do in order to be happy, so it must start with the realization that we already have everything we need. We just need to slow down, and become aware of that fact.

The workplace is generally not where we find that much expression of gratitude. While most people appreciate its value, most are hesitant to express it on the job. Just the simple act of saying thanks to a colleague or employee makes them feel so much happier and more fulfilled. Gratitude, though commonly thought of as a sign of weakness or vulnerability in the workplace, is really a sign of strength and leads to much more cohesion, motivation and productivity.

Gratitude is also an important individual quality for managers to cultivate, as being thankful improves their self-control and decision-making, and teaches humility. It involves less focus on the self and more on others, and an ability to see the value and strengths of their subordinates. The humility that stems from gratitude makes them a lot more open to criticism. Gratitude helps managers to want to become better and they start to view themselves more like a work in progress rather than an ego-driven finished piece of work. It also generates a sense of connection with all members of the organization and fosters better teamwork towards achieving common goals. When we realize we are part of something bigger than ourselves, we are inspired to raise the bar in our organizations. Gratitude is a gateway to a work environment that is full of connection, motivation and growth. It has a miraculous power to make us feel more positive about the past, hopeful about the future and motivated in the present. In a world that demands constant change and innovation, gratitude is a gift to everyone in the workplace that never stops giving.

Cultivating Gratitude

As gratitude does not usually come naturally to us, the first questions we should ask ourselves are: "Are we grateful in the present moment?" and "What are we actually grateful for?" and if not, "Why are we not feeling grateful?" For many of us the reasons we are not grateful may be because we are feeling bitter or resentful about something. This comes from the tension that develops by wanting our lives to be different than what they actually are or when our expectations are not met. It is very difficult to feel grateful under these conditions. This initial process of mindful awareness of our present state of mind forces us to recognize what mental state of gratitude we are in and all the reasons for it and directs our efforts to focus on what aspects of our life we can be grateful for.

It is then necessary to acknowledge all the things that we are grateful or not grateful for. We may even want to write them all down in a daily gratitude journal so that they are there in front of us to clearly see. For every negative entry or complaint about life, we try to see the other side of the coin, the positive side. We can ask ourselves if these negative aspects can have any positive benefits or reasons to be grateful.

Once we have acknowledged what we are grateful for, the next step is to be able to truly appreciate these aspects of our life. As we go through each one, we become aware of them and can contemplate our appreciation.

The final step is to practice expressing gratitude. We should not ignore this last step as it is often forgotten. Feeling gratitude is great but expressing it has the potential to be transformational and life-changing. How do we express our gratitude? Probably the best way is to voice our appreciation with others, in the form of compliments and thankful and kind words. Even a simple smile to someone can have significant positive effects. People are often amazed at not only how wonderful the recipient of our gratitude will feel, but what often is not realized is how our own level of happiness dramatically increases after we express gratitude.

Research on Gratitude

There have been hundreds of scientific studies linking gratitude with positive mind states. Studies by Dr. Robert A. Emmons and Dr. Michael E. McCullough, both psychologists, have clearly demonstrated the benefits of gratitude (Emmons, 2008). In one experiment, participants were divided into three groups, one group was asked to write every week about things that they were grateful for, the second group was asked to write about things that irritated them during the week, and the last group would write about anything that affected them whether good or bad. After 10 weeks, those who wrote about gratitude were much more optimistic and felt better about their lives. They were also motivated to exercise more and visited the doctor much less than those who focused on sources of irritation.

Another researcher in the field of gratitude is Dr. Martin E. P. Seligman, a psychologist from the University of Pennsylvania, who tested 411 people by getting them to write and personally deliver a letter of gratitude to someone who had never been thanked for his or her kindness. The participants in the study immediately exhibited huge increases in happiness scores, much higher than any other interventions and the benefits lasted even for a month later (Seligman et al. 2005).

MWMT Antidote 2: Meditative Contemplation on Gratitude

Find a comfortable, quiet place to be, either sitting on a chair on sitting on a cushion on the floor with your legs crossed. Place a pen and paper in front of you, which you will use at the end of the meditation session. Ensure that your back is straight and allow your body to settle and become grounded. Close your eyes and allow your facial muscles to relax. As you move your attention inside yourself, focus in on the gentle flow of your breath as it enters and leaves your body. Feel how you are connected to your breath as you inhale and exhale gently. Feel how you accept each breath and then let it go. Just observe your breath the way it is for a few minutes, not trying to change it or correct it, just leaving it as it wants to be. Let your breath find its own rhythm and its own pace.

Ask yourself what your mindset is at the present moment:

Do you feel grateful or not right now? If you do not, ask yourself why?

If you are angry or resentful or have an uneasy feeling of craving or jealousy in your mind, just observe your thoughts and the feelings that arise when you do. Ask yourself if you feel any tension in your body. Remember that any feelings you have are not permanent, they arise and then they pass away. Challenges that present themselves in our lives often have their positive sides and we can learn a lot from them. See if you can find any room to feel any gratitude even for those unpleasant experiences that your mind seems to be dwelling on right now.

Take a few breaths and as you exhale let go of any tension, any resentments, any anger or any uneasy feelings you may have. Notice how your breath calms down as you let go.

Now, contemplate on all the reasons for which you can be grateful. Think about all the people and all the circumstances that have arisen that have opened any doors for you to make you who you are today. Think of all the doctors and people who have cared for you so that you can be healthy and so that you can be alive today. Think of your parents or those who raised you and kept you safe and sheltered. Think of your friends and loved ones who have shared the good and bad experiences with you that come with life.

Take the next few minutes and go through a list in your mind of the things that you can be grateful for and for each contemplate your appreciation for each of them. Realize that without them, you would not be who you are or where you are today. Think of how each one of us is dependent on so many conditions that are out of our control.

Notice any feelings that arise when you think about all the things and people that you are grateful for in your life. Contemplate on how you can show your friends, family, co-workers, or acquaintances your gratitude for anything that they have done for you that has helped you during your life. In your mind, thank each one of them.

Spend the last few minutes observing your breath as you contemplate the feeling of gratitude.

As you slowly open your eyes, write down a list of all the people, things, and reasons for which you are grateful. You may wish to keep it as a Gratitude Journal and fill it in daily.

It can be in the form of:

**I am grateful to___________ for_______________
because___________________________**

Find some ways to express your gratitude to those who have helped you in your life. Write them a short email or letter or say something to them personally. Give one compliment every day to someone. Give people a smile when they do something thoughtful or kind for you. Remind yourself that expressing your gratitude has miraculous effects on the happiness of the recipients and for your own level of happiness. By expressing your gratitude you have the power to transform yourself and the world around you.

PATIENCE: THE NATURE OF ACCEPTANCE

Patience guards us against losing our presence of
mind so we can remain undisturbed, even when
the situation is really difficult.

— His Holiness the 14th Dalai Lama

The Buddha praised patience and considered it to be one of the sublime mental states that an awakened person has perfected. Along with generosity, patience is one of the *paramis,* which are perfections or virtues in Buddhist philosophy. Patience is a mind that is able to accept fully and happily whatever occurs. It is a lot more than just gritting our teeth and putting up with or suppressing the situation. Being patient means welcoming whatever arises, and giving up on the idea that things should be other than what they are. Patience gives rise to equanimity, that supreme state of mind that leads to less stress, peace, well-being and happiness. It is always possible to exercise patience. There is never any situation that is so bad that it cannot be patiently accepted with an open and peaceful heart. When we understand patience, it is really just the nature of acceptance.

According to the dictionary definition, patience is the capacity to accept or tolerate delay, difficulty, or annoyance without getting angry, anxious or upset. We tend to expect the environment to conform to our expectations, such as seen in our aversion to waiting in long lines, our anger at late food served at a restaurant, our frustration during traffic jams or our impatient habit of interrupting someone while they are speaking. We also tend to expect people to conform to our expectations as well. We expect that they should behave the way we think they should behave. These expectations are often unrealistic especially when it comes to what goes on in our minds. We think we should be able to control what thoughts and what emotions enter the mind, but unwelcome thoughts and emotions arise all the time.

Our society today expects everything to be presented instantly. We are constantly being told that time is money and efficiency and productivity have unfortunately taken the place of our well-being and happiness. Our lives have been constantly put on the fast track with high speed internet, social media, quicker transportation and fast food. These conveniences however come at a price. When our high expectations are not met, we only get more frustrated, lose our patience and become angry. In a lot of ways, we have lost our ability to be patient.

Most of the time our impatient response not only hurts us, but also the person we are impatient with, as well as our reputation. In fact, we often categorize people who are impatient as those that are arrogant, insensitive, impulsive, judgmental or poor decision makers. It is therefore always beneficial for us to cultivate patience, because we know we cannot control the ups and downs of our external world and it is inevitable that things will often not go according to our plans. We know the world is constantly changing, nothing is permanent and it is not possible for us to control things as we often think we can. We need to be open to change and gain this wisdom. Allowing this constant impatient battle in our mind where we expect something to happen and cannot accept that it is not happening, causes us a lot of unnecessary pain, stress and suffering. For this reason cultivating patience is so important and that is why in Buddhism, it is used primarily as an antidote for combating anger, but also for aversion, craving, resentment and greed. As we know by now, these are all non-beneficial emotional states of mind that prevent our happiness to be uncovered and experienced. Patience is also used as an antidote to our delusions about the nature of reality, especially helping us understand about causes of suffering, and the impermanence of emotions, and other mental constructs that we hold.

Cultivating Patience

We cannot always trust our mind, as it is often corrupted by our judgments, opinions and our past experiences, so we need to realize that we may be wrong in our thinking sometimes. We may not always have the complete story, so we need to keep an open mind.

There is an interesting example about patience that relates to how our mind can often be so wrong. This story is about an event that occurred at a post office. There was a man who was waiting in a long line becoming more and more impatient as time dragged on. He could see that what was holding things up was apparently a woman carrying a baby that was in a prolonged conversation at the front of the line with the female post office cashier. As he was already late and in a hurry, he could start to feel the anger inside him reaching a boiling point. His mind began to go over and over how unfair this woman was in holding everyone up and how disrespectful she was to all these people who are waiting in line. During his entire wait he could feel all the stress and impatience making him suffer incredibly. When he reached the front of the line, he felt frustrated, exhausted and extremely angry. The cashier apologized to him and told him that the baby that he thought belonged to the woman in line was actually hers. Her friend had been taking care of her baby, because she could not take the time off. Her baby had become suddenly sick and this woman just came to ask her advice and to report on her baby's condition. Suddenly all the anger, frustration and impatience, that burdened this man's mind was instantly transformed into a much peaceful state of understanding and compassion and he could feel all his suffering instantly disappear.

The moral to this is that we never know what the actual story may be. The food ordered in the restaurant may be late because one of the cooks is sick. There is a traffic jam because someone got killed in an accident up ahead. The person walking extremely slow in front of us recently suffered a heart attack, and the list goes on and on. We may often be completely wrong in our thinking and assumptions, so it makes sense to approach each situation we encounter in life with wisdom and patience.

There is no doubt that the world is getting more and more fast-paced and our minds are struggling to cope with dealing with so much information and tasks, often becoming overwhelmed in the process. If we can find ways to slow down our thought processes, become more grateful and accepting for the way our lives are right now, and understand that we may not always be right in our thinking, we will be able to cultivate patience with an open mind.

Since our minds constantly jump from one thought or worry to another, we really need to slow down. This is where meditation has its place. When we find a quiet place, sit down comfortably, close our eyes and place awareness on our breath, we are able to bring ourselves into the present moment and that is where we can see things a lot more clearly. When our minds are open, we are able to change and naturally become more patient. As we calm down the mind, our irritation and frustration will let go of its hold, and it will be much easier to cultivate patience. Before we get angry at someone for not doing things our way, the slowing down of our mind will allow us to consider not just our point of view but their point of view as well. With regular meditative contemplation, we start to feel an inner calm which we will later be able to carry out into our daily lives. It gives us space to respond to a situation with wisdom and not just blindly react to it. We will be able to see situations the way they really are with an open mind and not with one that is distorted with all our emotions. A calm mind is one that has the wisdom of clarity. It is not one that is fighting, judging or controlling the situation. It is one that accepts peacefully every situation as it presents itself in the present moment. This is what patience is all about.

Patience is also a form of self-compassion, an act of being kind to our self. We know that we suffer when we are impatient in life, so cultivating patience is an act of self-compassion. We are being kind or compassionate to ourselves so that we do not suffer the stress and suffering that comes with impatience.

Patience is not a process of resigning to the difficulties of life or just shrugging things off. It also does not mean suppressing or putting up with something which is irritating us until it goes away. A person may appear patient but may only be suppressing it, but still caught in a state of wanting something to cease or change. We should not be in the mind state that we should just hold on as eventually things will get better, or we will get our way in the end if we are patient enough. This is impure and will only temporarily deal with our impatience. It does not deal with the root cause which is our resistance or desire. Pure patience means we accept things as they are, bearing with the suffering without any expectations that it will go away. We do not add anything to it or try to cover it up. It is supported by the insight that when we have clarity of mind, suffering can be understood. It is this suffering that stirs up anger, hatred, greed and resentment and by cultivating patience through contemplative meditation, the reactivity of the mind which is a conditioned reflex can be stopped. A real patient person is one that can create a mind state that is completely free of that defilement. This frees the mind of suffering.

The Three Types of Patience

The *parami* of patience trains us to be calm and accepting when we face difficult people or circumstances. Patience entails cultivating skillful courage, mindfulness, and tolerance. In general, when we feel that others are hurting us or creating an inconvenience for us, we react with various forms of anger and irritation, instantly looking to strike back. When it comes to patience, however, we remain unwavering, solid as a mountain, neither seeking revenge nor harboring deep resentment. Patience is a very powerful antidote to anger. The three categories of patience include patience with interpersonal relationships, patience with life's hardships and patience with the daily ups and downs of life.

When it comes to interpersonal relationships we can often experience harm or insults by our enemies. This is part of life as we cannot please everyone. By cultivating patience we can avoid any acts of cruelty or revenge, avoid competition and arguments, and avoid harboring jealousy or resentment. We learn to not take insults personally.

Regarding life's hardships, we must accept that they are a part of the human condition and that things do not always go according to our plans. Patience teaches us not to expect immediate results but to focus instead on compassion to others, without becoming discouraged or frustrated when we encounter hardships. When we encounter them, we should avoid trying to escape from the present moment and imagining a better future or dwelling on the past. This will only cause us to miss our life in the present.

With the ups and downs of life, they are inevitable, and patience teaches us to accept them with courage and equanimity. Experiencing pain, disappointment or frustration gives us an opportunity to cultivate patience. In this way, these negative experiences give us an opportunity to learn and transform our impatience into patience.

Some science behind patience

Baylor University psychologist Sarah Schnitker, who has been studying patience for more than a decade, found that people who are more patient also tend to be more hopeful and satisfied with their lives (Schnitker, 2012). They are less likely to be stressed or depressed and less prone to health issues like headaches and ulcers, which are typical of Type-A personality types who exhibit low levels of patience. She found that patient people also experience less negative emotions and can cope better with upsetting or stressful situations. They also are able to feel more gratitude and connection to the world. She measured 3 types of patience (interpersonal, life hardship, and daily hassles patience) which relate to well-being. She found that patience facilitated pursuit of goals and satisfaction especially in the face of obstacles in life. She also found that after participants underwent a training program in patience, it led to increased patience, less depression and less negative feelings.

MWMT Antidote 3: Meditative Contemplation on Patience

Find a quiet place, sit down comfortably, close your eyes and place your awareness on the breath. Spend a few minutes just observing the in-breath and out-breath of your breathing.

Recognize in your mind that impatience has arisen and be mindful of its presence. As you recognize it, label it and say to yourself, "impatience, impatience." Ask yourself how you responded to this impatient situation that you encountered. Did it benefit you or others around you? Ask yourself what triggered this feeling and whether you have encountered this trigger before.

At first you may feel that the cause of your impatience is external to you. Remind yourself that the impatience you are suffering from is caused by your response to the circumstances that you are facing, not because of any person or situation itself. Make the intention to contemplate on the impatience that is arising in your mind and that the cause of it is because you are not getting what you want right away.

Remind yourself that human life is full of situations and people that will not always conform to your expectations. It is therefore inevitable that you will not always get your way and if you expect this is it will just make you suffer. Remind yourself of this reality.

Remind yourself too that it is possible that you may not be right. Open your mind and try to see the situation from a different point of view, other than your own. Try to find a positive view or outlook on the situation.

Allow yourself to really experience how impatience feels in your mind and in your body. What thoughts are coming up? Are they repeating over and over? Is your mind calm or agitated? Do you feel any physical or mental tension, pain or other sensations anywhere? Are they pleasant or unpleasant? Label every physical or mental feeling that you discover and repeat it to yourself: "tension, tension," "pain, pain," "frustration, frustration," What does impatience feel like in your body? Go through your body and locate any areas that you feel these sensations. Do not suppress these sensations or push them away but allow them to manifest themselves and allow yourself to feel them fully with acceptance.

Remind yourself that this is how impatience feels. It is most often an unpleasant feeling. Remember that feelings and sensations are never permanent; they arise and then pass away. The same is with impatience, it grabs a hold in our mind but it never lasts.

Now as you inhale, breathe in your acceptance to the reality of the situation, and as you exhale let go and breathe out all the unpleasant feelings you are feeling. Let go of any tension, frustration, or painful feelings. With every inhalation and exhalation your mind will feel lighter and the burden of your impatience will slowly dissolve. Observe how you feel as you let go with each exhalation.

Continue observing your breath as you contemplate the impermanence of impatience and the unnecessary suffering it creates. As you accept the present reality as it is, observe how much calmer and in control you feel when you let go of any expectations that you have created in your mind. Observe how it is possible to transform impatience into patience through acceptance.

Now ask yourself if there is anything you can do to change the situation without making matters worse for yourself or for others involved. If you cannot, then ask yourself if there is anything positive that you have learned from this experience. Keep this in mind for the next time you encounter a similar situation.

Take a few deep breaths and on the final exhalation let everything go. Spend the last few minutes of your meditative contemplation just observing your breath, as you slowly become aware of your surroundings and open your eyes.

FORGIVENESS: ESCAPE FROM
AN IMPRISONED MIND

To forgive is to set a prisoner free and discover that the prisoner was
you.

– Lewis B. Smedes

The weak can never forgive.
Forgiveness is the attribute of the strong.

– Mahatma Gandhi

One of the greatest obstacles for achieving happiness is the inability to forgive. When we cannot forgive we choose to hold anger and resentment in our minds and these deep seeded negative mental formations, cause us great pain and suffering and are sometimes very difficult to transform. Having the wisdom to understand what forgiveness means and how to train our minds to cultivate forgiveness is an important Buddhist practice. As with meditative contemplations on compassion, gratitude and patience, forgiveness is another effective antidote to combat one of the root causes of our unhappiness, anger.

The key to forgiveness is not to bring the memory of the past into the present moment, but to leave the past where it belongs. Forgiveness is the capacity to move on, to let go and learn from our experience and not to become lost in the dramas of our life. It is the process of releasing our suffering and burdens of the past. This definition is movingly illustrated in a well-known Tibetan Buddhist story about two monks who meet each other several years after being released from prison where they had been tortured by their captors. The first one asks "Have you forgiven them for what they did to you? The second one replies. "I will never forgive

272

them! Never!" The first one says, "Well, I guess they still have you in prison, don't they?" When we are able to let go, our mind is able to be free from suffering. It is only through contemplative practice that we can realize how heavy a burden we hold in our heart when we cannot forgive. Through training our mind, we open the door to an enormous potential for transformation.

We may find when we are in the grips of grief, that it is impossible to forgive what is usually deemed unforgivable. Many mistakably believe that if you practice forgiveness, you are accepting or pardoning some terrible act. Others believe that you are a weak person if you forgive and do not stand up to those who perform evil actions and that you are abandoning justice for them.

Forgiveness is not about surrendering to defeat, giving up, or helplessly accepting the situation. It does not mean being weak, or not standing up to justice. What it really is about is the way we hold a terrible wrong inside our heart while we engage to correct that wrong and prevent it from happening again. Forgiveness practice is about liberating our own feelings and finding meaning in the worst of life's events. To practice forgiveness is to be free of the inner violence of our rage. Forgiveness does not mean we condone what happened in the past, it is not to forgive and forget like a simple "I forgive you" and everything is fine. Forgiveness is a deep healing process of the heart and mind that purifies and releases us. For some, this process can take several years or even a lifetime.

The Buddha taught to abandon thoughts of revenge and resentment and said, "Hate never yet dispelled hate. Only love dispels hate." To be able to transform hatred and loss with love and a giving heart as we do when we forgive is the most difficult practice we can imagine. Buddha's teaching acknowledges that a corrupted and ignorant mind full of defilements is the cause of wrong or evil actions. With wisdom and patience, we can learn to show compassion and be able to forgive someone who acts wrongly under delusion. According to Buddhist philosophy, when we are compassionate or forgiving to someone who has harmed us, we do not remove the karmic consequences of their actions, but we are not drawn into the karmic cycle ourselves. So the act of forgiveness does not mean that this person is not going to suffer the consequences as life makes sure by karmic law.

Remember the mind is like a blue sky, and emotions and delusions are like clouds that are only temporary. Dwelling on other peoples faults is the source of much of our negativity and inability to experience happiness. We need to remind ourselves that people are not the enemy, their delusions are. When we choose to forgive those who have hurt us, we take away their power. When we forgive, we heal, when we let go, our happiness grows.

Part of the reason why we often cling to hate and fear so stubbornly may be because we sense that if are not able to project our pain on anyone anymore, we will be forced to deal with our own pain. We often resent or cannot come to forgive the bad qualities that people in the world have that we do not like. When we contemplate on this we often find that these bad qualities that we see in others are often the same ones that we are guilty of ourselves, yet cannot face. We also have the tendency to be unnecessarily loyal to our suffering and this makes it very hard to forgive. Buddhist science teaches us that it is just not worth it to live day to day with a mind full of hatred. It is not helpful to us nor does it serve to define us. Anger and resentment tend to harden our emotions, cloud our judgment and narrow our options in responding to situations in life. Why would we choose to live in this manner? Take the Dalai Lama as an example; he lost everything, was exiled from his home country of Tibet, but today he still remains happy and compassionate.

When we suffer from a great disappointment or tragic act, we are entitled to feelings of loss and grief and to ask for and expect an unfair situation to be rectified. According to Buddhist science though, there is no place or entitlement for any hateful revenge, or right to think our grief and loss are unique which gives us permission to torture another or make them suffer. Each of these factors arises out of our own aversion and delusion, and they only degrade our life. When we lust for revenge and are filled with hate, we create mind states that lack compassion and wisdom and are just the opposite of being loving to ourselves. This kind of behavior only forces us to engage in a form of self-affliction. Unfortunately we are constantly inundated with media and movies and television shows that depict the sweetness of revenge and payback. Our emotions are often manipulated to really hate the bad guy in the film and to wish them a long and tortuous death. This is not condoned by Buddhist philosophy as it does not teach real forgiveness and only propagates the transmission of hate, which keeps us trapped in the wheel of karma.

The three directions of forgiveness

When we speak about cultivating forgiveness, there are three directions where we can focus our meditative efforts on; forgiving ourselves for what we have done to others, forgiving ourselves for what we have done to ourselves and forgiving others for what they have done to us.

When our actions have inflicted pain or suffering on others, we can ask forgiveness for what we have done and form the intention that we will right whatever wrongs we have made in the past if possible and resolve to not repeat them again in the future.

We may be holding a lot of guilt within for the ways that we have harmed or betrayed ourselves, not loved ourselves or not lived up to our own expectations. This has caused us a lot of suffering. Out of our own confusion, misunderstanding, hatred or fear, we may have abused our body or our own physical health. We may have engaged in practices that have harmed our state of mind. We may have made many mistakes in our lives that we regret. Being forgiving to ourselves, allows us to let go of any unkindness that we hold within and to vow to correct any mistakes that we have made if we can and not to make them again.

Finally, we suffer a great deal from the wrongdoings of others. If we can understand with wisdom that these acts of betrayal all stem from ignorant and deluded minds, the same as our minds when we harm or betray others, then we need not take them personally and we can then find the strength to cultivate compassion and forgiveness.

Scientific research on forgiveness

Several scientific studies have found that there is generally a positive relationship between forgiveness and subjective happiness (Batik et al., 2017), (Sudirman et al, 2019), (Amanze, R. 2022). Being forgiving to ourselves and others may have benefits for mental health that can protect against stress, anxiety and depression. Unresolved conflict can greatly affect our physical health and some studies are finding that the act of forgiveness may even lower the risk of heart attacks, improve cholesterol levels and the quality of sleep as well as reduce chronic pain and high blood pressure. Research on forgiveness is still in its early stages but is showing a lot of promise in this area.

MWMT Antidote 4: Meditative Contemplation on Forgiveness

Find a quiet place, sit down comfortably, close your eyes and place your awareness on the breath. Spend a few minutes just observing the in-breath and out-breath of your breathing.

Recognize in your mind any unpleasant feelings and be mindful of their presence. Do not push any of these feelings away or suppress them, accept them for what they are, let them arise. If you feel any unpleasant feelings, label them and say to yourself, "unpleasant, unpleasant."

Observe how these unpleasant feelings affect your body. Try to locate any areas of the body that feel tension, tightness or pain. You many feel sensations in any part of your body, such as the heart, stomach, back, head or chest. Label them as well and say to yourself, "tension, tension," "tightness, tightness" or "pain, pain," each time you come across a sensation in the body. As you observe them, notice how they arise, stay for a while and then pass away. Feel the sense of weight they have when you hold on to them.

Observe any thoughts in your mind that you are having. Notice if the same thoughts are repeated over and over. If you feel any emotions that are generated from these thoughts such as anger or resentment, label them and say them to yourself, "anger, anger" or "resentment, resentment."

Contemplate on the benefit of having a loving heart, one that is not burdened by unpleasant feelings or negative emotions. Imagine that all the negative feelings you have are released and you let them go. Imagine how light you would feel and how relaxed and peaceful you would become.

Understand that you may not feel at all right now like forgiving or letting things go and that is alright. Just be aware that the act of forgiveness is a process that can be trained slowly step by step in your mind. Imagine that the job of forgiveness is like unfinished business that you have in your mind and heart that may take some time.

Start with thinking about anyone who is really close to you, someone that you trust dearly. Allow your heart to open as wide as possible to that person. Imagine that you are with that person and observe how that person makes you feel.

Take a few deep breaths. As you inhale imagine the feelings that come to mind when you think about the person that is close to you. As you exhale, release any negative feelings you have for anyone that has hurt you. Observe how this makes you feel. Notice if any tension, pain or discomfort is released in the parts of your body that had them before.

Notice how any negative thoughts you have or negative emotions arise and pass away. They are not permanent. They are like passing clouds in the sky. Observe the connections between your thoughts and your emotions and the sensations you feel in your body. They too, arise and pass away and are not permanent.

Remember that our human life is full of people in the world that will often disappoint us, harm us or deceit us. When their minds are deluded with negative emotions, they are capable of evil acts, the same as we are. Just as they have hurt or harmed us by their thoughts, words or actions, so too have we hurt or harmed others and ourselves by our thoughts, words or actions. Contemplate on the fact that it is not the person that hurts us but their delusions and it is our aversion to what they have done or said that makes us suffer.

Direct your forgiveness first to all the ways that you have hurt or harmed others in the past. Feel the weight of the burden that you carry. Contemplate on all of those who you have hurt by your thoughts, words and actions, because of your anger, hatred, fear or confusion. Imagine the pain and suffering that they experienced. Feel your regret and sadness for what you have done and make the intention to try to not repeat this again in the future.

Gently repeat these words to yourself several times and direct them to each one of those that you have hurt:

I recall so many ways that I have hurt or harmed you, out of my own anger, hatred, fear or confusion.

I ask for your forgiveness.
Please forgive me.

Next, direct your forgiveness to all the ways that you have hurt yourself. Feel the weight of the burden that you carry. Contemplate on all the ways that you have hurt of harmed yourself through thoughts, words or actions, because of your anger, hatred, fear or confusion. Remind yourself what you have done. Remember the pain and suffering that you have experienced. Feel your regret and sadness for what you have done and make the intention to try to not repeat this again in the future.

Gently repeat these words to yourself several times and direct them to yourself:

I recall so many ways that I have hurt or harmed myself, out of my own anger, hatred, fear or confusion.

I forgive myself.

Finally direct your forgiveness to all those who have hurt or harmed you in the past. Feel the weight of the burden that you carry. Contemplate on all those who have hurt you through their thoughts, words or actions, because of their anger, hatred, fear or confusion. Remember the pain and suffering that you have experienced and the burden that you carry. Understand that you may not be ready to forgive them yet.

Gently repeat these words to yourself several times and direct them to each one of those who have hurt you:

I recall so many ways that I have been hurt or harmed by you, out of your own anger, hatred, fear or confusion.

To the extent that it is possible for me right now, I offer you my forgiveness.

To the extent that it is possible for me right now, I forgive you.

Forgive yourself if you are not able to completely forgive at this moment. Give yourself time to allow your heart to soften, open and become more accepting. Allow your mind time to release all the tension, anxiety and anger that you are holding. With this meditative contemplation on forgiveness, your ability to forgive and to let go of any negative emotions will slowly but surely develop.

Take a few deep breaths and on the final exhalation let everything go. Spend the last few minutes of your meditative contemplation just observing your breath, as you slowly become aware of your surroundings and open your eyes.

SYMPATHETIC JOY: OUR UNLIMITED SOURCE OF HAPPINESS

The more we practice sympathetic joy, the more
we come to realize that the happiness we share
with others is inseparable from our own
happiness.

— Sharon Salzberg

Along with compassion, loving kindness (metta) and equanimity, sympathetic joy or *mudita* in the Pali language, is one of the four *brahmaviharas*, those purifying Buddhist virtues that are immeasurable or boundless and which should be cultivated as much as possible. Sympathetic joy is the practice of feeling genuine, untainted happiness and joy for other people. It is to delight in the happiness and good fortune of others. This not only applies to our loved ones and those close to us but also to strangers and even enemies. It is used especially as an antidote to jealousy, envy, egocentric competition and for minds that have a tendency to compare or judge. It is very helpful also for those overwhelmed with greed and those that tend to delight in other people's misfortunes. Sympathetic joy allows us to reconnect to others by letting go of our ego and cultivating compassion by focusing on others rather than our own struggles and desires.

The Buddha said that sympathetic joy was the most rare and difficult mental state to achieve. We can see why. Most of us do not have a problem experiencing sympathetic joy when our children or family members and friends have success or when something great happens to them in their lives. It is more common but also not guaranteed to feel happiness when those people that are close to us have success. Think of the pride a parent feels in their child's success. But, on the other hand it can also be absent as we often find in sibling rivalry which can even cause a lifetime of unnecessary suffering.

The more difficult and challenging task is experiencing the same joy when a stranger or an enemy of ours has a stroke of luck or has success in their life. Most of us find it especially hard if those people are successful at something that has some relevance to us, such as a co-worker who gets the promotion that we thought we deserved. We may even at times feel a combination of being happy for them while at the same time somewhat envious or jealous. However, when we are negative, this robs us of our own happiness and has a tendency to isolate us. If we can understand the law of impermanence, we can also appreciate that whatever success and good fortune others experience, it is never permanent and this applies to all human beings. And if we let go of our strong attachment to the self, then we can appreciate that we are all interconnected. The doorway to *mudita* or sympathetic joy is compassion, when we realize that we are all one and the same, and experience the same ups and downs in life.

Finally, if we can realize that even those who have more than we have also suffer, we inevitably feel closer to them and much more connected. According to Buddhist science, there is no real wisdom in comparing our achievements to others, feeling jealous or envious or experiencing joy in others misfortunes. Practicing and experiencing *mudita,* releases us from these negative mind states. Our ability to cultivate this virtue often relates to how well grounded or centered we are in our lives and how we have internalized these Buddhist teachings in our minds.

In some ways sympathetic joy is a form of generosity that not only helps others but one that can also multiply our own happiness. The Dalai Lama once stated some years ago with some humor that "there are so many people in this world; it simply makes sense to make their happiness a source of our own. Then our chances of experiencing joy 'are enhanced six billion to one,' he says. 'Those are very good odds."

The science on sympathetic joy

Scientific studies have shown that offering sympathetic joy when someone shares their success with us, increases our happiness even more than the actual successful event and that it contributes to improving and strengthening relationships. Thus both sides benefit in increases in happiness. Research by Dr. Shelly Gable, a professor of psychological brain science at the University of California in Santa Barbara, has supported the idea that sharing in the joy of others good fortune has many benefits (Gable and Reis, 2010). If we are able to actively respond to others successes with enthusiasm, with our full attention and with excitement, this greatly benefits the person who shares the good news with us as well as strengthens our relationship with that person. It seems to be that it is the nature of our mind to be compassionate. We often receive the greatest joy and meaning in our lives from helping and sharing with others as opposed to only our self-centered pursuits which only reinforce our sense of separation from others.

Studies show that sympathetic joy meditation has all kinds of mental health benefits, including reducing jealousy and increasing compassion (Caioppo, 2019). Training our mind to produce a rush of joy whenever we see someone else succeed connects us to an unlimited source of happiness. At any given moment, someone, somewhere in the world, is feeling profoundly happy and enjoying success. If we seek out those people and allow ourselves to share their joy, we can conjure up a genuine sense of happiness through sympathetic joy meditation, even when our own life is not going as we would wish.

MWMT Antidote 5: Meditative Contemplation on Sympathetic Joy

To practice Sympathetic Joy meditation, sit in a comfortable and relaxed manner, with your back and head straight and close your eyes. Allow your facial muscles to relax and adopt a slight smiling facial expression. Take a few deep breaths. Let go of any concerns or preoccupations. For a few minutes, observe the breath as it moves through the center of your chest into the area of the heart.

Please be aware that sometimes during Sympathetic Joy meditation it is possible that opposite feelings such as envy, jealousy or resentment may arise. It is important to take these as signs that your heart is softening and adjusting, which can cause other emotions to be uncovered. Just try to be mindful of them, without any judgment and accept them with patience and compassion.

First extend sympathetic joy toward yourself, by recalling something wonderful that has happened to you, such as winning an award or meeting your partner. Imagine all the details during that moment and allow yourself to fully feel the joy that you experienced.

As you sit quietly, mentally repeat, slowly and steadily, the following phrases:

I am delighted with my good fortune
I celebrate my joy
It makes me very happy
May it continue in the future

Allow your heart to slowly soften and open up to the meaning of the words. Allow yourself to accept this celebration of joy and to feel that you deserve this good fortune.

After a period of directing sympathetic joy toward yourself, bring to mind someone close to you in your life, one who deeply cares for you. Then slowly repeat these phrases to them:

I am delighted for your good fortune
I celebrate your joy
It makes me very happy
May it continue in the future

As you say these phrases, again contemplate their intention and heartfelt meaning. Imagine something happening to them that makes them feel very happy and focus on the joy that they would feel. If any feelings of sympathetic joy arise within you, connect the feelings with the phrases so that the feelings may become stronger as you repeat the words.

Next, as you continue the meditation, bring to mind an acquaintance or stranger that you have neutral feelings for and slowly repeat these phrases toward them:

I am delighted for your good fortune
I celebrate your joy
It makes me very happy
May it continue in the future

With every repetition, be aware that even people that we do not know very well or do not mean anything to us, also experience good fortune and can be a source of joy for us.

Again, as you say the words to yourself contemplate their intention and feel their meaning.

Next, as you continue the meditation, bring to mind a person who you may dislike or even hate or have very negative feelings towards. Imagine them feeling truly happy and try to feel equally as joyful for their successes. Even though it may feel difficult to do this, find the courage and understanding and remember that everyone deserves to be happy and have success in life, even though they make mistakes and suffer from delusions of the mind, just like we often do. Slowly repeat these phrases toward them:

I am delighted for your good fortune
I celebrate your joy
It makes me very happy
May it continue in the future

With every repetition, be aware that even people that we do not like or have conflicts with us, no matter what they have done, they too, just like us, wish to be happy and deserve good fortune. Again, as you say the words to yourself contemplate their intention and feel their meaning.

Next, bring to mind the person who is close to you, the person who is neutral and the person who you dislike and imagine that they are all in a room together with you. Slowly repeat these phrases toward them:

I am delighted for our good fortune
I celebrate our joy
It makes me very happy
May it continue in the future

Finally, expand your sympathetic joy and include all the people on this planet and send them this wish, silently repeating it to yourself for the next few minutes:

I am delighted for your good fortune
I celebrate your joy
It makes me very happy
May it continue in the future

With every repetition, be aware that all people in the world have a common wish and that is to be happy and to enjoy success and good fortune, and you can celebrate their successes with them.

As you come to the close, take a few last breaths and with your exhalation, let the phrases of sympathetic joy go, along with all the images and feelings associated with them. Return to just observing your breath for a few minutes before you close your meditation session.

Try in the future, when someone shares a success with you, to listen and respond in an active and constructive manner. Give that person your full attention and direct eye contact and show them that you are interested in what they have to share. Express positive emotion by smiling and making enthusiastic comments such as, "that sounds great," "you must be so excited," or "your hard work is definitely paying off." Ask constructive questions to find out more about what they have achieved and comment on the positive implications and potential benefits of what they have shared with you. This will enhance their experience and your relationship with them, leading to increased happiness for both of you.

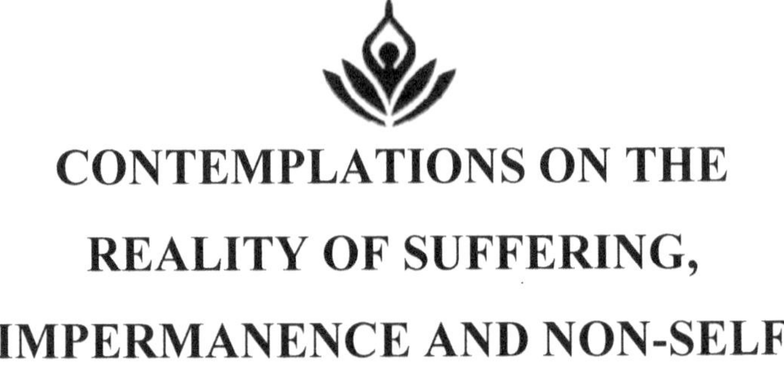

CONTEMPLATIONS ON THE REALITY OF SUFFERING, IMPERMANENCE AND NON-SELF

Within the stillness of meditation we see the
unreality of thought.

— Jack Kornfield

One of the most poisonous afflictions of the mind, as stated by the Buddha, is our ignorance of the true nature of our reality. It is our inability to see reality as it really is that is one of our greatest sources of our unhappiness. We have seen many examples throughout this book, where we often find it hard to accept that human life is inherently unsatisfactory, as we age, get ill and encounter death. We tend to turn a blind eye and resist this reality of suffering whenever we have the opportunity. The same applies to failing to accept the fact that everything in life, even our own bodies, our thoughts, feelings and opinions are not permanent and subject to change and pass away. This is what we have referred to in Buddhist science as the law of impermanence. Finally by grasping so strongly to a self that is only an illusion and constructed by our ego, we isolate ourselves from others and fail to realize that we are all intimately interconnected. We create unnecessary barriers and conflicts through this duality as we separate ourselves from others and from our external world. A lot of our pain and loneliness stems from this delusion.

No matter how much we try to fight against or show aversion to these natural laws of our reality (suffering, impermanence and non-self), the fact remains; they still remain part of the reality of our human condition. In fact, as we have seen, our failure to accept or internalize reality as it really is, takes away a lot of our sense of inner peace and happiness. We fail to realize that this ignorance or delusion is an affliction of the mind.

It becomes increasingly necessary then, for us to allow our mind to open up to the true reality that we as human beings are faced with. If we can overcome this ignorance and delusion, Buddhist science teaches us that we can eliminate all of our suffering. As we know, an intellectual understanding of reality is not enough. Through meditative contemplation though, we can gradually internalize these marks of our existence and let go of those mental habitual patterns that plague our minds and prevent us from seeing reality the way it really is. It has the promising potential to truly allow the happiness we already hold within, our very nature, to shine through and be uncovered and fully experienced.

MWMT Antidote 6: Meditative Contemplation on Reality

Find a comfortable, quiet place to be, either sitting on a chair on sitting on a cushion on the floor with your legs crossed. Ensure that your back is straight and allow your body to settle and become grounded. Imagine your body is a mountain, stable and solid, but at the same time relaxed and accepting.

When you are ready, close your eyes. Allow your facial muscles to relax and adopt a slight smiling facial expression. As you move your attention inside yourself, focus in on the gentle flow of your breath as it enters and leaves your body. Feel how you are connected to your breath as you inhale and exhale gently. Feel how you accept each breath and then let it go.

Move your attention from your breath and think about the First and Second Noble Truths, the truth of suffering and its cause, craving. Remind yourself that we as humans are subject to birth, aging, sickness and death and that no one can escape this reality. No matter how much success you achieve, or how much material wealth you have, you can never attain sustainable happiness. This should lead you to understand that true happiness is not found in the external world, it can only be found within your mind. Craving for something you desire or showing aversion to something you do not want, will only bring suffering.

Repeat this phrase silently to yourself:

"The source of happiness is not found in the external world. The source of happiness is only found in my mind. When I can let go of my craving, I will achieve inner peace and happiness."

Take a moment to reflect on this thought.

As you return to observing your breath, as you exhale, release this thought and let it go.

Now notice how each breath arises and then passes away. Your breath is a flow, a process that changes with each moment. Just like everything around you.

Move your attention from your breath and think about some of the objects in your room, such as a chair or table. These objects appear to be solid and permanent, but that is only an illusion.

If they are examined under a microscope they are actually made up of small moving particles of energy that are constantly in a state of flux and changing.

With time, even the chair or table and all objects will slowly break down and pass away. Even the largest mountains will erode and pass away with time.

Take a moment to reflect on this thought.

Focus your attention now to your body. Your body is also in a state of constant flux and change. Your body is different right now than it was a minute ago. Your cells in your body are in a constant process of change. They arise and pass away.

Ponder on the thought, that nothing in this world is really permanent.

No matter what you try to do, you cannot stop this flow of change. Sooner or later, even your body will age, break down and pass away. This is the natural order of things and this teaches you how precious each moment in your life really is.

No matter what you have accumulated in life, how many friends or family members you have, no matter how much money you have made, what work you have accomplished or what comforts you have in this world, you cannot hold on to them forever. Just like everything else, they will also one day pass away and you will have to let them go.

Repeat this phrase silently to yourself:

"Nothing in life that I hold is permanent."

As you repeat these words several times, pay close attention how your breath and body feel. Notice any changes or tension.

As you exhale, release this thought and let it go. Return to being aware of your breath and relax.
Even your thoughts and feelings are impermanent. They arise and pass away. When something negative happens to you, or you experience a tragedy in your life and you hold on to these negative thoughts and feelings, you only suffer.

Reflect on this thought with understanding and courage. As all things in life are impermanent including your thoughts and feelings, there is no need to hold on to them.

Repeat this phrase silently to yourself,

"Negative thoughts and feelings are not permanent. Holding on to them will only cause me to suffer."

As you repeat these words several times, pay close attention how your breath and body feel. Notice any changes or tension.

As you exhale, release this thought and let it go. Return to being aware of your breath and relax.

Now move your attention to how you see your "self."

Remember, your identity is created by your ego and only a construct in your mind. Your identity is subject to change. Nothing that you can call your "self" is really permanent.

Just like everything else in this world, your body and your mind are in a constant flux and always changing. There is no point then to become attached to your ideas, opinions and beliefs or to hold on to a concrete view of your "self" as all this is impermanent. You are like a wave in an ocean. You are interconnected with everything and everyone around you.

Reflect on these thoughts with an open awareness that you are a changing process interconnected with all that is around you.

Repeat this phrase silently to yourself,

"Nothing that I call my "self" is permanent. My body, identity, ideas, opinions and beliefs are all subject to change and there is no need to become attached to them."

As you repeat these words several times, pay close attention how your breath and body feel. Notice any changes or tension.

As you exhale, release this thought and let it go. Return to being aware of your breath and relax.

The opportunity to be kind, to forgive, to let go is right here, right now. The opportunity to give thanks and to be present is right here, right now.

The past is gone, the future is uncertain; the only time you have to live is in the present. Each moment is a chance for a brand new start. Holding on to things in the past that you cannot change or grasping on to how you want things to be in the future has no real purpose.

Reflect on this thought and silently say to yourself,

"I choose to live and be happy right here, right now."

As you repeat these words several times, pay close attention how your breath and body feel. Notice any changes or tension.

As you exhale, release this thought and let it go. Return to being aware of your breath and relax.

Now that you realize that nothing is permanent in this life, ask yourself, how would you like to spend your time that you have? What should you spend your time on right here, right now?

Reflect on this thought and silently say to yourself,

"My opportunity for growth, for healing and for letting go, is right here, right now."

As you repeat these words several times, pay close attention how your breath and body feel. Notice any changes or tension.

As you exhale, release this thought and let it go. Return to being aware of your breath and relax.

No matter how frustrated, angry, fearful, sad, lonely or stressful you feel right now, it is not permanent, just like everything else it arises in your mind and it passes away. All you have to do is let it go. This is the nature of all things.

Reflect on this final thought and silently say to yourself,

"I accept that nothing in this life is permanent. I have the opportunity to become a brand new person with each brand new moment that arises in my life."

Now it is time to bring this meditation exercise to a close. Take one last breath in and exhale and let go. Slowly bring your awareness back to your surroundings, and slowly open your eyes.

MANTRA MEDITATION: VIBRATIONS AND NEURONAL PATHWAYS

Mantras are passwords that transform the
mundane into the sacred.

— Deva Premal

Mantra meditation is the process of calming and focusing the mind using a phrase, word or sound which is called a *mantra*, by chanting it repeatedly out loud or silently to oneself. The word "*mantra*" originates from two Sanskrit roots, "*man*" meaning "mind" or "to think" and "*tra*" meaning a "tool" or "vehicle" to "protect" or "release." A mantra was intended to be used as a vehicle to release or protect the mind from all the suffering of life. Mantras go back thousands of years and originated in India and early examples are found in the ancient Vedic scriptures. The purpose of reciting a mantra, using the vibration of sound, is to relax the mind to achieve a state of restful alertness. Our entire world is in a state of vibration and when we are in a natural, resonant vibration, we are in a state of good mental and physical health.

Mantras can be used to open the channels of energy that have become blocked, allowing us to return to a natural state of resonance. The process of positive intention and internalized sound through chanting, oxygenates the brain, reduces heart rate and blood pressure and creates calm brainwave activity. The vibrations of vocal harmonics produced by mantra meditation have the power to change our brain chemistry, creating new neural pathways in the brain, altering its patterns and heightening our consciousness and awareness.

When we chant a mantra, we are creating the energy of vibration within ourselves and around us. As we repeat the sound or phrase over and over again, we begin to feel more connected with the universe. Our minds become quieter and calmer, and we start to see things differently. Chanting mantras also helps develop self-awareness, compassion, patience, love, and wisdom. The power of mantra meditation is its ability to focus our mind, and stop negative thought loops that often persist in our mind. One of the best uses of mantras is to prepare our mind for meditation, especially when we are very agitated, or under a lot of stress.

There are many mantras that have been used throughout ancient Buddhist societies and in many other religions and cultures. They have the ability to focus our agitated mind to achieve deep states of relaxation when repeated for long periods of time. They can even induce an almost hypnotic-like trance. In Buddhist science they are used to affirm our connection and resonance with the entire universe and with all beings.

Like prayer and affirmation, the repetitious use of mantras can have powerful effects on the mind, body, spirit, as well as our emotions. The mental benefits can include increased concentration, reduced stress and better balanced emotions and even improvements in memory and focus. Physical benefits can include lowering of the heart rate, reduction in blood pressure, and activation of the relaxation response which allows healing and regeneration to occur.

One of the most common and well known mantras is the one syllable mantra, Om or Aum. It is believed by many to be the first sound that originated on earth, the original primordial tone of the universe. Interestingly, astrophysicists have detected echoes of the Big Bang that happened at the beginning of time and the sound they detected was a deep humming sound very similar to that of the sound of Om. According to some sound theorists, when Om is chanted, it vibrates at the same frequency found throughout everything in nature. The Om or Aum mantra is composed of three sounds, A-U-M, pronounced "ah, "oo" and "mm." When Om is chanted and the three consecutive sounds are repeated slowly, it is possible to feel its entire vibration throughout the body, the "ah" felt first in the lower part of the body, then the "oo" in the center of the body and then the "mm" in the head area. Om chanting has been used for centuries for spiritual awareness and even for mental and physical healing purposes.

Another well known Buddhist mantra is "Om Mani Padme Hum" which translates to "praise to the jewel in the lotus." The lotus flower in Buddhism is considered pure as it has the ability to emerge from murky waters and represents the purity of speech, body and mind.

A final example, the Sanskrit mantra, "Lokah Samastah Sukhino Bhavantu" translates to "may all beings everywhere be happy and free." It is used as an affirmation or blessing of compassion, generosity and kindness for our self, and for all others. It reminds us of our own innate goodness or Buddha nature.

The science on mantras

Farmers in the village of Liangshan in East China's Fujian Province have claimed that playing soothing Buddhist mantras in the fields has helped them to dramatically increase their rice production. According to the Global Times newspaper and an article by the BBC (2014), after residents of the village installed 500 lotus-shaped speakers in the rice paddies that played mantras, rice output increased 15 percent, yielded larger grains, and suffered much less from pests, while the paddies nearby that played no music, yielded no such results. While there is no scientific consensus on what the effect of music can have on plants, researchers at the China Agricultural University have backed up this experiment saying that the sound waves that emanate from the rhythmic chanting of mantras have the ability to stimulate the pores on the leaves of a plant to assist it to absorb more sunlight. (BBC news article, 2014)

Another research study also found that various forms of music at different frequencies, especially rhythmic chanting music does have an influence and positive effect of seed germination, plant growth and development (Munasinghe et al. 2020). The rate of water that transpires out of leaves was found to be affected by sound waves. In 2014, in India when plants were exposed to chanting, they showed a maximum elongation of the shoot, maximum number of flowers and highest diameter of flowers (Chivukula and Ramaswamy, 2014). It has been postulated that using sound stimulation on plants could enhance disease resistance and even decrease the requirements for chemical fertilizers and biocides. It seems that sound certainly has a promising future in terms of enhancing the growth of plants.

There is some evidence from research studies that has found that practicing Mantra Meditation is effective in relieving stress and in bringing high blood pressure down (Lynch et al. 2018). Other reports have shown potential decreases in anxiety and increased immunity with mantra meditation but as of yet, they have not yet proved conclusive as they require more long-term studies to support this claim, but it does look very encouraging.

MWMT Mantra Meditation

Find a comfortable, quiet place to be, either sitting on a chair on sitting on a cushion on the floor with your legs crossed. Ensure that your back is straight and allow your body to settle and become grounded. When you are ready, close your eyes. Allow your facial muscles to relax and adopt a slight smiling facial expression. As you move your attention inside yourself, focus in on the gentle flow of your breath as it enters and leaves your body. Feel how you are connected to your breath as you inhale and exhale gently. Feel how you accept each breath and then let it go.

Choose any mantra of your choice, and either repeat the mantra out loud or to yourself. There is no set number of times you should repeat a mantra. Often, mantras are repeated a minimum of 108 times, as the number 108 has been a revered and sacred number for thousands of years. The symbolic number 108 has been used in mantra meditation to ward off planetary influence. This is because in astrophysics, the diameter of the sun multiplied by 108 gives the distance from the earth to the sun and the diameter of the moon multiplied 108 times also happens to give you the distance from the earth to the moon. In Ayurveda, its significance is found in that there are 108 *marma* points on the body, 107 on the physical body and 1 in the mind. Many people use a mala bead necklace that usually comes with 108 beads so you can use it to count and keep track of the number of repetitions you make.

You can also find many versions of mantras on the internet that you can recite along with. The important thing is that you focus on the word or phrase with its correct intent or meaning. In most cases, 10 minutes of mantra chanting is enough to quiet and relax your mind in preparation for your meditation session.

PROBLEM MEDITATION AND
SENSATIONS IN THE BODY

*We cannot solve our problems with the same
thinking we used when we created them.*

— Albert Einstein

We learned back in Part III that problems according to Buddhist science are only mental constructions; they are really only illusions of the mind. We also learned that rather than confronting them with aversion and negativity, it helps to analyze them as potential opportunities for inner growth. This can be difficult in the moment when we feel stress and anxiety while confronted with a difficult situation that we cannot immediately resolve. We should know by now that we cannot control everything that happens in our external world. Therefore, we are bound to encounter many instances when things do not go according to our wishes. The fact that things do not go according to our plans all the time should come as no surprise. Instead of pointing the finger on someone or some situation as the cause of our problems, we need to take responsibility ourselves because we are the ones that create the problems in our mind.

Each time our sense organs connect with our external world and we experience a non-pleasant feeling, we have a tendency to reject it and show aversion. As we battle with this non-pleasant feeling, it often develops into the mental construction of a problem and causes us to suffer. As our mind ruminates on non-beneficial thoughts, the ego gets involved and we begin to take things personally. A minor problem can sometimes escalate quickly into a full-blown catastrophe, and we can overreact in non-beneficial ways if we allow our mind the freedom to do so. When our minds clarity is agitated with a problem, it is almost impossible to see things clearly or to be happy. Negative emotions take over and we can often feel the stress manifest into tension or physical pain.

What do we do during times like this? Meditation techniques teach us that we should not suppress our problems but to allow them to surface so that we can observe them and peacefully accept them for what they are. As we learn to apply mindfulness to what is happening in our minds, we can see how a problem is created, how we have a tendency to grasp onto it, and how it is also possible to let it go.

Through meditation and mind training, we create space between our self and the thoughts and emotions that revolve around our problem. We begin to see that it is only a creation in our mind, one that arises and also passes away. Problems, just like thoughts and emotions are not permanent. When we come to this realization we learn that we need not hold onto our problems. Just as it is possible to create them in our own minds, it also becomes possible to let them go. As we learn to train our mind to be mindful of the thoughts, feelings and sensations that we experience, accept them and release them from our grasp, our suffering will significantly diminish. Negative thoughts will dissipate and clarity and peace of mind will return. We begin to see the problems we have for what they are and for the opportunities for growth that they offer. This is an important key to uncovering and experiencing more happiness.

MWMT Problem Meditation and Mindfulness of Sensations Instruction

Find a comfortable, quiet place to be, either sitting on a chair on sitting on a cushion on the floor with your legs crossed. Place a pen and paper in front of you, which you will use at the end of the meditation session. Ensure that your back is straight and allow your body to settle and become grounded. Close your eyes and allow your facial muscles to relax. As you move your attention inside yourself, focus in on the gentle flow of your breath as it enters and leaves your body. Feel how you are connected to your breath as you inhale and exhale gently. Feel how you accept each breath and then let it go.

Just observe your breath the way it is for a few minutes, not trying to change it or correct it, just leaving it as it wants to be. Let your breath find its own rhythm and its own pace. If your mind wanders to different thoughts or distractions, don't worry, that is the nature of the mind and it is normal, especially at the start of your journey. Just be aware when your mind wanders with peaceful acceptance and return again to observing the breath.

While keeping your awareness of your breath in the background and keeping your eyes closed, move your attention to the worst problem you currently have and that is taking most of your happiness away right now.

As you focus in on your main problem that you have, pay close attention to the thoughts that come up in your mind. Remember thoughts are always passing through the mind like clouds passing in the sky. They arise and then they pass away. They are not permanent. Try to be an observer of whatever negative thoughts are occurring at the moment when you think about your problem. When you come across any negative thoughts just let them be as they are, do not suppress them. Just let them arise with calm acceptance and realize that they will not last, they are impermanent just like all thoughts. Do not try to solve your problem in your mind or try to find solutions, just accept it as it is and let your mind let go of its hold on your problem.

Spend the next few minutes just observing your thoughts as you think about the problem you have.

Now, as you focus closer on your problem, pay close attention to the feelings it evokes. Do not try to push away these feelings and emotions or suppress them in any way. As these are usually unpleasant feelings, your mind has been habitually trained to push unpleasant feelings away with aversion.

But now, you want to investigate, you want to observe these feelings as they arise. Let them arise naturally and try to see them as they actually are. When you identify a feeling or emotion, label it right away. If you feel anger, repeat to yourself twice, "angry, angry", if you feel sadness, say to yourself, "sad, sad", if you feel fear, say to yourself, "fear, fear." Do the same thing for any other emotion that you feel when you think about the problem that you have.

As you observe the feelings you have, remember, that emotions also arise and pass away, they are impermanent.

Spend the next couple minutes observing and labeling your feelings as you think about your problem.

Now, when you identify an emotion you feel when you think about your problem; try to scan the body for any sensations that are associated with this emotion. You may feel tightness or tension somewhere in the body, or even pain, try to find the location of this sensation. You may feel sensation in the head, or chest or stomach or back or any other part of the body. If you do not feel a sensation right away, start from the head and scan the body from head to toe, going through each part until you find a place where you feel a sensation. Sensations can arise such as tension, pain, tingling, pulsing, warm or cold sensations or even sensations of pressure, vibration or any other type.

When you locate a sensation, whether it is pleasant or unpleasant, accept it as it is, placing no judgment on it whether it is good or bad, positive or negative; only let it be as it is. Just observe the sensations in your body with calm acceptance. Even these sensations arise and will pass away. They too, are impermanent.

Spend the next few minutes observing these sensations in your body and as you inhale, breathe in the sensations and emotions and as you exhale, release your hold, breathe them out and let them go.

Finally, now that you have let go of focusing on your problem, return your attention back to only your breath. Again, observe your breath as you inhale calmly and exhale calmly.

As it is time to slowly end this exercise, take one last deep in-breath and with your final out-breath, exhale and let everything go and relax. Slowly bring your awareness back to your surroundings and slowly open your eyes.

EQUANIMITY: THE TRUE TEST
OF WISDOM

Equanimity: It is evenness of mind, an inner
equipoise that cannot be upset by gain or loss,
honor and dishonor, praise and blame, pleasure
and pain.

— Bikkhu Bodhi

*A*s we were first introduced in Part III, equanimity or *upekkha* in the Pali language refers to a state of unshakeable mental stability. It is like a mountain; strong, solid, sturdy, unmoved and grounded, resistant to any of the harshest seasons or inclement weather patterns. We could really say that equanimity is the ultimate measure of success for Middle Way Mind Training because if we can achieve this prized state of mental composure, we can truly be prepared for anything that happens in our life. We will be ready to meet each experience bravely with even-minded acceptance and calm understanding. Equanimity is the last of the four immeasurables, the *Brahmaviharas*, prized by the Buddha. The other three we have already discussed in previous chapters being compassion, loving kindness and sympathetic joy. As we know, these divine abodes as they are often referred to, are highly valued in Buddhist teachings and meant to be developed to the greatest extent.

We can be sure that there will always be fluctuations in our life. In most cases, our mind is subject to a rollercoaster of emotions as we respond and react to life's events. Equanimity counters any indifference, anxiety or pride and has the ability to see things as they truly are. It takes into account the natural laws of human existence, including the laws of suffering, impermanence and non-self. Equanimity escapes the grasps of craving for pleasure, the aversion to what is unpleasant, and the unending demands of the ego.

In life we are constantly presented with its dualities. The Buddha taught that we are constantly being pulled in either direction by things or conditions we either want or hope to avoid. As a result, because we view life in a dual nature, we experience gain and loss, praise and blame, success and failure, along with pleasure and pain. Buddhist science teaches us that these states are all impermanent. Equanimity teaches us how to deal with them in a balanced, non-reactive, non-judgmental and non-resentful way. If we can understand that our tendency is to look at life through the lens of duality, we can gain some appreciation of equanimity. We usually view life's events as either one or the other. When we are pulled by greed to gain material possessions, we end up suffering because we find that they do not ultimately satisfy us and we can lose them just as easily. We can gain a member of the family by the birth of a child, but we can also suffer incredible loss when someone dies who is close to us. If our mind is pulled to grasp onto praise from others for something we have accomplished, and our ego lets it grow into pride and arrogance, we suffer because it too does not endure forever. We can quickly suffer when the exact opposite happens and we get blamed for something we have done. When we grasp onto pleasurable experiences, the feeling never lasts or we experience the pain or fear of losing something or not being able to regain it again. We can experience the giddy heights of success in our lives only to fail and lose everything at another time. In each of these situations, our minds are not in balance, we are not at peace, because we allow our mind to be pulled in one direction or to the other.

For these reasons, equanimity is one of the most difficult states for our minds to attain. Because the pulling forces are so strong, we allow our ego to engage and take over and we fall into the trap of believing that we are in control of everything that we do.

We also tend to take things very personally when events occur in our external world. We can suffer when it rains on our wedding day even though there is no way to control that occurrence. It is like we live within two different realities. One reality is that we take things personally; the other reality is that the experience is often out of our control and is impersonal because we had absolutely nothing to do with it.

Let me offer a few more examples. We may be a parent and our child is a drug addict. He or she comes home high on drugs and lies to us and even steals from us which can deeply hurt our feelings. We take it extremely personally because it is our child and we feel it is our fault for the condition. The other reality is impersonal as we cannot guarantee no matter how well we raise our children that they do not end up with difficulties like this. On top of that, it is well known that addicts in desperation will lie, steal and do anything to get their drugs.

We may be at work and our boss starts yelling at us for no reason, and we take it personally and as a result suffer the entire evening. The alternate reality is that our boss is dealing with a bad divorce and is frustrated and angry with his situation and is lashing out at us only to vent his anger. Again this is out of our control.

Our partner decides to leave and tells us that he does not love us anymore and has fallen in love with someone else. We take it very personally; our mind may even convince us that we are not good enough. The other side of the reality is that we cannot control what happens in life sometimes, whether our partner meets someone else. It is not our fault and may have absolutely nothing to do with us at all.

A final example is a boy who is in a foster home and has to deal with the reality that his mother suffers from substance abuse, has become a prostitute to support her habits and because of her poor mental health had to give him up for adoption. The boy believes that it is his fault and he is not worthy to be loved and convinces himself that is why he was given away. In one way this situation is very personal because it has affected his whole life and affected his self-worth. The other reality is very impersonal; his mother's problems have nothing to do with him at all.

The way to handle these situations, even though they are all very difficult to accept calmly, is to change our perception in a way that it matures and sees reality the way it really is. We need to first acknowledge that we often live in two different realities. We need to ask our self how our situation is personal and how it can also be seen as impersonal. We need to analyze our feelings and assess if we are only being influenced by our emotions that are telling us a story that is far from reality.

We tend to think that the world revolves around us, but the other reality is that it really does not. Buddhist science teaches us that we are interconnected with the world and with all other beings. The more we can mature in our perception, the less personally we take each experience and the more we can see the other side of reality. If our mind pulls us in one direction, we need to release our grasp and avoid making up stories, such as, "I am great," or "I am someone special," when someone praises us or when we experience success. On the other hand, we should also not fall in the trap of thinking that "I am useless or "I can never do anything right" when someone blames us or when we fail. All the stories that our mind constructs cause us to grasp onto a false narrative that in reality is impermanent and will not last. This kind of behavior will only lead to suffering in the future. It is much wiser when we receive praise to appreciate it, but not to hold onto it and realize that it too will not last and will pass. The same goes when we are ridiculed, blamed or laughed at. With equanimity, we do not take these things personally, whether they are positive experiences or negative. Both will pass in the mind as they are both impermanent.

The realization of the reality that one day we will not be so great, will not be invincible, will not be so beautiful anymore, or will not be so idolized or loved, is often difficult to accept. People who experience a lot of fame, wealth or success and lose it, often suffer bouts of alcoholism, drug abuse and other vices, as they cannot deal with this reality.

Like a glass of water that is clear, pure, refined and holds no impurities, with equanimity we see through the nature of reality. Middle Way Mind Training guides us so that we can become detached from the mind states that make us suffer and that sway us from one direction to the other. With equanimity, comes eradication of defilements that disturb our mind so we can achieve inner peace and happiness.

Training our mind contributes greatly to the cultivation of equanimity. Any mental training exercise that develops our ability to be directly aware and conscious of the changing and unsatisfactory nature of human existence, that everything arises and passes away, and that serves to connect us together, makes us much less vulnerable to be shaken up by the pleasant or unpleasant aspects of life.

We need to realize both intellectually and internally the true wisdom of the phrase "this too will pass." We can then realize the futility of attempting to grasp onto what we cannot hold onto forever. We learn with equanimity that we are all interconnected, that we all have in common the struggles and suffering that characterize human existence and we no longer need to get entangled with the stories that our minds and ego tell us. If we understand equanimity, we accept whatever comes.

This does not mean that we should go through life being apathetic and emotionless, nor does it mean complete detachment and to just withdraw and not engage in anything. We need not be like Dr. Spock in the Star Trek series and be void of any human emotion. It is just that we should experience life with the cleanest emotions, those that are beneficial to us and others around us. Some may argue that through this process of equanimity or position of neutrality, we lose our human nature because we are not allowing the other sides of our emotions to be freely expressed like anger, hatred, fear, greed or jealousy. However, according to Buddhist science, in reality, those non-beneficial mental states are all just delusions in our mind, and do not reflect our true human nature. What truly makes us human, are the beneficial emotional states of mind such as love, generosity, gratitude, patience, kindness, forgiveness and joy. Are these not the true aspects that really make us who we are?

How do we develop equanimity? Through the meditation of observing the breath, through mindfulness meditation, compassion meditation and through all the contemplative meditation techniques we have discussed that are antidotes to agitated mind states. Understanding the theory behind them is not enough. We need to train the mind to internalize them in order to allow this transformation to occur.

Equanimity is really the measure of whether Middle Way Mind Training is working. If we prevent craving, be mindful of our sense doors and not allow greed, anger and delusion to develop and see reality as it really is, then we will not let things entangle our mind. As we know, it is our agitated and untrained mind that leads us to making non-beneficial choices in our thoughts, emotions and actions. If we learn not to overreact emotionally every time we experience a tragedy or painful event, or get overcome with greed or envy when someone has more that we do, then we approach life with equanimity. The benefit to us is that we achieve inner peace, and our happiness and compassion shines through. Equanimity, according to Buddhist science, is really the ability to achieve an elevated and balanced mind state which is the true test of wisdom. Equanimity is the key to the end of our suffering, which opens the door to experiencing happiness.

SUMMARY OF MIDDLE WAY
MIND TRAINING

I will teach you the Truth and the Path leading to
the Truth.

— The Buddha

As we come to the end of Part V of this book about practical exercises for Middle Way Mind Training, it is a good time now to summarize the key teachings in Buddhist science that we have learned throughout our journey into our understanding of happiness. It is worthwhile to spend some time on each concept to ponder its importance.

Here is an overview in point form:

- Everything we do in our lives, we do to be happy and to avoid suffering.

- Happiness is a state of mind that is not dependent on our external world but is inherent to our inner nature.

- In order to transform our mind, we need more than just an intellectual understanding. We need to apply our knowledge and experience it internally by training our mind through contemplative meditation.

- Everything that we experience begins through contact of our six sense doors with our external world (sight, smell, hearing, taste, touch and thought).

- Initial contact of our sense organs with a sense object in our external world, creates either a pleasant, unpleasant or neutral feeling, which if unguarded can often lead to craving, aversion or delusion.

- The three root causes of our suffering stem from greed, hatred and delusion.
- We are not our thoughts, as thoughts are often distorted through our sense doors by our ego, feelings, emotions, memory and perceptions. Believing all our thoughts and the stories our mind tell us, lead us to react in ways that are often not beneficial to ourselves or to others, and to not see reality the way it really is.
- We prevent our ability to experience happiness by grasping on to non-beneficial emotions such as greed and hatred that cloud our inner nature and cause us to suffer.
- These non-beneficial distorted states of mind are due to craving for pleasant experiences, aversion to unpleasant experiences and ignorance of our true reality.
- We spend far too much time dwelling on the past or dreaming and worrying about the future. Happiness is only found in the time that we are living and that means right now in the present moment.
- According to the Buddha's First Noble Truth, the truth of suffering, we need to understand the reality that there is always an undertone of dissatisfaction or suffering in human life as we are subject to birth, aging, sickness and death.
- The Buddha's Second Noble Truth teaches us that the cause of our suffering is craving.
- The Buddha's Third Noble Truth states that if we can eliminate craving in the mind, then we can eliminate suffering.
- The Buddha's Fourth Noble Truth reveals that there is a way to achieve this goal. It is called the Eightfold Noble Path or Middle Way, which we can develop to achieve lasting and sustained happiness. It involves cultivating morality, concentration of the mind and wisdom.
- Middle Way Mind Training is a method that is based on Buddha's Noble Eightfold Path and that extracts all its necessary elements and places them in a practical and logical program for us to follow.

- Through cultivating each of the 8 Foundational Principles of Middle Way Mind Training we can all dramatically increase our level of happiness.

- We need to cultivate a solid ethical or moral foundation. This includes ensuring our speech does not harm others and that we mindfully listen to what people are actually saying (The First Principle), that our actions do not harm ourselves or others (The Second Principle) and that we engage in meaningful work that benefits all of us (The Third Principle).

- We need to direct our efforts to cultivate and maintain wholesome mind states while abandoning and preventing unwholesome ones (The Fourth Principle). We can do this through Mindfulness meditation, Compassion meditation (Metta) and Meditative Contemplations such as Generosity, Gratitude, Patience, Forgiveness, and Sympathetic joy that serve to act as antidotes to negative unwholesome mind states and as mind training exercises to reinforce and develop our positive wholesome states.

- We need to concentrate and focus our mind (the Fifth Principle) so we can calm our "monkey mind" which brings clarity to our thoughts, emotions and actions. One of the most effective ways to accomplish this is through the Meditation of Observing the Breath.

- We need to develop a non-judgmental bare awareness, which we call Mindfulness. (The Sixth Principle) Mindfulness meditation trains our mind to slow down to create space for us to observe so we can free our selves of habitual emotions and uncontrollable non-beneficial reactions. It allows us to see reality the way it really is in the present moment, without grasping to the past or the future. We need to be mindful of our entire experience. This includes training in mindfulness of what is happening in our body, what feelings we experience and what cognitions and thoughts we construct. As we cultivate mindfulness step by step, we will develop a deeper insight into the nature of reality.

- Mindfulness will lead us to be able to view reality as it truly is (The Seventh Principle). We need to have clarity in our view on reality. As we observe our thoughts, emotions, feelings and movements of the body we start to see that the things that we initially thought were stable, controllable and satisfying turn out to be impermanent, unsatisfying, unpredictable and unmanageable. We come closer to seeing the real truth of suffering, and then with time, we can see that things are unsatisfying, impermanent and contain no-self. This right view of reality brings us wisdom and peace of mind.

- In order to achieve wisdom, we must not only have the right view of reality but also hold the right intentions (The Eighth Principle). Our intentions should be based on goodwill and we should avoid any thoughts of attachment, hatred or harmful intent. Mindfulness meditation, Compassion (Metta) meditation, and Contemplative Meditations as antidotes for any negative thoughts will help us maintain the right intentions.

- Wisdom in Buddhist science means to see reality without ignorance or delusion, the way it really is and not what we want it to be. It involves understanding and internalizing the meaning of suffering, impermanence and non-self.

- All things in life are impermanent so there is no use in grasping on to them. This will only cause us to suffer.

- Our "self" is an identity that is constructed by our ego. In Buddhist science it has no real true substance and considered just a delusion. There is nothing about us or what we are composed of that we can identify as our self. Holding on to what we believe is a concrete self that is constantly changing and impermanent is futile and will only cause us to suffer.

- Buddhist science and Quantum Mechanics agree that we are all interconnected to each other and the world around us. We are more like waves in an ocean. Reducing our emphasis on our "self" brings us closer to this realization of our reality. The more we de-emphasize our self or become less selfish, the more we become happier and feel our connection to others and the world around us.

- All of the 8 Foundations of Middle Way Mind Training need to be cultivated and maintained for lasting and sustainable happiness.
- It is recommended to train in the core meditations; Meditation of Observing the Breath, Mindfulness Meditation and Compassion (Metta) Meditation daily in our meditation practice.
- We need to be aware of the five obstacles to meditation and not allow them to become hindrances to our meditation practice. These are, the wanting mind, the not-wanting mind, the slow and drowsy mind, the restless mind and the doubting mind. Remember, these are states of mind that are impermanent, they arise and pass away and can be eliminated by various meditations and meditative contemplations.
- We need to ensure that we develop each of the Middle Way Mind Training Foundational Principles by following the recommended meditation exercises for each.
- We should utilize the Contemplative Meditation exercises as antidotes to negative emotions. For example, if we have a mind full of anger or hatred, we apply Compassion (Metta), if we have a mind of greed, we apply Generosity. It we find that we are complaining about life often, we apply Gratitude. If we feel that we have no success in our life, apply Sympathetic Joy. Remember, all these negative mind states are impermanent and with practice can be transformed to positive and beneficial ones.
- Through Middle Way Mind Training we can ultimately cultivate a mind of equanimity, the calm even-minded acceptance to every experience that presents itself in our lives, whether positive or negative. A mind of equanimity will eliminate our suffering.
- Middle Way Mind Training can help us to eliminate non-beneficial mind states such as hatred, greed, envy and fear and to accept and internalize the nature of our true

existence. This will allow us to access our true inner nature, which is peace and compassion.

- If we can access our inner nature, this will uncover and allow us to experience sustained happiness.

PART VI

REAL WORLD APPLICATIONS OF MIDDLE WAY MIND TRAINING

Get the inside right. The outside will fall into
place.

— Eckhart Tolle

FEEDBACK: HOW WILL I
KNOW IF MWMT IS WORKING?

All that we are is the result of what we have
thought, what we think is what we become.

— The Buddha

Now that we hold the necessary tools according to Buddhist science to transform our mind and achieve lasting and sustainable happiness, we need to take a realistic approach and re-evaluate what we have learned and apply it to what we call our real world. After all, the average person is not destined to become a monk nor has the luxury to meditate in an isolated cave, free from any distractions and worldly influences for the rest of their life. We need a pragmatic and down to earth approach to achieve happiness. Amidst the daily challenges that life presents, we need to first realize that most of us are far off the middle of the road that leads us to our destination. Middle Way Mind Training (MWMT), provides a way to allow us to get back onto that road to happiness. Meditation teaches us not to set any goals, as the mere setting of a goal, such as achieving happiness, changes our minds into "wanting minds" that crave a future that is away from the present moment. However, we do need some way to monitor and evaluate our progress, otherwise many of us may quit before we even have a chance to experience any beneficial results.

A common question asked after we focus our training on all the foundational principles and put them into practice is how will we know if MWMT is really working? One of the hindrances to our practice is the "doubting mind" and this common question is a prime example. It is especially difficult for most us to be absolutely certain about what we are doing at the beginning of our journey. The reality is that we need some measure of progress so that we have the encouragement to continue because our minds are often attached to the realization of goals.

The Buddha approached his quest to eliminate suffering by adopting a mind similar to a scientist and his teachings were based on a scientific method. If we are to approach the science of the mind it should not be any different. Initially, we should make an observation, then pose a question, propose a hypothesis, make a prediction based on that hypothesis, perform an experiment to test our hypothesis, and then analyze the results so that we can come to a conclusion. Similarly, the Buddha first made an observation (There is much suffering in the world), then asked a question (What is the cause of suffering?). He then proposed a hypothesis and made a prediction (Training our mind to let go of craving will eliminate suffering). He tested his hypothesis by experimenting on himself by following his Noble Eightfold Path. Finally, after analyzing the results, he made a conclusion; that craving is the cause of suffering and by following his path we can eliminate suffering and achieve lasting and sustainable happiness (He achieved nirvana).

As we know, the Buddha advocated that we should not believe his words but experience his method for ourselves. Each time we endeavor to train our mind through Middle Way Mind Training, we are performing an experiment on our mind. MWMT should not be based on any kind of blind faith, but on reality. We need to monitor and analyze our results to provide feedback so we really know whether our efforts have provided the desired results. As our ultimate goal is happiness, we need to know what happiness really means. In the first three parts of this book, we learned that happiness is found internally, not externally and that it is something that we hold inside. It means a feeling that it true to our inner human nature, which is that of inner peace and compassion. As we peel away the layers of negative emotional mental formations, and let go of the cravings that obscure us from happiness, we begin to change and react differently to others and to the world around us.

As we progress in our personal experiment, and especially in the early stages, we often need some gentle reassurance that we are really on the right path. Instead of being obsessed with getting someplace fast during our meditation, which often slows progress, an open curiosity or ability to notice and appreciate small changes is healthy and can be very encouraging.

I have included a list of some common things that we may notice or become aware of as we progress with time in our MWMT meditative practice. We should not feel discouraged if we do not experience any or all of them right way. Even small changes amount to profound progress. For some, it may take many years or a lifetime to fully develop them all. Instead, throughout our journey, we should remain calm, accepting, patient and non-judgmental and our efforts are bound to be successful.

Common changes we may experience during MWMT:

- We become less bothered by things that have commonly annoyed us in the past.
- Our friends and family notice, even if we do not, that we are different and that we have changed, become less reactive, more relaxed and friendlier.
- We become more and more aware of our breathing, even outside of our meditation sessions and how this awareness brings us calmness.
- Initially breathing may feel boring when we observe it, but with time it becomes much more interesting.
- We become more mindful of new sensations in the body that we have never noticed before.
- We start to enjoy doing simple things in life, and we have less desire to grasp onto or desire big things.
- Our sense of concentration and focus improves with time and our mind drifts less into the future or past.
- We begin to notice more things in our outside world as we slow down our thoughts.
- Colors, shapes and the beauty of the world around us become more noticeable.
- We become more aware of our body and posture even outside of meditation.
- We begin to experience feelings of joy and appreciation much more often.
- We become less selfish and more concerned about others.

- We become more aware of our non-beneficial thoughts and thought patterns and realize that we do not need to keep thinking those thoughts.
- We come to a realization that we have a choice in whether we follow our thoughts or become prisoners of them.
- We become more aware of our intended actions earlier and we prevent non-beneficial actions to play out.
- We become more mindful of our speech and there are fewer instances when we regret what we have said.
- Instead of dragging ourselves to our meditation sessions, we begin to look forward to them and start feeling much more relaxed during them.
- When we start to enjoy our meditation, we will notice that time passes quickly rather than the initial feelings when our meditation session feels like forever.
- We begin to desire to meditate longer than we have initially and may even have a reluctance to end our session.
- We become more aware of the things about ourselves that we would like to change which may feel uncomfortable at first but is useful for our transformation.
- We begin to feel a softening of the heart with more warmth and openness.
- We become more open to new ideas and opinions other than just our own.
- We may begin to experience interesting or odd things during our meditative sessions such as unusual body and mind experiences, seeing patterns of light or feeling periods of extreme calm or bliss.
- We start to see a shift from the "wanting mind" that craves for progress to a more calmer and accepting mind that is not so bothered or obsessed about getting anywhere.
- We begin to understand and accept that we will have good meditations on some days and distracting meditations on other days and that there are ups and downs along our journey.
- We become more creative and better at problem solving.

- We may experience deeper sleep and more ease in falling asleep as we calm the mental chatter in our minds.
- We are less prone to stress and anxiety and the feeling of being overwhelmed.
- Our physical health often improves and we find we experience less days feeling sick.
- Our communication improves as we get more mindful of our thoughts and speech, which improves our relationships and connection with others around us.
- We become more adaptable to changes in our life and we become more patient and calm and able to embrace uncertainly much better.
- We find it easier to forgive others than before.
- We start to let go of our tendency to control things in our life and loosen our reign on how things should be.
- We are less frequently disappointed when things do not go according to plan and much more accepting and equanimous.
- We experience feelings of inner peace and happiness more often and we are able to show more compassion and empathy for others.

MWMT AND PSYCHOLOGICAL DISORDERS

I think Buddhism should open the door of
psychology and healing to penetrate more easily
into the Western world.

— Thich Nhat Hanh

One of the most exciting real world applications for Middle Way Mind Training is in its promising future to assist many psychological disorders that plague modern society.

Buddhist science originated with the Buddha's search for an answer to the problem of suffering, that which comes from a human life of birth, aging, sickness and death. The Buddha identified suffering to be associated with, aversion to things that we do not like, being separated from things that we do like and not being able to get what we want. Human life is unavoidably linked to situations which are distressing. In Buddha's second noble truth of the cause of suffering, his teachings describe the progress of mental distress and how through our senses we construct psychological defenses which lead to destructive mind states in response to afflictions.

When trouble occurs, we habitually seek distraction and comfort, initially in the form of aversion or attachment at the level of sensory contact with our external world. We have seen how we tend to build our reality in the mind and hence our self, through this process of attachment, and that it can take beneficial or non-beneficial forms. All these reactions are often habitual and form the basis of our mental being and how we respond to the world around us. They lead to mental formations which we often identify with and hold onto very strongly. These can lead us to

318

non-beneficial ingrained views and behaviors that can hurt us or others around us.

By training the mind to become aware of these processes without judgment and with acceptance, we gain profound and deep insight and can begin to observe these processes for what they are. We learn that there is no purpose to hold onto them as they are impermanent; just like everything, they arise and pass away.

Buddhist teachings and the experiential knowledge that comes from over 2500 years of study and practice has clearly much to offer by way of guidance for those working in the field of mental health. There have been a number of significant attempts to draw on Buddhist teachings and apply them to psychology and psychotherapeutic practice. Early Western theorists like William James and Carl Jung were very much influenced by Eastern thoughts and more recently we have seen an influx of techniques incorporating meditation and mindfulness, all of which have their roots in Buddhist science. They are now being used more and more to deal with a variety of mental health problems. Recently there have been various interventions that have come into prominence, such as Mindfulness Based Stress Reduction (Kabat- Zinn, 1990), scientifically shown to be very effective for stress and anxiety and Mindfulness Based Cognitive Therapy (Segal et al. 2001), which is gaining a lot of inroads into dealing with depression. Mindful eating (Aamodt, 2016) along with Compassion meditation (Salzberg, 1995) is being used to positively assist those who suffer from eating disorders and obesity to improve their relationship with food. New branches of psychology, such as Buddhist psychology (Tirch et al., 2016) and Buddhist Psychotherapy (Ennenbach, 2014) are emerging. Numerous research studies are currently being conducted using these methods, particularly on those that incorporate meditation and mindfulness techniques and the scientific results show much promise.

Middle Way Mind Training (MWMT) involves not just meditation, mindfulness and contemplative techniques. It cultivates all the other foundational principles that are deemed essential according to Buddhist science such as ethical behavior and the wisdom of reality. Digesting the meaning of each of the MWMT principles intellectually as well as experiencing them internally often has a positive effect on mental health.

While this book has focused primarily on understanding and increasing the level of happiness in our lives, many psychological disorders that cause immense suffering, may naturally become lessened or even resolved through this mind training process. This is not to say that MWMT should replace professional psychotherapy or psychological counseling. Many patients will always need professional supervision, guidance and counseling by experienced mental health professionals and many are incapacitated and require medication. However, the staggering growth rates of people suffering from stress, depression, anxiety, phobias, addictions and many other mental health problems in recent decades and the questionable effectiveness of drugs such as antidepressants to treat them, mean that novel approaches need to be considered and better researched as traditional methods of the past do not seem to be working as well as expected.

It does seem reasonable to believe that if our mind can be trained to resist being consumed by obtrusive thoughts, to see reality as it really is and to accept with calmness and patience every experience that we are confronted with, we will be much better equipped psychologically to deal with any difficult challenge that presents itself. As we learn to guard our sense doors and become aware of our entire thought process, we can learn to live more in the present moment instead of grasping to the past or future. We can train our minds to let go of non-beneficial mind states that bind us to habitual responses. A well trained mind has the resilience and wisdom to deal with our human condition and all the hardships, tragedies, and blessings that are a part of it, with equanimity and without succumbing to harmful mind states that are detrimental to our mental health.

According to Buddhist science, we are all considered emotionally unbalanced and delusional. We believe our thoughts and often let them control us and we certainly do not see or accept reality the way it really is. We are all caught in varying states of delusion and confusion. These states may differ in form or degree. This realization should allow us to better relate to those who suffer from high distress and have serious mental health issues, with a sense of compassion and understanding that arises from our shared human frailty. Buddhist science teaches us a view that encompasses a sense of commonality between all humans. Each one of us, whose mind is not prepared or trained, is vulnerable and each one of us is maybe only a step from falling into the extremes, into what society would call psychotic states of behavior.

The Middle Way Mind Training approach to improving mental health is based on becoming less caught up with maintaining our sense of identity and the world view that supports it. It is grounded in the importance of looking for the reality in things, shifting away from our rigid views and encouraging a much deeper connection with others and with the world around us. A person who has developed a mind that is mentally healthy is not self-centered or self-preoccupied, but has compassion and interest in the people around him or her.

Middle Way Mind Training offers an opportunity that no matter how far we may deviate from the middle of the road, no matter how deluded or psychotic our mind becomes in response to life's events and tragedies, there is always a way back. This comes with the realization and comfort that we already have everything we need to be happy and mentally stable and healthy; we just need to uncover it. As we already know, Buddhist science teaches that each one of us holds within an inherent nature, our inner core, or what is called Buddha nature. We can think of this as our default mode, that which makes us who we really are. With the training of the mind, we have the ability to access that inner core, unravel and let go of all the layers of disruptive mental formations so we can gain access to the very essence of our humanity, that which is inner peace and happiness.

MWMT AND PHYSICAL

HEALTH PROBLEMS

If you just allow your body and mind to rest, the
healing will come by itself.

— Thich Nhat Hanh

Throughout this book, we have focused primarily on the mental health benefits of Middle Way Mind Training, but naturally along with them, it is common to discover many physical improvements that often arise as well. While the goal of meditative contemplation should not be focused on just ridding ourselves of our physical health problems, we know that there is definitely a mind-body connection that leads to favorable results. The question that is often posed is whether training the mind can also heal our body. Often the body indirectly benefits when the mind becomes free of negative emotional states especially stress, anxiety, fear, anger, and depression.

We know that these mental states are linked to so many physical health problems. Many of them are risk factors to some of the most serious diseases that we have in society.

Chronic stress and anger are often cited as major risk factors for heart disease as well as inflammation of the heart muscles and the coronary arteries, due to the development of an unhealthy level of stress hormones. When we are stressed or angry, our body produces an influx of hormones that increases the heart rate and causes blood vessels to narrow. This often results in a temporary spike in our blood pressure. When this occurs often, damage to blood vessels, heart and kidneys may result.

Inflammatory Bowel Syndrome is a common chronic disorder that affects the large intestine and causes cramps, pain, bloating, and diarrhea or constipation. Often it can flare-up when those people are under stress. Those who suffer from IBS often experience mood disorders such as anxiety, chronic anger or depression, so there seems to be some link (Alhan and Ibiloglu, 2016).

Higher blood sugar levels and possibly even diabetes may be caused or affected by extreme stress. When we feel stressed, our body wants to make sure we have enough energy to deal with the cause of stress. As a result it releases more glucagon and adrenaline, as well as glucose, from our liver. Insulin levels fall, and growth hormones and cortisol levels rise, which make our body less sensitive to the insulin we do have. This means more glucose is available in our blood stream, and we have higher blood sugar levels. Consistently high blood sugar levels can be very detrimental to our health.

Stress can also alter the immune system and result in changes in its ability to fight off infections. For example, people who are under severe, long-term stress are much more likely to catch a cold when exposed to a virus than people under milder stress.

Those who suffer from stress or anxiety tend to turn to emotional eating or binge eating where they indulge in foods that are high in fat and sugar, in an attempt to make them feel better. In this way a habit of overeating can occur increasing the risk of the person developing obesity. Research also has shown that people with high levels of cortisol, weigh more, have a higher body mass index (BMI), and a larger waist compared to those that have lower levels of cortisol (Aamodt, 2016).

Stress, anxiety, fear and depression also have detrimental effects on sleep patterns and quality of sleep. Chronic insomnia may occur with difficulty in falling asleep or staying asleep or sleep apnea where there is a recurring collapse of the upper airway during sleep causing heavy snoring and choking episodes during the night.

Doctors are yet to prove the connection between stress and Alzheimer's disease, but stress is thought to cause inflammation of the brain, making it more susceptible to these kinds of health issues in general. Stress is also associated with depression, which is known to increase the risk of developing Alzheimer's.

People under constant fear, stress and worry often develop ulcers, tension headaches and migraines, muscle aches and pains and even breathing difficulties such as asthma. The stress response as well as depression is linked to increased body pain, increased tension in the muscles, increased perception of pain and can make existing pain even worse. Chronic fatigue is also very common, with decreased interest in sex and decreased appetite.

In this book, we have presented much research on meditation and mindfulness and its positive effects on stress, anxiety, fear and depression. We have described how Buddhist science deals with these non-beneficial mind states. As we learn to train the mind with Middle Way Mind Training to cultivate inner peace and equanimity, our reaction to life's events will not lead us to hold on to them. We learn to let them go so they do not have a chance to develop into destructive mental patterns.

With meditation and mindfulness, our sympathetic nervous system calms down, along with heart rate, respiratory rate and blood pressure (Deepak et al. 2012). As we reduce the stress on the mind, headaches and migraines are often reduced. Our sleep patterns and quality of sleep improve. By training the mind to understand and deal with stress, anger and anxiety more effectively, we reduce our risk of coronary artery disease, strokes and cancer, which are the leading causes of death in our society. Even mindfulness of eating has shown to be very effective to curb cravings for food, reduce emotional eating and binge eating, as we become more aware of our eating behaviors and habits (Aamodt, 2016). Scientific studies on mindfulness and meditation on chronic pain management have shown positive results (Kabat-Zinn, 1990). It seems that pain is worsened when we are under stress or suffer depression and anxiety and assisting these conditions with mind training using mindfulness and meditation techniques, may lessen the perceived pain or even increase our perceived pain threshold.

As we experience pain during mindfulness we begin to see that it is not permanent, that it arises and passes away, and our aversion to it, often makes it a lot worse than it actually is in reality. This gives hope to those that suffer from fibromyalgia, rheumatoid arthritis and chronic musculoskeletal pain.

Finally, there are a small but growing number of studies that are looking at the effects of meditation on telomere length, which is a biological marker of cellular aging. Telomeres are structures made from DNA sequences and found on the ends of chromosomes. They are affected by many lifestyle factors such as stress and tend to shorten as we age. The shorter the telomeres, the greater association with bad health outcomes such as cancer, heart failure, diabetes and coronary heart disease. Meditation seems to help to preserve or lengthen telomeres (Jamieson, 2017). Though in its early stages, this research may demonstrate that meditation may help slow the aging process and may protect the brain from normal cortical thinning which is a sign of cognitive aging, as well as improving cognitive performance in the elderly.

We cannot help but notice how the mind is intimately related to the body and that methods which can train the mind to alleviate mental health problems, will definitely benefit our physical health. Understanding the mind through the help of Buddhist science and Middle Way Mind Training and putting the foundational principles into practice is the key to developing a health mind for a healthy body.

MWMT AND RELATIONSHIPS

In most of our human relationships, we spend
much of our time reassuring one another that our
costumes of identity are on straight.

— Ram Dass

$\mathcal{O}$ ne of the most common reasons why we seek out the help of a therapist is because of problems in our relationships. Whether they involve a romantic partner, a family member, co-worker or a friend, relationships often become strained and frequently lead to disagreements, bitter conflicts, separations and even divorce. These events end up causing us a lot of suffering in our lives. It is certainly beneficial to take a look at how Middle Way Mind Training can be applied to these kinds of troubling situations and how Buddhist wisdom can be used to assist them.

As we know, our untrained mind tends to make the mistake of searching for happiness outside of ourselves in our external environment. We have learned from Buddhist science that sustained happiness cannot be found there, yet we still mistakably believe that grasping onto material wealth and success can fulfill this need. In the same way, we develop relationships with people and make the mistake and look to them to make us happy. When we train our minds, we learn that we already have everything we need to be happy. Our unhealthy attachments can then be alleviated and we can allow our innate compassion and happiness to extend out to our relationships instead of trying to extract happiness from them. Many of the conflicts we have in our lives are due to our desire to be fulfilled through our lovers, friends, and family. This is not a wise or sustainable path and this leads to constant frustration, disappointment and suffering. If we can realize and internalize this, we don't have to fall into what are often called needy or clingy relationships, those where we become addicted or dependent on others for our happiness.

Striving for perfect relationships is impossible. The more we set high unrealistic expectations of how our relationship should be, the more we are bound to suffer. We need to accept the other person and reality as it is, so that we can experience love and acceptance from moment to moment. If problems arise, we deal with them when they present themselves. Buddhist philosophy teaches that suffering is caused by attachment and craving. The same can be said of our intimate relationships. Instead of embracing what the moment brings to the relationship, what often happens is that fear arises, and we become terrified of losing the relationship or our partner. This attachment often negates the presence of love that exists in the present moment. There is a big difference between needing someone and consciously making a choice to be with them. When we consciously choose to be with someone, we appreciate and embrace their presence, but we also don't mind their absence as well.

A solid moral foundation is needed for happiness and also for a trusting relationship, whether with a friend, family member or romantic partner. As most relationships break down due to poor communication, it is important to ensure that we are mindful of our speech so that we do not hurt others. Effective and honest communication is essential to relationship success. Many couples seek out help with communication. We know that using the right speech and active listening dramatically benefits communication and they are both important for happiness in relationships. Following the ethical foundational principles of Middle Way Mind Training will definitely build quality relationships and friendships that will be based on trust, mutual appreciation and effective communication and listening skills. Misunderstandings will then be avoided, senseless arguments will be reduced and a sense of harmony will be instilled. Relevant debates are healthy and important for self-expression in relationships but when they lead to heated or spiteful arguments, they can be very hurtful and serve no real purpose. Couples should refrain from lies and gossip as well as using profanity, harsh words or name-calling. It is useful, before we speak or react, to utilize the Pause of Wisdom that we discussed earlier in the book. As we develop our skills in mindfulness and meditation, before we say something we learn to be aware of how we are actually feeling, so we can express ourselves peacefully, with respect, instead of reacting with negative emotions such as anger.

Everyone who is in any kind of relationship enjoys feeling appreciated for their efforts, so it is very important to regularly show our gratitude and not to take the other person for granted. Whether we have a demanding career, or whether we take care of the home, it is important to feel valued for the things we do that make our partner's life more enjoyable. Expressing appreciation regularly can ensure that both sides feel more noticed in the relationship, even if it is just for something simple.

One of the main challenges to relationships is that situations in life are always changing. As much as we would like to have control of our external environment, we certainly do not. Not only do things in life change, but we ourselves change. Our ideas, plans, feelings, thoughts and opinions are not permanent. If we hold on to the expectation that things will also be the same as they have been before, we are setting ourselves up for a lot of disappointment. We can see this very clearly in the classic evolution of most romantic relationships. When we fall in love, we assume that the euphoria we feel at the beginning will last forever. When bad things happen, we become disappointed and try to hold on to the good moments. Each relationship has its happy moments; however, there will inevitably always be some issues that arise. Initially, we see our partner through the lens of rose-colored glasses and are often blinded by the true reality. That stark reality strikes us usually a bit later after the initial honeymoon period is over, when we discover that our partners are not perfect after all and come with their own individual faults and imperfections. It is inevitable that after some time in marriages or relationships that both people change. It is certainly not realistic to expect that people will stay the same throughout their entire life.

People age, grow, adapt, and are fundamentally changed in various ways by their life experiences. This is the law of impermanence. Some of what used to seem so important might begin to not even matter anymore. Change does not mean that long term relationships cannot continue working. Change in a healthy relationship can even be exciting and can breathe a breath of fresh air into the relationship. It just means that we need to make the intentional effort to spend some time rediscovering one another and talk with each other and discuss how we see the future evolving. There is a need to develop tolerance for our emotions and to instead develop curiosity and an ability to just be with them and mindful of them. That on its own will decrease their intensity. In many cases marriages and friendships evolve to a point where there are so many differences which we refuse to accept. It then becomes very challenging to stay together anymore and many of us simply give up. However, what often happens even after a divorce and after finding a new partner, we just fall into the same trap again. Buddhist science teaches us that the solution is to realize that true sustainable happiness can only be found within ourselves, not with a new partner.

Another factor that gets us into trouble is holding tightly onto our identity. It is amazing how often we feel the need to prove something to each other. We hold on so tight to our opinions and views, often isolating ourselves in the process. We need to be right; we need to have the answers to everything, when in reality we are far from understanding the answers to life. When we learn to let go of our identity, that which is just a construct of our ego, and embrace our imperfections and our failures and flaws, things don't seem as unmanageable as before as we find a common bond. This is where the Buddhist concept of non-self can help us in realizing that we are a part of a whole, interconnected world and none of us are as special as we make ourselves out to be. We all experience suffering throughout life, no matter who we are, how wealthy or successful or famous we are and that is common to all of us.

Training the mind in meditation, mindfulness and meditative contemplations such as generosity, gratitude, forgiveness, loving kindness and sympathetic joy, will combat negative emotions and instill beneficial behaviors. These techniques will develop our ability to guard our sense doors and will not allow negative non-beneficial emotions to escalate to a point where relationships and friendships could be threatened.

Middle Way Mind Training will lead to acquiring the wisdom to truly understand the nature of suffering, impermanence, and non-self and with time will eliminate our attachments to our opinions, egoistic behavior and selfish motives. Placing our partner, relative or friend ahead of our interests more often, will lead to the development of compassion, empathy, loving kindness and mutual respect. As we let go of arrogance and curb our pride, we eliminate factors that often lead to resentment, anger, and disharmony in relationships, and we generate equanimity. We react more even-minded, avoid overdramatizing situations and find the strength to remain level-headed even during difficult times in a relationship. We become much more accepting and we confront problems as they are, not as we often make them out to be. One thing we can take from Buddhist science is how important it is to be aware of our habitual reactions to things that annoy us and perhaps to challenge them if they are really true to reality. The beauty of training the mind to cultivate this awareness is that no matter how lonely, angry, frustrated or unsatisfied we are in a relationship, there is always hope because these feelings are not permanent, they can pass away or become beneficial ones that have the power to transform a bad relationship into a happy and flourishing one once again.

MWMT IN THE WORKPLACE

The best way to find your self is to lose yourself
in the service of others.

— Mahatma Gandhi

There is certainly much that businesses and companies can learn from Buddhist teachings and from Middle Way Mind Training. Many large corporations face serious problems such as high turnover, high absenteeism and suboptimal productivity. There are so many employees today that are experiencing a lot of dissatisfaction and unhappiness in their workplace. They often feel frustrated, unmotivated and stressed which is contributing to a trend in cases of burnout that are reaching epidemic proportions. Employees often report unfair treatment, unreasonable workload, low autonomy, lack of social support and poor communication from management. As a result, team work, productivity and goal setting suffers.

A growing body of evidence indicates that there are now unprecedented levels of employee turnover along with high absenteeism which are often due to stress and burnout. As a result, companies are now much more aware of the costs associated with an unhealthy workforce. The number of sick days due to health issues has increased dramatically in the past decade and mental health is now one of the leading causes of sickness-related absences from work.

It seems reasonable that employees today demand a lot more from their jobs than just a paycheck. I am sure that we know this already as receiving a raise or a bonus for our extra efforts is great but the feeling fades quickly with time and will not be enough to keep us happy in our job. Making money and earning a living is certainly important and motivates us to some degree but our work needs to also have a purpose and benefit others. This attribute leads to greater satisfaction, fulfillment and personal happiness. We all need a strong sense of purpose in our work along with meaningful interpersonal connections with our colleagues and managers. We also want to feel a sense of shared identity and to be valued by our managers and the organization.

In recent years, many innovative global companies have or are in the process of introducing corporate wellness programs which include meditation and mindfulness training. They have discovered that they benefit wellbeing and decrease stress levels. Many have confirmed that this investment is paying off as their employees have demonstrated that they can focus and concentrate better, are more resilient to stress, have less absenteeism and reduced turnover. In addition, they are finding that they are more open to new ideas as well as becoming more compassionate and empathetic towards their colleagues and managers. It stands to reason that if employees feel good in their environment and are not stressed, they will be much more motivated and their productivity naturally will increase.

Resilience to stress and the ability to deal with difficult situations is critical to happiness and wellbeing. During stressful periods, employees with high levels of resilience will be able to persevere and remain engaged and productive. Meditation and Mindfulness programs at work can support resilience by equipping employees with the training and ability to understand their emotions, their level of stress and their ability to influence them.

Implementing the foundational principles of Middle Way Mind Training in the work environment can assist both management and employees. We already know that healthy working relationships are a cornerstone of employee happiness. Cultivating a solid ethical foundation in the workplace is also important. Middle Way Mind Training will also assist businesses and organizations to build honest and trustworthy business practices that not only provide them with financial gain, but are responsible to the environment and provide benefits to society as well. Developing ethical speaking and listening skills that do not harm others, will reinforce teamwork, reduce conflicts and strengthen interpersonal relationships. Profitable companies can also exhibit their generosity through charitable donations. By training the mind to cultivate gratitude, both employees and management can become aware of the wonderful opportunities that are available in their workplace and can show appreciation for the chance to work together to achieve a common objective.

Managers can learn to get the best out their employees without the need to inflate their ego or uphold their pride. They can choose instead to create a non-threatening peaceful working environment that leads to increased engagement from employees. The more mindful and aware the boss is, the less emotionally exhausted the employees are and the higher their job satisfaction. This kind of environment is one that welcomes new ideas and solutions to problems. Creativity is essential for innovation and problem-solving. Without creativity, new products and services will not be developed and the organization will not improve. When people are in better control of their emotions, they experience less stress and can be much more creative. Mindfulness can assist in creative thinking by providing increased focus, greater idea generation, and improved receptiveness to new ideas. As workers learn to live in the present moment, they can attend much more effectively to the matters at hand.

Training in meditative concentration and mindfulness will reduce impulsive emotional reactions from both managers and employees, reducing unnecessary conflicts and leading to informed and wise responses. If there is equanimity in the workplace then emotions never get out of control, problems can be quickly resolved and more goals can be accomplished.

Increasing a sense of connection amongst workers is also vital and will assist in developing a team that is in harmony and shares common goals. It will result in feelings that each has something useful to offer or contribute to the whole. Conflicts amongst co-workers decrease once they become more compassionate and empathetic, when effective speaking and listening skills are cultivated and when sense doors are watched where emotions are able to be observed and regulated.

If companies and organizations are to move forward and withstand the competition, remain profitable, attract top-notch talent, and become innovative leaders in their industry, the needs of their employees must be addressed. Working and cooperating as a team with others will never be easy, the same as with any one-on-one relationship. It will always present challenges as it involves individuals with diverse backgrounds, experiences, desires and opinions. Following the path of Middle Way Mind Training and incorporating it into the corporate environment will ultimately increase the happiness of everyone who is involved. If the key elements we have discussed in this book are implemented, who knows what such companies could actually accomplish and how they could benefit our society in the future.

CONCLUSION: AN OPPORTUNITY

FOR TRANSFORMATION

We are fascinated by the words, but where we
meet is in the silence behind them.

— Ram Dass

*I*t has been more than a year that has passed, since I began to put down the first words to this book, yet it has been a lifetime of learning and making a lot of mistakes, to even get to this point. I remain a work in progress and still don't claim to have all the answers, but grateful to be where I am now, nonetheless. Now, as I come to complete this conclusion, I cannot help but feel that I have gained so much throughout this writing process. While composing every chapter, I was reminded time and time again of the infinite wisdom that the Buddha shared with the world. He certainly understood the workings of the mind far better 2500 years ago, than most of us do today. I will be forever indebted for his teachings and it is an honor and a privilege that I can share this practical application that I call Middle Way Mind Training, with you all.

If you have made it here all the way to the end of this book, I sincerely congratulate you. I believe that you now have at least the necessary intellectual understanding and practical tools of how to proceed with a transformation of your mind in order to experience lasting happiness. It is now up to you to begin to apply the foundational principles of Middle Way Mind Training and internalize them by putting them into practice.

What is unfortunate is that even though our civilization and technology has advanced incredibly and we have come a long way since the time of the Buddha, the way our mind works really has not progressed very far. We unfortunately still succumb to and suffer the perils of greed, jealousy, envy, hatred, fear, loneliness and grief that we have always endured for thousands of years. Those same untrained emotions that have led to terrible acts of violence, murder, crime, deceit and destruction were evident in Buddha's time, and are still alive and well today. In addition, we see the startling rise in recent decades of rates of depression, stress and anxiety.

As I observe the current state of affairs in the world, I am faced with a very gloomy prognosis, one which involves many wars and conflicts, economic troubles, famines, disease, growing materialism and escalating levels of psychological problems. It seems to me that we just cannot keep living this way and perhaps it is high time for the needed paradigm shift in our way of thinking. The sad realization is that there are just so many of us that are unhappy despite having more material wealth and modern conveniences than we have ever had in history before.

I hope that Buddhist science has convinced you by now that experiencing sustained happiness is an opportunity that is freely available to everyone who seeks to really understand it and uncover it in their mind. There is no need to earn vast amounts of money, or spend years of study in university to achieve happiness. It does not require the biggest house or the priciest car. It does not depend on having the most loving family or the largest network of friends. It does not matter if we have undergone the saddest of tragedies, lost a loved one, or have been diagnosed with a terminal disease. No matter how tragic or hopeless the external world has presented itself, we can always revert back to our default mode, that inner core of happiness that is inherent to every human being. That is our Buddha nature.

The ability to uncover and experience the happiness that we already have is available to each one of us. Unfortunately, for most, it usually takes a long time for things to sink into our minds before we realize what is really important in life. Sometimes it takes a tragedy or an accident to even begin to appreciate things that we seemed to ignore before. Opportunities for transformation often pass by unnoticed because we are just not aware of them. When an abnormal event occurs in our lives, one that we are not prepared for, it usually pulls us out of our passive state, and we are forced to suddenly live in the present moment. We have always had the chance or opportunity to change, to transform and to get back onto the middle of the road, so that we can progress on our journey of discovery of who we really are. The law of impermanence states that change is constantly occurring, so the possibility of a transformation is certainly attainable.

Middle Way Mind Training is like performing a slow yet steady surgical operation of our mind. We disrupt existing habitual patterns and instill new and beneficial ones, ones that can gradually extinguish the layers of negative non-beneficial emotions that cover up our inner Buddha nature, that which is the source of our inner peace and happiness. Training the mind requires patience, courage, constant vigilance and dedication.

In recent years there have been promising and hopeful signs that the teachings of the Buddha are finally starting to hit home and become part of the mainstream. Society is starting to see the benefits of meditation and mindfulness and many programs are being offered now for companies, individuals, even children, and finding its way into psychological counseling and psychotherapy. Meditation and mindfulness have, after 2500 years, become popular and trendy. However, trends tend to come and go and always come with the risk that they become a passing fad and fade away like the next fashion wave. If we are to experience sustained happiness, training the mind needs to go beyond this and become firmly entrenched into our daily lives. It is a fundamental requirement and we need to understand its vital importance.

Imagine if everyone underwent this transformation of the mind. What would the world look like then? The Dalai Lama once stated that "if every 8 year old in the world was taught meditation, we would eliminate violence from the world within one generation." Just think of our history and the thousands of years of wars and violence, crime, murder and abuse that continue right up to this day. The realization and internalization that happiness is found within us and not in our external world would certainly change the entire focus of mankind. Every action, discovery or invention would be assessed whether it can help others and the environment, rather than being based on just selfish motivations of greed or status or arise out of fear or hatred. Cooperation amongst us would have an entire new meaning when we actually understand that we are all interconnected, not separated from one another, and what affects one, affects the whole. Just imagine how much more could be accomplished and how much less time would be wasted if we all learned to live in the present moment. Think of how much suffering we go through when we linger in the past and the future.

While this kind of mass transformation will certainly not happen overnight, the seed, or the dharma, the truth of the nature of our reality has already been planted. The Buddha planted it 2500 years ago and it has been passed on throughout his lineages, preserved and cultivated right up to this present day. Each of us has the opportunity to access this wisdom. In some ways the content of this book is also like a seed, one which can be planted in our own mind. Whether we decide to nurture it, and see it grow and bear fruit, is entirely up to us. Middle Way Mind Training is an opportunity to finally gain control of our mind, eliminate all unnecessary suffering that we habitually go through and become genuinely happy. If it is true that everything we do in life is to seek happiness, then this certainly is a worthwhile endeavor.

It is now time to put all that we have learned into practice and no amount of words in this book can do that for us. In the famous quotation by Ram Dass, he describes how "we are fascinated by the words, but where we meet is in the silence behind them." We need silence much more than we think. In silence we can find peace, and with peace we uncover happiness. We often become too preoccupied by words that we miss the deeper meaning and intention behind them. We get lost in the intellect and forget to put things into practice and experience them. We need to see beyond the words and penetrate their deeper essence. I hope that it is evident now how Middle Way Mind Training can offer a reliable passage, a raft to traverse the turbulent waves we encounter, to reach an ocean of calm that lies beyond the everyday noise of our mind. I believe that it offers a practical way through the art of understanding the mind and a systematic scientific method to reach and experience a much greater sense of sustained happiness than the majority of us can imagine.

We need to ask ourselves now; what are we prepared to do to reach that higher state of mind? I hope that this book has at least provided some food for thought to answer this question. I wish all of us the courage and strength to realize that inner peace and happiness is always within our grasp, it is within us, as it has always been.

Thank you for embarking on this enlightening journey with me. Perhaps we can get closer to an understanding of who we really are and why we are all here together, right here and right now. I am sure that we are destined to meet one day, somewhere amidst the silence, that which lies beneath all of these words that I have written.

May we all be happy.

Namaste,

Frank Navratil

REFERENCES

Aamodt, S. (2016). *Why Diets Make Us Fat: the unintended consequences of our obsession with weight loss*. Melbourne: Scribe

Alhan, C., Ibiloglu, A.O. (2016). Irritable Bowel Syndrome, depression and anxiety. *Eastern Journal of Medicine.*

Amanze, R. (2022). Forgiveness and Happiness; Links, associations and relationships *University of Bolton*

Batik, M.V., Bingol, T.Y., Kodaz, A.F. (2017). Forgiveness and Subjective Happiness of University Students. *International Journal of Higher Education.* 6(6):149

Bernstein DM, Loftus EF. (2009) The Consequences of False Memories for Food Preferences and Choices. *Perspect Psychol Sci.* 2009 Mar; 4(2):135-9.

Bodhi, B. (2003) *A Comprehensive Manual of Abhidhamma.* Onalaska, WA: Pariyatti

Booker, C. L., Skew, A. J., Kelly, Y. J., & Sacker, A. (2015). Media use, sports participation, and well-being in adolescents: Cross-sectional findings from the UK household longitudinal study. *American Journal of Public Health*, 105, 173-179

Brandon, Hl, Hidaka, B.A. (2012). Depression as a disease of modernity: explanations for increasing prevalence *Journal of Affective Disorders* 140(3): 205–214

Brasington, L. (2015). *Right Concentration: A Practical Guide to the Jhanas.* Boulder: Shambhala

Brickman, P., Coates, D., Janoff-Bulman, R. (1978) Lottery Winners and Accident Victims: Is Happiness Relative? *Journal of Personality and Social Psychology* 36(8):917-27

Casioppo, D. (2019). The cultivation of joy: practices from the Buddhist tradition, positive psychology, and yogic philosophy. *The Journal of Positive Psychology* 15(1):1-7

Chivukula, V., Ramaswamy, S. (2014). Effect of Different Types of Music on Rosa Chinensis Plants. *International Journal of Environmental Science and Development* 5(5):431-434

Cole, J.M., Scrivener, H. (2013) Short Term Effects of Gossip Behavior on Self-Esteem *Current Psychology* 32(3)

Davidson RJ, Lutz A. (2008). Buddha's Brain: Neuroplasticity and Meditation. *IEEE Signal Process Mag.*2008 Jan 1;25(1):176-174.

Deepak.D., Sinha. A.N., Gusain, V.S., Goel, A. (2012). A study on effects of meditation on sympathetic nervous system functional status in meditators. *Journal of Clinical and Diagnostic Research* 6(6):938-942

Emmons, R.A. (2007). *Thanks! How Practicing Gratitude Can Make You Happier.* New York: Houghton Mifflin Harcourt

Ennenbach, M. (2014). *Buddhist Psychotherapy.* Twin Lakes: Lotus Press

Feldman, R.S., Forrest, J.A., Happ, B.R. (2002) Self-Presentation and Verbal Deception: Do Self-Presenters Lie More? *Basic and Applied Social Psychology* 24(2):163-170

Fermelia, A. (2017) The One Second Brain Thought *CLM Report,*

Gable,S.L., Reis, H. (2010). Good News! Capitalizing on Positive Events in an Interpersonal Context. *Advances in Experimental Social Psychology* 42:195-257

Gard, T., Hölzel, B.K., Lazar, S.W. (2014) The potential effects of meditation on age-related cognitive decline: a systematic review. *Annals of the New York Academy of Science.* 2014; 1307 (1):89-103.

Gilbert, D.T., Wilson, T.D. (2005) Affective Forecasting: Knowing What to Want. *Current Directions in Psychological Science* Vol. 14, No. 3 (Jun., 2005), pp. 131-134

Goleman, D., Davidson, R.J. (2018). *Altered Traits: Science Reveals How Meditation Changes Your Mind, Brain and Body.* New York: Avery

Greenberg, J., Pyszczynski, T., Solomon, S. (1986). The Causes and Consequences of a Need for Self-Esteem: A Terror Management Theory. In: Baumeister, R.F. (eds) *Public Self and Private Self. Springer Series in Social Psychology.* Springer, New York, NY.

Hanson, R. (2009). *Buddha's Brain: The practical neuroscience of happiness, love, and Wisdom.* Oakland: New Harbinger Publications

Hart, W., Goenka, S.N. (1987) *Vipassana Meditation as taught by S.N. Goenka*. New York: Harper & Row

Horowitz, S. (2010). Health Benefits of Meditation: What the Newest Research Shows. *Alternative and Complementary Therapies* 16(4):223-228

Hunt, M. G., Marx, R., Lipson, C., & Young, J. (2018). No more FOMO: Limiting social media decreases loneliness and depression. *Journal of Social and Clinical Psychology*, 37,751-768.

Jamieson, K. ((2017) The Effects of Meditation and Mindfulness on Telomere Length and Telomerase DOI:10.13140/RG.2.2.21267.37927 Conference: *Association for Applied Psychophysiology and Biofeedback*

Kabat-Zinn, J. (1990). *Full catastrophe living: Using the wisdom of our body and mind to face stress, pain, and illness*. New York: Delta.

Kaur, H., Tee, E.Y.J. (2013). A Laboratory Experiment on Loving-kindness Meditation and its Undoing Effect on Anger.

Kelly, A., Wang, L. (2012) Science of Honesty Study *University of Notre Dame*

Killingsworth, M.A., Gilbert (2010) A Wandering Mind Is an Unhappy Mind. *Science*, 2010; 330 (6006): 932

Killingsworth, M.A., Kumar, A., Gilovich, T. (2020) Spending on doing promotes more moment-to-moment happiness than spending on having. *Journal of Experimental Social Psychology Volume 88, May 2020*, 103971

Kuhn, P.J., Kooreman, P., Soetevent, A.R., Kapteyn, A. (2008). The Own and Social Effects of an Unexpected Income Shock: Evidence from the Dutch Postcode Lottery. *NBER Working Paper* No. w14035,

Leanos, S., Kurum, E., Strickland, C.M., Ditta, A.S., Nguyen, G., Felix, M., Yum, H., Rebok, G.W., Wu, R. (2020). The Impact of Learning Multiple Real-World Skills on Cognitive Abilities and Functional Independence in Healthy Older Adults. *The Journals of Gerontology: Series B*, Volume 75, Issue 6, Pages 1155–1169.

Le Nguyen KD, Lin J, Algoe SB, Brantley MM, Kim SL, Brantley J, Salzberg S, Fredrickson BL. (2019) Loving-kindness meditation slows biological aging in novices: Evidence from a 12- week randomized controlled trial. *Psychoneuroendocrinology*. 2019 Oct; 108:20-27.

Luberto CM, Shinday N, Song R, Philpotts LL, Park ER, Fricchione GL, Yeh GY. (2018). A Systematic Review and Meta-analysis of the Effects of Meditation on Empathy, Compassion, and Prosocial Behaviors. *Mindfulness* (N Y). 2018 Jun;9(3):708-724.

Leung MK, Chan CC, Yin J, Lee CF, So KF, Lee TM. (2013) Increased gray matter volume in the right angular and posterior parahippocampal gyri in loving-kindness meditators. *Soc Cogn Affect Neurosci.* 2013 Jan;8(1):34-9.

Lin, L. y., Sidani, J. E., Shensa, A., Radovic, A., Miller, E., Colditz, J. B.,& Primack, B. A. (2016). Association between social media use and depression among U.S. young adults. *Depression and Anxiety*, 33, 323-331.

Lynch, J., Prihodova, L., Dunne, P., Carroll, A. (2018). Mantra Meditation for Mental Health in the General Population: A Systematic Review. *European Journal of Integrative Medicine* 23 (3)

Mora-Ripoll R. (2010). The therapeutic value of laughter in medicine. *Altern Ther Health.* Med. 2010 Nov-Dec;16 (6):56-64. PMID: 21280463.

Munasinghe, S., Weerakoon, S., Somaratne, S. (2020). Biological responses of Sri Lankan rice (Oryza sativa L.) varieties to rhythmic sound patterns (music and religious chants) *Nusantara Bioscience* 2020 Vol 12 (2)

Navratil, F., Navratilova, J. (2022). *Stranded on a Desert Island: A collection of poems to rescue and enlighten lost souls.* Ricany: Frank Navratil

Park SQ, Kahnt T, Dogan A, Strang S, Fehr E, Tobler PN.(2017). A neural link between generosity and happiness. *Nat Commun.* 2017 Jul 11;8:15964. doi: 10.1038/ncomms15964. PMID: 28696410; PMCID: PMC5508200.

Prater, T., Kiser,S. (2002) Lies, Lies, and more lies. *Sam Advanced Management Journal 67(2):9-36*

Provine, R. (2000). *Laughter: A Scientific Investigation.* New York: Viking

Ricard, M., Thuan, T.X. (2001). *The Quantum and the Lotus.* New York: Crown

Robbins, M. L., & Karan, A. (2020). Who Gossips and How in Everyday Life? Social *Psychological and Personality Science*, 11(2), 185–195.

Rosner, F. (2002). Therapeutic efficacy of laughter in medicine. *Cancer Invest.* 2002; 20 (3):434–6.

Salzberg, S. (1995). *Loving-Kindness: The Revolutionary Art of Happiness.* Boston: *Shambhala

Schnitker,S. (2012). An examination of patience and well-being. *The Journal of Positive Psychology* 7(4):263-280

Schmidt, A. (2005) *Depa Ma: The life and legacy of a Buddhist master.* New York: Bluebridge

Segal, Z.V., Williams, J.M.G., Teasdale, J.D. (2001). *Mindfulness-Based Cognitive Therapy for Depression: A New Approach to Preventing Relapse.* New York: Guildford Press

Seligman ME, Steen TA, Park N, Peterson C. (2005). Positive psychology progress: empirical validation of interventions. *Am Psychol.* 2005 Jul-Aug;60(5):410-21.

Sharabi, L., Caughlin, J.P. (2018) Deception in online dating: Significance and implications for the first offline date *New Media & Society* 21(1):146144481879242

Smythies, J. (2005). How the brain decides what we see. *J R Soc Med.* 2005 Jan; 98(1): 18–20.

Stefan, S., Hofman, S.G.(2019) Integrating Metta Into CBT: How Loving Kindness and Compassion Meditation Can Enhance CBT for Treating Anxiety and Depression. *linical Psychology in Europe.*

Stevenson, I., (1997) *Where Reincarnation and Biology Intersect.* USA: Praeger Sudirman, S.A., Suud, F.M., Rouzi, K.S., Sari, D.P. (2019). Forgiveness and Happiness through Resilience. *Al-Oalb*

Suzuki, S. (1970). *Zen Mind, Beginner's mind.* Boston: Weatherhill Press.

Tirch, D.,Silberstein, L.R., Kolts, R.L. (2016) *Buddhist Psychology and Cognitive-Behavioral Therapy: A Clinician's Guide.* New York: Bantam.

Tonelli ME, Wachholtz AB. (2014). Meditation-based treatment yielding immediate relief for meditation-naïve migraineurs. *Pain Manag Nurs.* 2014 Mar;15(1):36-40.

Tromholt, M. (2016). The Facebook experiment: Quitting Facebook leads to higher levels of well-being. *Cyberpsychology, Behavior, and Social Networking,* 19, 661-666.

Tucker, J.B. (2006). *Life Before Life: A Scientific Investigation of Children's Memories of Previous Lives.* London: Piatkus

Twenge, J. M., Sherman, R. A., & Lyubomirsky, S. (2016). More happiness for young people and less for mature adults: Time period differences in subjective well-being in the United

States, 1972-2014. *Social Psychological and Personality Science,* 7, 131-141.

Twenge, J.M., (2019) The Sad State of Happiness in the United States and the Role of Digital Media. *World Happiness Report* Chapter 5. San Diego University

Twenge, J. M., Martin, G. N., & Spitzberg, B. H. (2019). Trends in U.S. adolescents' media use, 1976-2016: The rise of digital media, the decline of TV, and the (near) demise of print. *Psychology of Popular Media Culture.*

Twenge, J. M., & Campbell, W. K. (2018). Associations between screen time and lower psychological well-being among children and adolescents: Evidence from a population-based study. *Preventative Medicine Reports,* 12, 271-283.

Umberson, D., Montez, J.K. (2010). Social relationships and health: a flashpoint for health policy. *J Health Soc Behav.* 2010 ;51 Suppl (Suppl):S54-66.

Weiss, B. (1988): *Many Lives, Many Masters.* New York: Simon and Schuster

BOOKS BY FRANK NAVRATIL

MIND TRAINING / HEALING BOOKS

- MIDDLE WAY MIND TRAINING: THE ART AND SCIENCE OF UNCOVERING THE HAPPINESS YOU HOLD WITHIN
- STRANDED ON A DESERT ISLAND: A COLLECTION OF POEMS TO RESCUE AND ENLIGHTEN LOST SOULS

NATURAL MEDICINE BOOKS

- THE EYE FOR AN EYE DIET
- EAT WISE BY READING YOUR EYES
- FOR YOUR EYES ONLY: A FASCINATING LOOK AT THE ART AND SCIENCE OF IRIS DIAGNOSIS, THE DIAGNOSTIC METHOD OF THE NEW MILLENNIUM
- BOWEN THERAPY: TOM BOWEN'S GIFT TO THE WORLD

CHILDREN'S BOOKS

- KARMA KYLE THE CROCODILE: WHAT GOES AROUND WILL COME AROUND
- KARMA KYLE THE CROCODILE: ANGRY CLOUDS
- KARMA KYLE THE CROCODILE: FRIENDSHIP IS THE GREATEST TREASURE
- THE BIGGEST ICE CREAM CONE EVER

To have Dr. Frank Navratil speak at your engagement
or for more information on MWMT courses, books,
audio meditations, online consultations and webinars,
please contact us on our web site:

www.middlewaymindtraining.com